I0796671

Napoleon's Line Infantry – From the Invasion of Russia to Waterloo

To Yves Martin

Thank you for your friendship and support of my endeavours

Napoleon's Line Infantry – From the Invasion of Russia to Waterloo

Uniforms and Equipment

Paul L. Dawson

Frontline Books

First published in Great Britain in 2025 by
Frontline Books
An imprint of Pen & Sword Books Limited
Yorkshire – Philadelphia

ISBN 978 1 03615 054 9

A CIP catalogue record for this book is available from the British Library.

Typeset by Mac Style

The Publisher's authorised representative in the EU for product safety is Authorised Rep Compliance Ltd., Ground Floor, 71 Lower Baggot Street, Dublin D02 P593, Ireland.
www.arccompliance.com

For a complete list of Pen & Sword titles please contact

PEN & SWORD BOOKS LIMITED
47 Church Street, Barnsley, South Yorkshire, S70 2AS, England
E-mail: enquiries@pen-and-sword.co.uk
Website: www.pen-and-sword.co.uk
or
PEN AND SWORD BOOKS
1950 Lawrence Road, Havertown, PA 19083, USA
E-mail: uspen-and-sword@casematepublishers.com
Website: www.penandswordbooks.com

Contents

Acknowledgements

This book sets out to describe what the various regiments of line infantry wore during the last years of the 1^{e} Empire. Our goal is to chart the dress of every regiment from previously unused archive sources to answer a perennial question: Did the famous Bardin regulation exist? This book lays the facts bare warts and all.

Yves Martin's unfailing support and friendship and his most generous assistance in the provision of research material and illustrations has been invaluable: without him this book would not exist.

I am also indebted to Sally Fairweather and Jean Charles Lair for their assistance with, and photographing of, archival material at the Archives Nationales and Service Historique de la Défense Armée de Térre, in Paris. As the world stepped out of the Covid lockdown, Jean stepped up to the plate and completed the last pieces of essential research to ensure this book was completed in 2021: travel restrictions and quarantine prevented travel to Paris. *Bravo mon ami!*

Martin Lancaster, Ben Townsend and Robert Cooper must be heartily thanked for their encouragement of this book and my research: their support and critical input to my thinking have kept this project progressing for the last seven years. I hope, Gentlemen, that the finished thesis lives up to your expectations and the thousands spent on air flights, hotels and dedicated patronage of Le Drapeau at Vincennes has been worth it.

Bertrand Malvaux is to be heartily thanked for allowing me to use images of his extensive collection.

Jerome Croyet must be thanked for his permission to reproduce the photographs I have taken of the former Brunon collection. He is also to be thanked for provision of research notes. Isabelle Artaud of the Musée de l'Armée Paris is also to be heartily thanked for also providing me with permission to use images of the collections of the Musée de l'Armée.

The staff at Service Historique de la Défense Armée de Térre as well as at Archives Nationales in Paris need to be thanked for answering questions and locating items of research that have made this book possible.

Lastly, the staff at Le Drapeau in Vincennes must be thanked for their hospitality for nearly twenty years.

Paris, 5 December 2024

Chapter 1

The Bardin Regulation is Born!

As our previous volume described, what the soldier wore, especially the infantry, was a constant headache for the War Ministry. With over 120 regiments existing by 1811, and ever-increasing costs, some way of organising order from chaos was needed. An idea of the problem facing the War Ministry in clothing the army can be found in a report from the war administration to the Emperor from September 1811. The report informed the Emperor that the ministry had clothed 644,782 men, of which 244,242 were conscripts from the class of 1810, 238,764 from the class of 1811 and 49,522 reservists, i.e., men conscripted but who had not yet joined up. The report continued to note, however, that unfortunately, 281,540 of these uniforms had been made with an inferior quality of cloth, which forced the regiments to replace them earlier than anticipated.[1] Indeed, by the end of 1810 it was increasingly apparent that the 'standard operating procedures' of clothing the army were not fit for purpose, and route and branch reform was needed. In January 1811 the Comte de Cessac complained to the Emperor that the 1806 reforms had been a failure:

> Sire,
> The current legislation of the clothing service was regulated by the decree issued by your Majesty on April 25, 1806. Four years of experience have made it necessary to make some changes to the administration system currently in force.
>
> The successive increase in the price of commoditys which has been the result of the ever increasing size of the army; arbitrary expenses that regiments have made as a result of the free rein given to them regarding their expenses which has resulted in abuses made in internal administration of the regiments; the disorder which exists in their accounts for the four years which preceded 1810; are the reasons which have led me to propose to your Majesty modifications to the present system of the clothing service.[2]

A few weeks later, a memo from Comte de Cessac revealed that the War Ministry had been busy reviewing the issue of clothing the army and reported that:

> The experience of several years has shown that the clothing fund, as fixed by the decrees of April 25 and July 6, 1806, was insufficient for regiments to meet all the expenses which this fund was to provide for. The increase in prices of raw materials and labour since these decrees were issued has completely destroyed all balance between income and expenditure on clothing, and many regiments were forced to take out loans to cover all their expenses ...[3]

The commission further reported:

> The quantities of cloth allocated for clothing, and in particular for the clothing of the line infantry, also warranted the attention of the committee. The old estimate adopted after many tests, allocated for the *habit* one metre seventy-one centimetres; and the decision of February 9, 1810, recalled in the circular of the minister-director, dated February 19 of the same month, reduced this quantity to one metre thirty-four centimetres. The committee section thought that such a reduction would reduce the size of the *habit* so much that it could no longer be large enough to adequately cover the soldier and leave him free in all his movements. They therefore asked the Minister-Director to have models made according to which it was possible to determine exactly the quantities of material that should be granted for the clothing of troops of all arms. His Excellency replied on February 2, that he was going to have the models in question made; but that he did not think that the lack of these models was an obstacle to the examination of the project by the committee; that further delays would jeopardise the good of the service, and that it was important that His Majesty was to have a quick answer.
>
> The commission noted, in the work used to determine the proposed mass for the cavalry troops, that there was a lot of uncertainty about the uniform of the different arms; the Minister agreed, moreover, that this work could only be considered provisional, until it had been pronounced on various changes which he had proposed to uniforms of the mounted troops.
>
> The commission felt if new regulations for just part of the army were created it would result in the fragmentation of the legislation on the general clothing fund; and felt it was very important to put an end to the lack of uniformity which reigns in the clothing of the troops of the same arm, following the arbitrary changes which had been introduced by regimental Colonels making requests to the Minister of War and to the Minister-Director.[4]

The War Ministry all but admitted that it had all but lost control of dress regulations. What was needed was total reform. The result of this was twofold: a commission was established to critically assess what the army wore and to draw up a new regulation for the entire army; second as a stopgap measure the War Ministry decreed that all *habits* worn in the infantry, artillery and dragoons would henceforth have short tails like those of the *légère* regiments, long gaiters would be abolished in favour of half gaiters, *pantalons de tricot* would replace *culottes*, and the *veste manches* would be replaced by a cut round *gilet manches*, again in imitation of the *légère* regiments, which were to be introduced to service from 1 October 1811 for replacement clothing for the year 1812.[5]

After adopting this stopgap measure, the commission set to work examining the infantry *habit* and the dress of the army in detail. In less than six weeks after being convened, the commission reported to Marshal Berthier on 30 April 1811:

[…] the commission has recognised that the line infantry's uniform *habit* is too tight and not large enough in the arms; the *habit* is too short and leaves the loins and upper hips uncovered, the pockets are too small and only allow the soldier to have access to them with great difficulty. Consequently, the *habit* fits badly and its general appearance is one of not clothing the soldier in a decent manner. Under the old specifications, a *habit* used 1m71 worth of broadcloth for the body. The directive of 9 February 1810 reduced that amount to 1m34. The materials used for these models were reduced further to 1m18. Both these reductions represent a loss of 51cm or two-thirds […]

With regards to the details of construction, the lapels are expensive and absolutely useless for their intended purpose since it is impossible for the soldier to close them across the chest. What is needed is:

that the *revers* are stitched directly to the *habit* in order to preserve uniform distinctions.
to adopt squared *revers*, that are cut lower to cover the top of the *pantalons*.
to get rid of the *revers*, by buttoning the *habit* down the centre.

Furthermore, the neckline of the *habit* is too low, due to a design issue. The collar itself isn't high enough, which is detrimental to the health of the soldier because of his short hair. The lining of the *habit*, which is made from linen, should be cut squarely to the top of the pockets and covered by a serge lining, in order to make it more durable … The madder red colour of the cuffs is often inconsistent, scarlet red should be preferred. The *culottes* are lined with linen, which makes them unbearably hot during the marches in the summer and difficult to keep clean. The lining of the *culotte* should be abolished and replaced by underwear. The sleeves of the *capote* seem to be a little narrow and a little too short.

The light infantry *habit* has the same disadvantages as the one for the line infantry. That is to say that it is too short and too tight … The neck line is also too shallow, the tails should be lined with serge as those lined with bay are chafed easily, which immediately gives the *habit* a ragged look. The use of *pantalons de tricot* in the light infantry has allowed some saving to be made and the extra cloth has been used on the *habits* to line the tails with wool broadcloth, which looks better and needs less maintenance.

Cavalry: the same general observations as those regarding the line and light infantry. This leads us to the conclusion that it is crucial to adopt a new model of uniform that will give the soldier greater freedom in his movements and dress him well. *Habits* of a larger size, cut longer and with squared *revers* descending over the waistband of the *pantalons* will satisfy these criteria and will better protect the soldier's health. With regards to certain proposed changes, it will not be permissible to allow them without the inconvenience of touching upon the uniform distinctions that certain units have benefitted from for a long time now.[6]

On the strength of the report, Berthier asked Bourcier in July 1811 to head a new commission that was tasked by the Minister of War to determine a new uniform for all branches of the army.

On 2 January 1812, the Minister of War wrote to Napoleon informing him that he had received the conclusions of the commission appointed to review changes in the army's uniforms.[7] The Emperor, seemingly in agreement with the proposed new uniform regulations, asked the war administration to draft a decree, which he signed on 19 January 1812 and a second decree of 7 February was issued that concerned the mounted troops for implementation by February 1813.

To illustrate the new clothing and equipment, drawings were prepared by artists working for the War Administration, and cost the vast sum of 150,000fr. The famous artist Carle Vernet was paid 16,000fr to paint each and every regiment of the army and every item of equipment at the scale of 1:10. Each item of uniform was drawn twice in full size or half size. The line drawings were engraved and printed. Initially, the full-size line drawings were printed as black and white drawings to accompany the written descriptions in the regulation, having been annotated with relevant dimensions. A second set of engravings was printed and hand coloured, which were presented to the Emperor for his approval. The plates by Vernet, in three volumes, are held by the French Army Archives and are on loan to the library of the Musée de l'Armée. The text was printed by Les Goupil at some stage in 1812, but as we shall see represents a state of the regulations that 'never made it'.

Donated by Madam Millot in 1901 to the Musée de l'Armée was Major Bardin's working copy of the manuscript. The text, after being presented to the Emperor, went through many edits, and it is filled with notes, comments and major changes to the regulations in April 1813. We have used Bardin's own notes as the basis for our work. We have endeavoured to present the text as it is written down by Bardin, including corrections and annotations. Where words are struck out in the text we have done so, ~~comment~~; where words are added in later, we have used superscript, ^{comment}; where Bardin has added in notes we have italicised these words *comment*. The heavy redaction appears to date from April 1813. In some places notes had been added with a date simply signed Bdn. It is hard to untangle the various edits to recover the original intention of Bardin, as in many places he pasted new sheets of paper over the original text. The text is therefore presented in its final form from April 1813, warts and all.

Chapter 2
Bardin-Regulation Clothing

So, what was the Bardin regulation? It was a root and branch reform of the dress of the army. For the line, Bardin codified the short gaiters, *pantalons de tricot*, round cut *gilets manches* of a year earlier, and provided new patterns of *habit* and *capote*. About the cut and fit of a soldier's clothing, the Bardin regulations commented that:

> Article 1. Dress of men.
>
> 1. The dress of the *sous-officier* and soldiers of our corps of infantry, artillery, sappers and veterans, shall be composed of a *habit-veste*, a *gilet manches* with sleeves, *pantalons de tricot*, linen *caleçons*, linen pantalons and a greatcoat, a *schako.*
> 2. The clothing will be made according to the proportions details as follows, except the items specific for each arm. The pieces made from broadcloth, which meet the proportions once made.
> 3. The *habits-vestes* and *gilet manches* shall be cut following the height and build of the men, so that the cut shall allow the men to perform with ease the movements ordered, without danger of ripping the seams. To this effect, the body shall be cut very large, the rear of the *habit* and *gilet manches*, and the sleeves, and arm holes shall equally be cut large. The measure shall be taken of each man on the body, the shoulders held well up and back, to take the measure of the back the arms are held forward. The *revers* are made so that a hand can be passed between the *habit* and the *gilet manches*; the collar when closed, shall be able to take two fingers behind it. The *pantalons* shall be cut large enough to easily contain the *caleçon*, and for the man to be able to place his knee on the ground with ease. When the measure cannot be made on the man, the *habits*, *gilet manches*, and *caleçon* shall be cut for three sizes for the infantry and two sizes for the artillery.[1]

A fusilier therefore had – in theory! – a *habit-veste* worn over a *gilet manches*, a pair of linen *caleçons* (underpants), a pair of *pantalons de tricot* (tight-fitting, ankle-length trousers with a fall front), a *schako* measuring 190mm tall, a *pokalem* (off-duty cap or *bonnet de police*) and a double-breasted *capote* (greatcoat) made from beige broadcloth.

As well as his uniform a soldier needed a myriad number of other items, ranging from his ammunition box and cross belt, to shirts, socks and shoes. These were paid for either by the state or from stoppages in the man's pay.

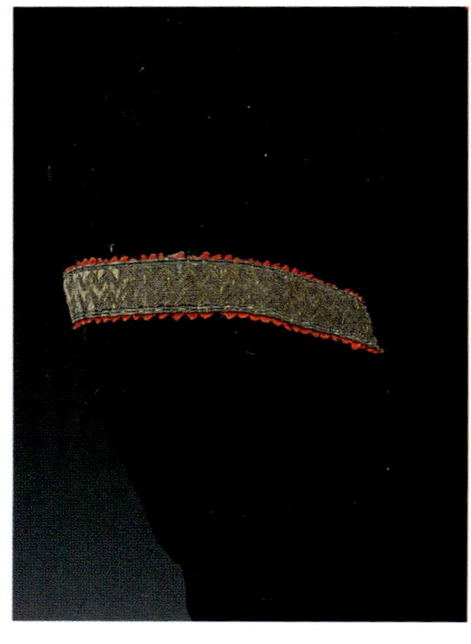

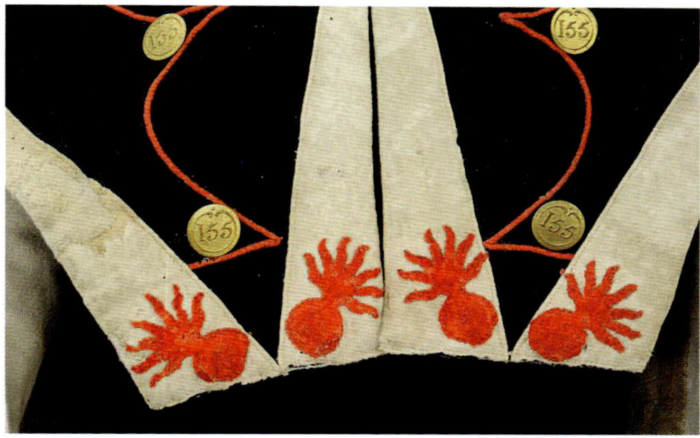
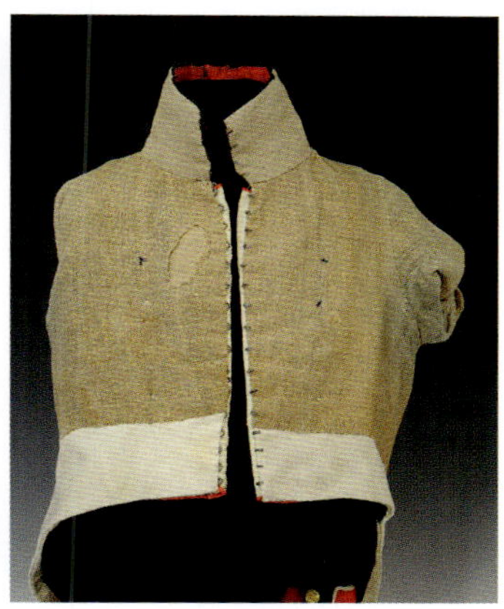

Incredibly well preserved example of the 'Classic' *habits-veste* of the Bardin regulation. This garment belonged to a *fourrier* of the 156e *de Ligne*. It dates to 1813–14. (*Photograph and collection of Betrand Malvaux*)

Grand Equipment

The soldier's '*grand equipment*' comprised a fusilier, a bayonet with scabbard, and *giberne* with belt. Corporals, *sous-officiers* and grenadiers carried a sabre and belt.[2] This was paid for by the state along with the soldier's weapons.

Two patterns of *giberne* were issued, that for the regular soldier and the other for the *fourrier* (quartermaster corporal who was the clerk to the company sergeant major), sergeants and sergeant majors, the company *sous-officiers*. The other ranks *giberne* was unchanged from previous decrees. The *sous-officier giberne* held two packets of ten cartridges, an oil bottle, a worm, screwdriver and a spring clamp, and was smaller than the model issued to the other ranks. It was little changed from the 1786 decree; under Bardin the top flap, rather than being closed by a tab and buckle, was fastened by a copper stud, which was screwed through the leather body into the wooden block.[3] The

Under the *habit-veste* and worn off duty, the men wore a *gilet manches*. This incredibly well-preserved example belonged to a *voltigeur*, denoted by the chamois collar. This item accords exactly to the November 1812 collation of Bardin, the third iteration issued in 1812. (*Photograph and collection of Bertrand Malvaux*)

gibernes of *sous-officiers* had no ornaments, but the grenadiers were authorised a copper grenade, 80mm tall; *voltigeur*s were allowed a copper hunting horn, 80mm wide; and fusiliers were allowed copper 'N' with separate copper cast crown, with a combined height of 80mm. For light infantry these devices were to be in white metal. The *giberne* belt for grenadiers, fusiliers and *voltigeur*s was 71mm wide, and was fitted with the bayonet frog. It came in three sizes. The *baudrier* was used by *sous-officier*, drummers and *sapeur*s and had both the frog for the sabre and the bayonet; their *giberne* belt had no bayonet frog.[4]

Only one instance of a *giberne* for a *sous-officier* has been located in the archive paperwork, ergo it is doubtful if they were ever made in any number. Yet they were an integral part of the Bardin regulation under the terms of the 17 September 1812 decree. On the march and on campaign the highly polished flap was to be covered with a black waxed linen cover.

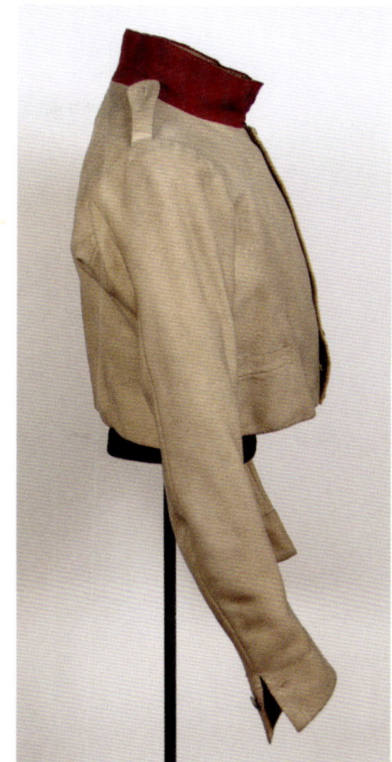

Grenadiers had a scarlet collar to their *gilet manches*. This item accords exactly to the November 1812 collation of Bardin, the third iteration issued in 1812. Fusiliers were authorised to have blue collars, but we know of no extant such garment. (*Swedish Army Museum*)

On campaign and in barracks men wore loose-fitting linen *pantalons* as shown here. (*Private collection, France*)

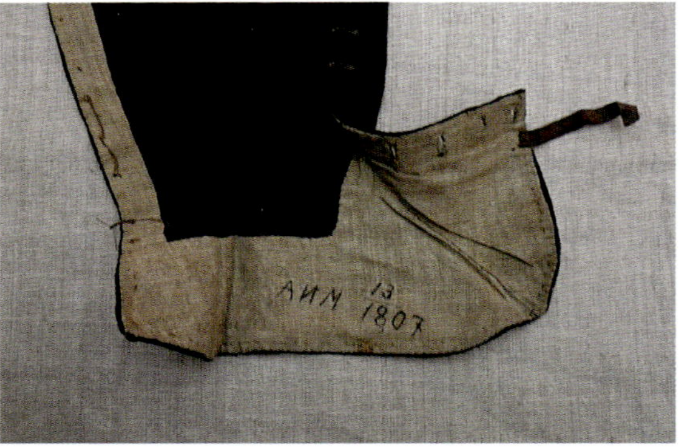

An innovation of the 1811 regulation was the use of shorter gaiters by the *ligne*. This gaiter matches both the 1810 and Bardin regulations.

Bardin regulation allowed *voltigeurs* a yellow horse *aigrette*. This is one of the few known original examples. (*Photograph and collection of Bertrand Malvaux*)

Linen and Shoe Fund

As well as his *habit-veste* and legwear a soldier needed other items of clothing, which the army also provided. About small clothes, Bardin regulations commented:

> **183. Composition of the Linen and Shoes.** A soldier shall have 3 shirts, 1 black stocks [*col noir*] with 3 *rabats*, two to be carried in the *trousse*, 2 pairs of socks, 1 pair of black half gaiters, 1 pair grey half gaiters, 1 pair of *pantalons* in linen canvas, 2 pairs of shoes, 2 handkerchiefs, 2 night caps.[5]

The soldier's shirt came in three sizes – like all items of kit – and Bardin's description merely confirms that of 1786: the shirt had cuffs fastened with links, the collar fastened by a 'Dorset button', a low collar made from superfine white linen and shoulders reinforced with 'epaulettes' made from a heavy-grade linen. An entirely new design of stock appeared in 1812. Bardin states:

> **No. 185. Stock and Rabat**. The stock is made from black *calomande* and lined with linen, to be 50mm tall. There will be attached a cord made from linen in the same colour, black, and will be used to tie the stock around the base of the neck. ~~The front will be embellished with 7 pleats, each pleat will be at the distance of {illegible} mm from one another.~~ ~~The part garnished with pleat.~~ The top edge of the stock will be covered by the *rabat* made from white linen and will be 6mm wide and the *rabat* is fitted into the entry in the top of the stock which will also allow the reception of the cardboard of the same height destined to stiffen it.[6]

The Bardin regulation did not allow *voltigeurs* to have their own-pattern *schako*. Yet incontestable proof that these items did exist comes from undeniably authentic original items, like this example. How common these items were in use we cannot tell as none appear in any archive document from the epoch. (*Collection de l'Office du Tourisme de Pontarlier. Dépôt au Musée municipal de Pontarlier, France*)

From this, we learn that the *col noir* was made of black *calomande* (polished horsehair) and had a cardboard interlining. The thin white edging at the top of edge of the stock was called a *rabat*. It was made from a piece of bleached white linen folded over and hemmed, to be 6mm tall. It was sewn into a 'gutter' at the top edge of the stock: the top edge opened to allow the card liner to be changed. The top edge was tack stitched closed, the *rabat* presumably reinforcing the leading edge. The stock was not reversable – the back face or lining was black linen. It was fastened with linen tape and not a buckle.

On campaign grey linen gaiters were worn under loose-fitting linen *pantalons*. The grey gaiters were made exactly the same as the black gaiters. These were not the ankle-length items that re-enactors use: these low gaiters existed only from 1822. The socks, Bardin notes, were knitted from wool, and covered the lower leg to mid-calf and were made from natural fleece. The night cap was made from linen, and fashioned like the *flamme* from a *bonnet de police*. The linen overalls have been described previously.

Petit Equipment

A soldier was also issued *Petit equipment*, paid for with a 40fr gratuity to the conscript by the state. The *petit equipment* comprised:

> **168**. Details of the first issue
> Under the name of first issue we will understand the petit equipment. Linen and shoes, the uniform, petit monture and items for maintenance.

The illustrations accompanying the Bardin regulation show *voltigeurs* with a simple fusiliers' *schako*. *Voltigeurs* were marked out by the chamois collar to the *habit*, and hunting horn devices to the tails of the *habit*:

> '**70 Distinctions des *Voltigeurs*.** The uniform of the *voltigeur* will be no different to the infantry of the line except that that their collar and their epaulettes will be in chamois broadcloth. The turnbacks are garnished with a hunting horn cut from chamois broadcloth. Their *schako* is to be the same as the fusiliers except that it is ornamented with a citron yellow chamois *aigrette* conforming to model No. 42.'

What does epaulette mean? The regulation reads that the *voltigeurs* used the same shoulder straps as the fusiliers, but cut from chamois, piped in scarlet, or as the plate accompanying the regulation shows, fringed epaulettes. The vagueness of the regulation presumably gave colonels a marked decree of latitude in adopting fringed epaulettes or not. These are not mentioned anywhere in the regulation, but archive documents show they were used. The regulation is very clear that the *voltigeurs* wore fusilier *schakos*.

This image shows a grenadier in the regulated full dress uniform as imagined by the Bardin regulation. Bardin is clear that grenadiers and *voltigeurs* did not carry sabres:

> '**Section 4. Armament and Equipment**
> **Art 1 Composition**
> **90.** The armament of the infantry will comprise a musket with bayonet. The dragoon musket will be used by *voltigeurs*. The *sapeurs* will use a *mousqueton* with bayonet. The *sabre-briquet* will be used by the drum major, the sergeant majors, *Vaugmestre*, chief workmen, sergeants, drum master, *fourrier*, corporals, *sapeurs*, musicians, drummers and *cornets*. There will also be issued to the *sapeurs* and *porte-aigle* a pair of pistols, a pole arm to the *porte-aigle* and also an axe to the *sapeur*.'

Yet the Vernet plates accompanying the text contradict this, as does the detailed description of sword knots for grenadiers as part of the regulation: we are left with an enigma of what was, or was not, allowed.

In undress, the *gilet manches* was worn, shown here. The 26 July 1812 decree allowed the *pokalem* shown here and the use of a fusilier *gilet manches* but with a cut-out cloth grenade to the sleeve by grenadiers. It also shows epaulettes were to be tolerated to be worn on this garment. The *pokalem* was swept away with the September 1812 collation of decrees relating to clothing. In its place the old *dragonne* style was kept in use. The November 1812 collation of decrees removed the blue cuffs and shoulder straps from the *gilet manches*, allowing just a blue collar for fusiliers, scarlet or madder red for grenadiers, and chamois for *voltigeurs*.

An incredibly well-preserved example of a grenadier *schako* that exactly accords to the Bardin regulation. (*Collection de l'Office du Tourisme de Pontarlier. Dépôt au Musée municipal de Pontarlier, France*)

A fantastic example of the Bardin-regulations *schako* for a fusilier, complete with the regulation plate. (*Collection de l'Office du Tourisme de Pontarlier. Dépôt au Musée municipal de Pontarlier, France*)

In wet weather, the *schako* was covered with an oil cloth cover. This is one of the few known original examples to exist. (*Photograph and collection of Betrand Malvaux*)

A major innovation of the precursor regulation to the Bardin regulation was the adoption of Imperial Livery for all musicians. This image by Rousselot gives a good idea of the theoretical appearance of drummers from the end of 1811 onwards. (*Collection KM*)

169. Distributed under the name of 1st Issue, it will comprise the petit equipment, and will comprise the items of dress, of petit monture [illegible] the petit equipment will comprise the havresac, the linen *sac à distribution*, the *aigrettes* Viz. no. 42 et 43, pompoms for fusiliers viz No. 41, the cockade, the ~~stock buckle,~~ sword knots for grenadiers and sous-officier, small canteens. These objects will be renewed at the expense of the clothing fund ~~the linen and shoe fund~~ with the exception of the havresac as well as the sac a toile, the major part of which will be still funded from the linen and shoe fund. The small canteen will be supplied from the campaign fund *and then renewed at the expense of the battalion.*[7]

Perhaps the only contemporary image from the epoch showing Imperial Livery in use. (*Collection KM*)

Regulation drawing for the dress of the drum major and drum master. The regulation colpack was only issued to two regiments as far as we can tell. (*Collection KM*)

Bardin designed a new-pattern *sac de peau* – also known in the period as *havresac* – but it was never put into mass production.[8] The *sac à distribution* is also known as the *sac à toile*. It was not a shoulder bag that re-enactors and artists claim it to be. This was the French soldier's bread bag. It was made from a coarse heavyweight canvas. It had several purposes, the main one being for holding food and rations that were distributed to a squad. This is confirmed in the Ordonnance sur l'habillement of 1786, article 11, as well as Service de Campagne 1791 section 1, which also confirmed it could be slept in. In 1801 it was regulated to be made from a double thickness of canvas and measure 157cm long by 76cm wide.[9] The Bardin regulation stated that the *sac à distribution* was 1m 50 long, 50cm wide, was closed by two tapes, and was made from heavy linen.[10]

Rather than drummers, *voltigeur* companies retained *cornets*, as shown here.

Musicians dressed according to the first iteration of the Bardin regulation:

> '**Art. 5 Dress of the Musicians**
> **89.** The clothing of the musicians will comprise that same as the soldiers. Their headdress and footwear will be the same as the soldiers Viz No. 30 and 187. Their pompom will be the same as for the *etat-major*, and their *bonnet de police* will be cut from green broadcloth in the same model as the men. The *habit* will conform to that described No. 790. The collar and cuffs will be ornamented with a lace the same as used by the drummers. ~~The musicians will wear veste and pantalons cut from green broadcloth in the same form as the men~~ ~~Their vestes and pantalons will be cut from white broadcloth~~ *for the regiments that have* pantalons *the same colour. The* vestes *and* pantalons *will be green for those regiments whose* pantalons *are of the darker colour*. They will be armed with the *sabre briquet* and *baudrier*.
>
> The Chef de Musique will be marked out by the same rank stripes as the sergeant major of their arm, and will be in gold or silver lace. The collar with be decorated with rows of gold or silver lace, the same as appears on the cuffs.'

Presumably line infantry had white *veste* and *pantalons* and light infantry green. (*Collection KM*)

Light infantry musicians dressed to the first iteration of the Bardin regulation. In its final form, from April 1813, bandsmen of *Ligne* and *Légère* were to be dressed the same as the drummers:

> 'The *habits* of the drummers, musicians, drummers and *cornets* will conform to the general model viz 83 to 88, their *bonnets de police* will be in green broadcloth. The ornaments of the turnbacks of the musicians will be a crowned N in green broadcloth the same as ~~the drummers of the grenadiers~~ the drummers of the fusiliers, ~~the same colour as their arm and their company. Their *vestes* and *pantalons* will be made from green tricot and the lining to the *vestes* will be white. The drummers of the line infantry will have white *pantalons* and *veste*.~~'

Therefore, we must imagine that the musicians, drummers and *cornets*, as well as the trumpeters, creating a single garment for ease of mass production. (*Collection KM*)

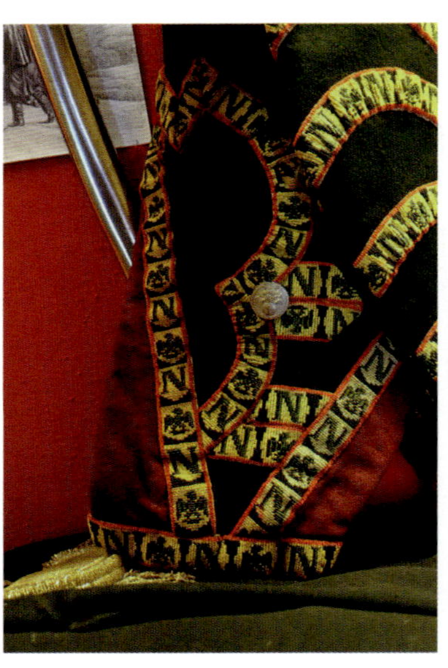

Despite being a reconstruction, albeit using original lace, this garment gives an excellent impression of the drummer, *cornets*, musicians and trumpeters' *habit*. (*Musée de l'Empéri, Collections du Musée de l'armée, Anciennes collections Jean et Raoul Brunon*)

An incredibly rare drum that reflects the Bardin regulation that standardised the use of brass shells. (*Photograph and collection of Betrand Malvaux*)

Petit Monture

As well as items of *petit equipment*, the soldier received items of *petit monture*. The *trousse* contained the items *petit monture*, which included according to regulations:

> **Art 8. Objects of clothing and *Petite Monture***
> 189. The objects of *petit monture* will comprise items for cleaning and carrying out necessary repairs, and will comprise a *trousse*, a brush for cleaning copper, a *vergette* for the *habit* and a shoe brush, needles and a box of grease.
> **190. The *trousse* and items of clothing**
> The *trousse* will contain linen thread for sewing, material for mending uniforms, a pair of scissors in a case, needles, an awl, two sets of gaiter foot straps, spare buttons for the gaiters, *habits* and breeches, a spare needle file for the *epinglette*, a piece of leather to protect the leg, two *rabats* for the stock, a button stick, a comb a razor.
> **191. *Petit Monture***
> A pay book contained in a white metal case, *giberne* cover in waxed linen, a cover for the *schako* made from oil cloth [funded by the clothing fund at the same time as the *schako*], a musket worm [provided by the magazines of the empire], a screwdriver, a piece of grease, lead to hold the flint, a wooden flint, a bottle of oil for the musket, every corporal will have these objects as well as a spring clamp for his squad.[11]

The case for the paybook appears to have been cylindrical, and carried from a cord. For personal hygiene, the soldier would have some soap and a linen towel and a comb (*peigne*). He would be shaved by the company barber twice a week.[12]

Chapter 3

Getting the Regulations into Service: the Bardin Collation of 1812

Signed into law on 19 January 1812, it has long been supposed that as soon as the decree was passed regiments began making Bardin-regulation kit. Not so. Bardin kit was being made in new year 1812 but for the National Guard only, and only from March 1812.[1] For the *ligne*, despite the decree being passed, the War Ministry had not yet issued orders to say 'go and make this'. This is understandable, as the desks of the War Ministry were snowed under with preparing the largest single army the French state had cobbled together in its history, and the officials had more important pressing needs to attend to.

No doubt the National Guard was a testbed for the new regulations.

The January 1812 decree in its original form allowed line infantry scarlet facings. This was rapidly changed to *garance* (madder red) on 21 March 1812 – the colour then in use. At the same time the cut was changed of the *gilet manches* – the front now closed with ten buttons, not the nine in the original decree, and the front was cut longer in consequence to make space for this additional button. The decree also states '*bonnets de police a la dragonne* in blue broadcloth, piped in vivid garance' were to be kept in service and made from materials recovered from old clothing. The tassel at the front was to be made from cut strips of cloth, the cavalry alone were allowed tassels made from worsted fringing.[2] As a cost-saving measure, it was much cheaper to cut up old *habits* to make *dragonne*-style *bonnets de police* than issue cloth for *pokalems*. Does this mean the *pokalem* was not adopted? The prints by Beyer from 1813 and 1814 clearly show the use of *pokalems*: The National Guard certainly had *pokalems*, and by inference the 135^{e}–156^{e} *de Ligne*. Were these the only regiments so adorned? Alas, without further documentation we cannot tell, but it seems very likely that the *pokalem* was never in mass production or use.

Despite these small changes, still nothing had been issued from on high about starting production of Bardin kit for the *ligne* and *légère*.

On 2 April, Comte de Cessac wrote from the War Ministry, warning colonels that he would be issuing instructions concerning changes to the uniform of the army. He requested that inspections be carried out for the number of new items needed for replacements for the year 1813, and no items were to be made until he issued instructions.[3]

These were issued ten days later and decreed that the replacement clothing for the year 1812 was to be the old model, i.e., more of what was already in use, and the replacement clothing for 1813 was to be of the new pattern.[4]

Incredible ensemble of an officer's *habit* and *schako* for the 75e *de Ligne*. The fringed epaulette on the right shoulder indicates the rank of capitaine-adjutant-major. (*Photograph and collection of Betrand Malvaux*)

We note that regiments were inspected annually between 24 September and 1 October, and had been since the days of the Revolution: under the Revolutionary calendar, New Year fell in this time window, and regiments were inspected on the first day of the new year. Despite the change back to the Gregorian calendar, this 'new year's day inspection' was fossilised in army regulations. At this inspection, the regimental clothing officer marked down the men who needed new clothing, and the number of new items needed for the allocated influx of new conscripts. Despite the Bardin regulation being signed into law, no one had yet said 'go and make this', and nothing would be made until the end of the year until the 1 October 1812 inspections had been submitted.

Months passed until finally from his desk in the War Administration, Comte de Cessac wrote to regimental colonels of the *ligne* and *légère* regiments on 21 July 1812 warning them that he would shortly pass an order requiring them to begin the production of a 'clothing reserve' as outlined in the decree of 3 October 1811, anticipating the

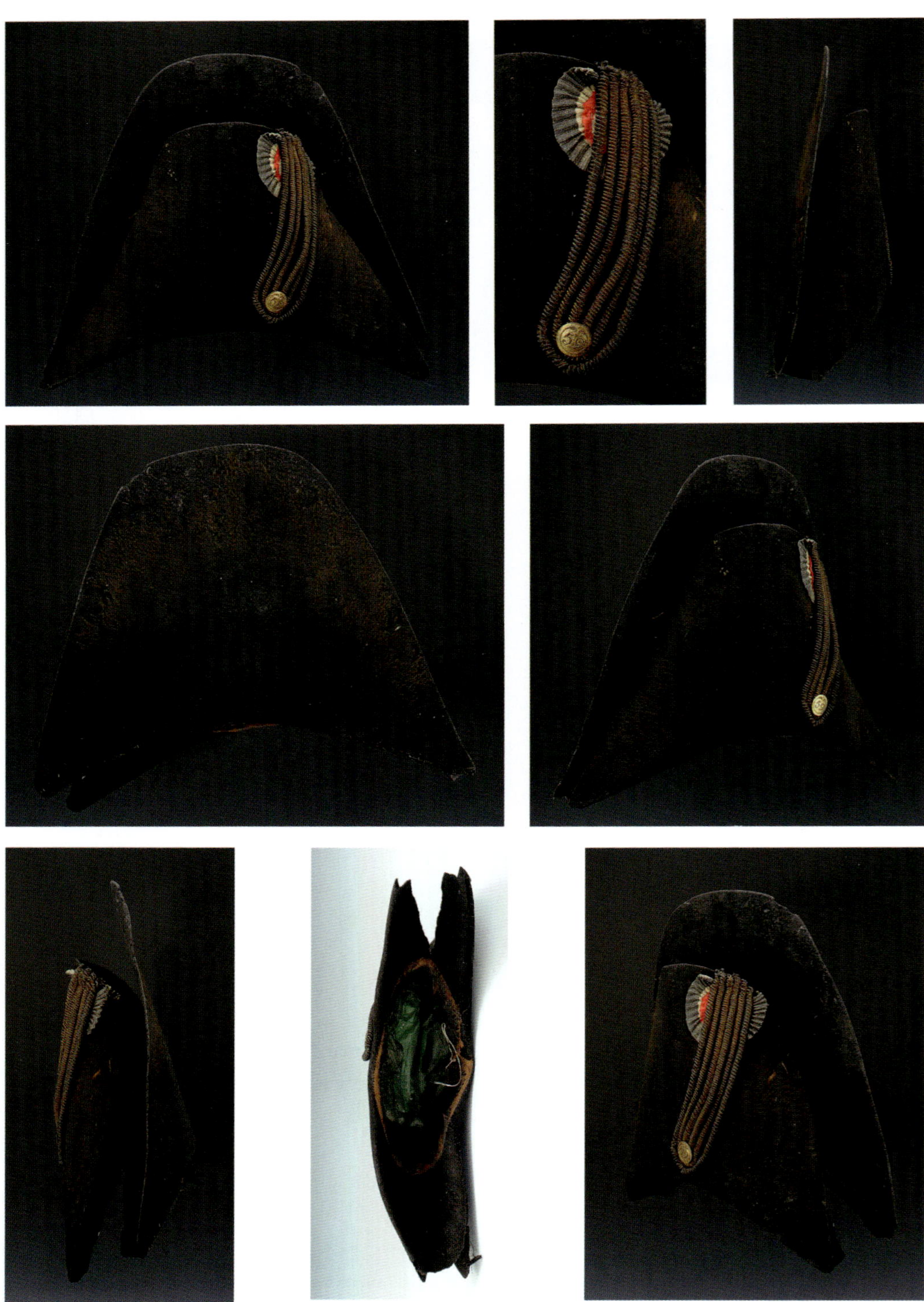

Off duty, officers wore a *chapeau*. Bardin designed a regulation model, but as officers supplied their own uniforms, we are not sure if any were made. This example gives an excellent impression of an officer's elegant off-duty headdress. (*Photograph and collection of Bertrand Malvaux*)

needs for 1813. All items were to be made according to the decree of 19 January and 7 February 1812.[5]

The War Ministry ordered three days later, the 24th, that as huge quantities of leather equipment existed in regimental stores, government stores and arsenals of the Empire, an immediate audit was to be carried out to assess just exactly how much kit existed, and issued orders that this stockpile was to be issued before any new equipment was to be made.[6]

Two days later, in a War Ministry circular of 26 July 1812, colonels of *ligne* regiments were ordered to begin the production of 200 *habits-vestes*, 200 *gilets manches*, 200 pairs of *pantalons de tricot*, 200 *capotes*, and 200 *bonnets de police* as a reserve stockpile. The colonels were also ordered to provide the same number of *gibernes*, *sacs de peau dit havresac*, etc – for issue in 1813.[7] Bardin regulation, a full six months after the decree had been passed, was at long last going into production, but in limited numbers.

Several months would pass before any more official utterances were made about clothing.

On 12 September 1812, the War Ministry stated that no changes were to take place to items of '*petit equipment*' and the regulation of 1801 was to remain in force for these items. After complaints had been received about the poor design of the new *havresac*, the order to make the new *sac de peau* was in essence rescinded.[8] Included in the '*petit-equipment*' were epaulettes: here was tacit approval for the continued use of epaulettes by not only grenadiers but also *voltigeurs*, which had been paid for by the regiment's officers since 1809.[9] The War Ministry, realising that hundreds of metres of madder red facing cloth lay in regimental stores, and that not using it would be a colossal waste of money, made orders to ensure that all stocks of *rouge-garance* (madder red) broadcloth were used before the new scarlet facing cloth was taken into use. The same circular ordered that long gaiters were no longer to remain in use and were to be replaced by short ones, once those in use had been worn out.[10]

Days later, on 17 September 1812, a second decree was issued. The decree authorised the production of new Imperial Livery for drummers, and silver lace for musicians. The same decree brought into use the new-pattern *schako* in two types: grenadier with red lace and red *aigrette* and the fusilier model for fusiliers and *voltigeurs*, along with the two new patterns of *schako* plate – grenadier and fusilier/*voltigeur* – *schako* covers and yellow *aigrettes* for *voltigeurs*. *Sous-officiers* were allowed *gibernes* and their *giberne* belts officially had no bayonet frog, and their *gibernes* lacked *giberne* plates. The decree also witnessed the introduction of the new crowned 'N' *giberne* plate for fusiliers, while grenadiers retained a flaming grenade and *voltigeurs* had a hunting horn. The decree notes grenadiers, *voltigeurs* and fusiliers all used the same-pattern *giberne* belt with the bayonet frog. *Sous-officiers*, drummers and *sapeurs* were allowed *baudriers* and sabres. *Sapeurs* under the terms of the decree were no longer allowed to wear bearskins. The decree again mentioned short black gaiters with copper buttons and short grey linen gaiters, and linen *pantalons*.[11]

With the army expanding exponentially since 1800, obtaining the raw materials from which to produce uniforms and equipment was becoming an issue. The first 'problem' arose in mid-September. Comte de Cessac explained to the Emperor on 15 September 1812 that:

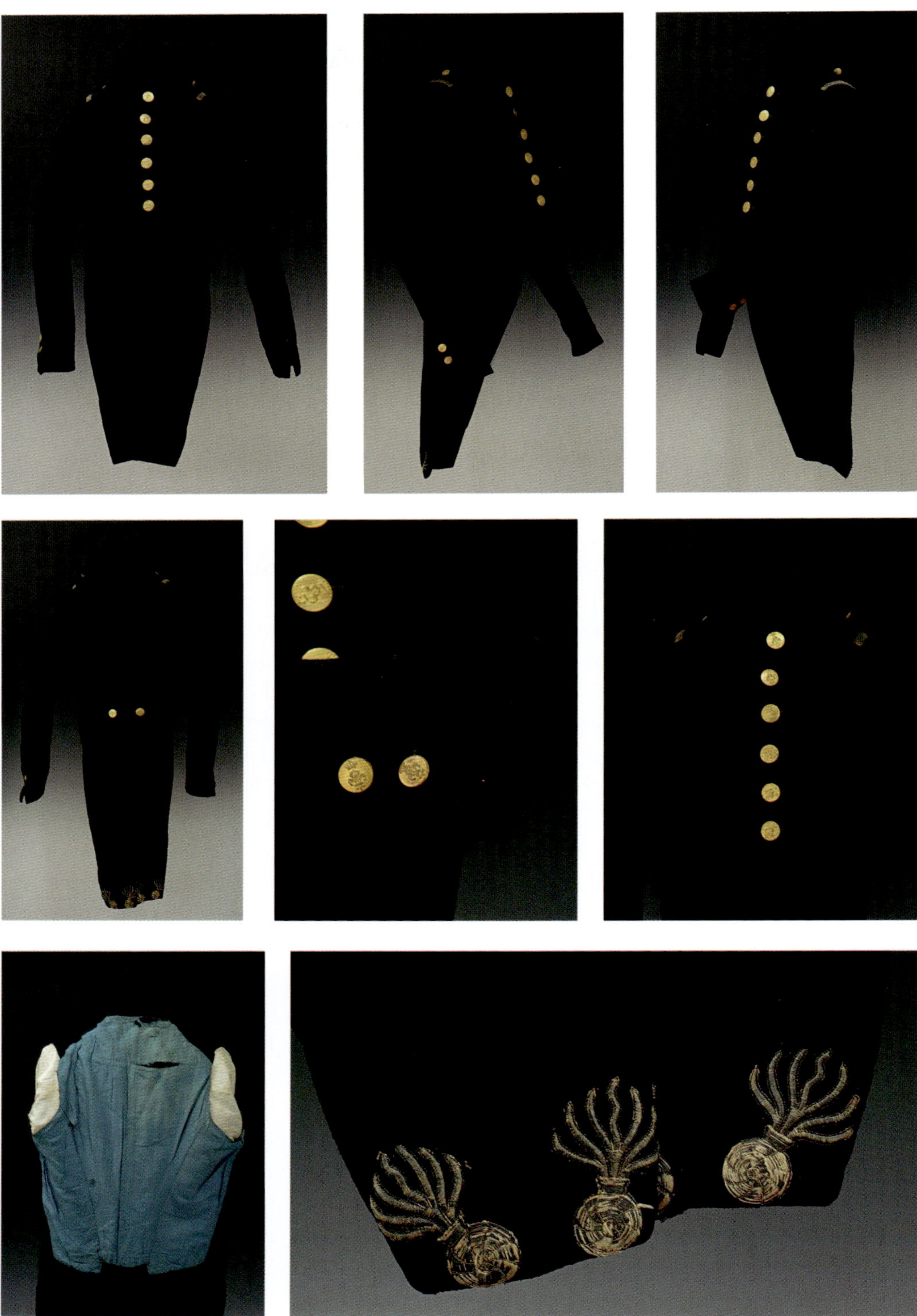

Rather than the *habit-veste*, on campaign and off duty, officers wore a sombre *surtout*, of which this is an outstanding example. (*Photograph and collection of Bertrand Malvaux*)

> due to the impossibility of acquiring white broadcloth to make the *gilets manches* and stable coats for both the cavalry and line infantry, His Excellency … has decided that for the year 1813, the conscripts' fatigue jackets for both the infantry and other corps assimilated to this branch of service would continue to be made from tricot; and that His Majesty shall have the explanations justifying the reasons why it was necessary to not follow the dispositions detailed within his Decree of 19th January.[12]

Thus, the *gilets manches*, like the *pantalons*, were now made from tricot and not broadcloth. This was just the first of many issues that would beset the production of clothing and uniforms.

Many officers were unhappy with the design of the new *habit*. Even after the signing of the decree, several senior officers continued to want to change the uniforms, as reported by the Minister of War to the Emperor on 23 September 1812:

> I have the honour to report to Your Majesty that the Comte de Cessac has sent me a new model of uniform for the infantry and submitted to me by the Chevalier de Saint-Hilaire, director-general of the Grande Armée's clothing.
>
> This model is different to the one sanctioned by the recent decree of 19th January for it has two double *revers* which cross one on top of the other. One lapel is in blue wool lined with canvas and the other is in white wool. The Chevalier Saint-Hilaire tells me that His Highness the Prince Major-General has given his approval for this new regimental jacket for it better protects the chest, thus protects the soldier from the wintery conditions of where the army is currently stationed, and avoids the disadvantages of badly sewn on hook and eyes.
>
> Comte de Cessac had this model examined by the clothing board, who were of the opinion that it shouldn't be adopted for the following reasons:
>
> 1° It is not within the dimensions and proportions prescribed by the Decree of January 19th;
> 2° it is more expensive;
> 3° The double *revers* joined together by a seam present no advantage and many disadvantages since they limit movement when they are crossed, create a type of pocket in the chest and are uncomfortable and awkward. Regardless of these reasons, I believe that it would be of a great inconvenience to continually change the uniform of the troops. I therefore don't recommend that Your Majesty approves Monsieur de Saint-Hilaire's model and I will inform H.H. the Prince Major-General likewise.[13]

We are dealing here with a *habit* that rather than fastening with hooks and eyes in the centre, the *revers* fastened across the *habit* – a *habit* made exactly like this exists in the Emperi collection for line lancers. We wonder how many were actually made.

Officers wore when on duty a *gorget* – in French *Hauscol* – the last vestigial remains of armour. (*Photograph and collection of Bertrand Malvaux*)

Yet the reality of the unfolding events in Russia brought about new demands on the production of clothing. The Emperor was faced with the realities of building a new army for the 1813 campaign.

To meet immediate manpower needs, a *senatus-consulte* was drawn up on 12 August 1812 with the aim of calling up 120,000 conscripts of the class of 1813. This was approved on 1 September 1812. A second *senatus-consulte* ordered another 17,000 men to be conscripted in order to make up the cohorts of National Guard. Both *senatus-consultes* were signed into law with a decree signed by the Emperor on 22 September and provided the army with 136,042 men. The majority of the conscripts of the 1813 levy had arrived at the *dépôt* in the last weeks of 1812 and the beginning of 1813; the best men were taken into the *Garde Imperiale* to fill out the ranks of the Young Guard.

These men all had to be clothed and equipped. Rather than equip these men in old-pattern clothing only to have to replace it in 1813, the War Ministry ordered that from 25 September 1812 all new clothing would be of the new pattern.[14] Rather than hoping that the master workmen would interpret the text correctly, each regiment was to receive from the War Ministry an example of each item of uniform for the master tailors of the regiment to copy, along with a written copy of the regulation.[15] We find sealed patterns, literally items '*de modèle*', in regimental stores.

Created in 1808, under Bardin the 2[e] and 3[e] *Porte-aigle* were issued:

> '**57. Distinctions of the Porte-Aigle.**
> The second and third *porte-aigle* will be distinguished by the colour of the pennant on the spontoon by their headdress, which will be a *carabinier* helmet and pennant; that of the second *porte-aigle* will be red; that of the 3[e] *porte-aigle* will be white; they will wear this and other distinctive marks, those of the sergeant major; there will also be placed four chevrons in gold or silver corresponding to the colour of the buttons, as for the service chevrons on each arm. Their will remain in usage the epaulettes of grenadiers garnished with scales. The remainder of the uniform is the same as the men.'

In addition, they carried a pair of pistols in a shoulder-mounted holster, which Bardin describes in great detail. Their sabre was carried off a black leather waistbelt that held in place the bottom of the pistol holster. In lieu of a musket they carried a spontoon. This helmet is presumably the second pattern, as in April 1813 Bardin ordered 'a helmet of particular form and by the colour of the *criniere*' on the helmet. By *criniere* we assume *chenille* is meant, we are unclear as to the chosen form of the helmet: many of these 'particular' helmets exists in museums, yet none have been recorded in any documentation from the epoch. (*Musee de l'Armée*)

The massive increase in demand resulted in dramatic shortages and in consequence caused prices to increase sharply. Since the summer of 1812 an entirely new army of over 300,000 men had to be raised, fed, trained, clothed and equipped. A monumental task.

On 14 October 1812, the war administration advised the Emperor:

> The decrees of 19 January 1812 and 7 February 1812 have brought about changes in the uniform of the troops. There now are large quantities of items from old uniform in some of the stores, especially those of Bayonne, Perpignan, Strasbourg, Wesel and Mainz, where I have been obliged to constantly keep up provisions in order to cover the needs of the armies in Spain and Germany, as well as the draft dodgers. Since

Vernet's plates accompanying the Bardin regulations show the initial concept of a *carabinier* helmet.

> the aforementioned decrees are to be put into effect from 1 January 1813, I have deemed it to be most appropriate for the good of the service, and for Your Majesty's interests, to supply these items to units that have battalions or squadrons on active service in Spain. I believe it is my duty to inform Your Majesty of this decision and I hope that I will have the honour of having your approbation.[16]

Therefore, one imagines that for a regiment with battalions in Spain, they received pre-Bardin clothing as a matter of course. For regiments that were solely deployed in Germany, they received Bardin clothing. Yet this plan was not easily put into action. Comte Daru, in charge of the army's intendance in Prussia, complained that:

One of the few depictions of an eagle guard is this image by Suhr, which shows the use of bearskins rather than helmets, and for an unknown reason, the *revers* of the *habits* match the band, who are not wearing Imperial Livery. What is shown is a hybrid of Bardin and earlier regulations.

[...] we are taking care of transporting the most important objects but the means at our disposal are far from being adequate for our needs. The siege artillery pieces and ammunition alone will tie the teams up for a long time before we can even hope to start moving the clothing, which is being issued whilst we have the opportunity to do so.[17]

Excellent example of a halberd carried by an eagle guard. (*Photograph and collection of Betrand Malvaux*)

Even issuing the stockpiled clothing, the army needed more clothing, so much so that by the end of 1812 or the beginning of 1813, the order is not clearly dated, Napoleon authorised regiments in great need of uniforms to issue the stockpile of 200 items authorised in July 1812 to be issued and ordered that reserves were to be replenished.[18] Yet it was clear that if the men were to be dressed by new year 1813 shortcuts would have to be made. In order to lessen the costs of clothing for the mass of new conscripts flooding into the army, the decree of 20 November 1812 for the clothing and equipment for the recently levied conscripts states that they were to be issued a *habit-veste*, *gilet manches*, *pantalons*, *capote*, *bonnet de police*, *and schako* and cover of the new model of 19 January 1812. Leather equipment was to be taken from the magazines of the Empire. The decree makes no mention of grenadier *aigrettes*, but makes provision for '*houpettes de grenadier*'. Again, no mention is made of epaulettes and instead grenadiers were

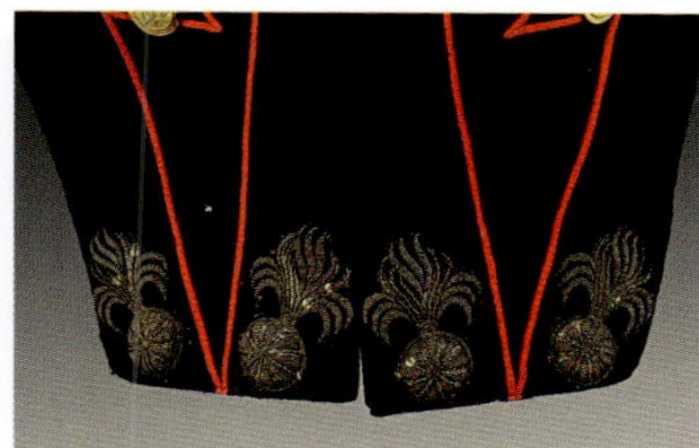
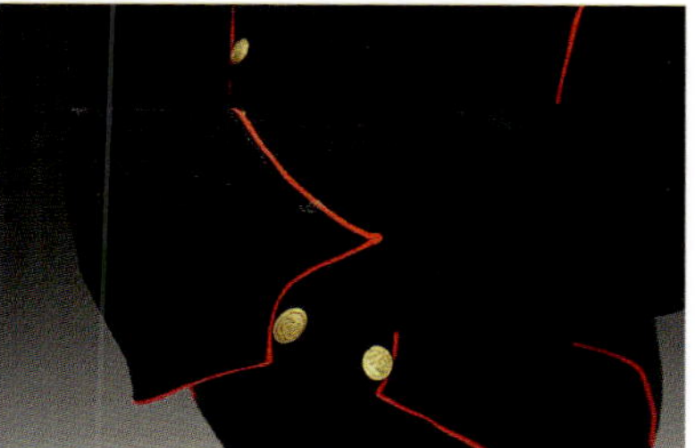

Enshrined with the Bardin regulation was the retention of regimental artillery. This *habit* is a superb and rare example of a regimental artillery officer's garment. (*Photograph and collection of Bertrand Malvaux*)

allowed red broadcloth shoulder straps and cut out grenades to the *habit*, and red collar and shoulder straps to the *gilet manches*. Nothing is said about sabres or *baudriers* for grenadiers. One can only assume as an economy measure they were discontinued, along with grenadier *schakos*. *Voltigeurs* were allowed chamois collar and shoulder straps to the *habit* and *gilet manches*.[19]

With this measure, combined with the distribution of the uniforms stockpiled in the general *dépôts*, a large part of the new army that would fight at Lützen and Bautzen was dressed in uniforms that followed both the old and new regulations.

Chapter 4

Change and Change Again

As the last men limped back from Russia, it was clear the Grande Armée was a spent force: a report dated 7 January for the 105e *de Ligne* merely notes that 'there is no one left'.[1] Needing a new army, Napoleon issued a *senatus-consulte* on 11 January 1813 calling for the recruitment of 350,000 additional men, of which 100,000 were to be drawn from the National Guard, 100,000 reservists from the classes of 1809, 1810, 1811 and 1812 and 150,000 from the class of 1814.

On 3 April 1813, Napoleon signed another *senatus-consulte* that called for a new levy of 180,000 men: which included the formation of the four regiments of Guards of Honour attached to the Imperial Guard, 90,000 conscripts from the class of 1814 and 80,000 reservists from the classes of 1807 to 1812. It is hard to imagine the huge efforts made by the staff of the Ministry of War to organise the conscript levies, to organise the formation of the new battalions, appoint thousands of new officers and to send the thousands of conscripts to all the different regimental *dépôts* across France and Germany: huge quantities of quills, paper and ink were used to draw up and dispatch orders. Slowly but surely the new Grande Armée was being raised.

As could be expected, acute shortages of materials were already having an impact on equipping the army. For example, on 9 February 1813, the adjutant of the 57e *de Ligne* recorded that he had authorised the production of 3,865 pairs of grey half gaiters and 3,544 pairs of black twill gaiters, but he added that due to 'the impossibility of obtaining grey linen, 3,110 pairs of gaiters and 3,653 pairs of *pantalons de route* had been made from white linen.' He added that due to a lack of linen, he had no option but to cut up underwear to line the linen and black twill gaiters of his regiment.[2]

A report, dated 18 February 1813, by the commander of the 12e Military District based at La Rochelle further illustrates the situation that regimental *dépôt* workshops found themselves in, and is no doubt representative of regimental *dépôts* throughout the Empire at this time:

> 26e *de Ligne*: Manufacture is progressing most actively.
>
> 82e *de Ligne*: The workshop has 40 military labourers and 15 civilian labourers. All available manpower has been more or less uniformed and equipped. The regiment is missing drums, which have been requested on several occasions from H.E. the minister.
>
> 132^{e} *de Ligne*: The workshop has 56 labourers, many of which are civilians. They are concentrating their efforts on the clothing but they will soon be inactive due to a lack of cloth.[3]

Martinets' impression of an officer wearing Bardin-regulation clothing.

The report concluded that due to lack of funds, materials and workmen, the process of clothing and equipping the army was almost at a total standstill. Clearly as the Emperor read these various reports, he no doubt characteristically flew into one of his habitual rages. We are sure that he made his feelings known to War Ministry, whose director responded in a letter dated 14 March 1813 to explain the causes for the delays in making and issuing clothing and equipment:

> [...] the lack of funds is paralysing, and continues to paralyse, the suppliers. Secondly, the dealings that the regiments have had with these same suppliers to dress the men sent from the departments. The result of these dealings has been that part of the resources that we were counting on to carry out my orders has now disappeared.[4]

Reading between the lines here, it seems that there were simply not enough raw materials to go round. Both regimental colonels and the War Administration were working against each other in obtaining materials: there was no cohesive planning. Both parties would approach the same supplier, and then bid against each other to get the required materials, increasing the price of the materials! Beyond reasonable doubt, the French state simply could not furnish sufficient cloth to dress the army, nor did it have the capacity to make the required numbers of uniforms. Unsuitable low-grade materials were pressed into use and even more corners had to be cut.

The 1813 Collation

By spring 1813, the French economy 'was on its knees': cloth and other materials were in short supply, and the desperate need to regenerate the army meant that the approach to clothing the army had been pragmatic. In an undated letter sent to the colonels of the 9^{e}, 35^{e}, 53^{e}, 84^{e}, 92^{e} and 106^{e} *de Ligne*, probably written in February or March 1813, the War Ministry stipulated that if there were not enough *habits* in the stores to equip the 1^{e} and 2^{e} battalions, the battalions were to be mobilised with *capotes*, *gilets manches*, *pantalons de route* and their equipment. The regiments were ordered to send *habits* and other items on to the men in June.[5] One wonders how many men were still in the ranks to receive their *habits*, if they ever did!

The greatest issue arose with the supply of leather equipment, as Comte de Cessac explained in a letter dated 12 April 1813:

> Perhaps more so than the high cost of the materials, it is the army's urgent need that has given the suppliers an excuse to demand a price increase to the general rates of 2 August 1812 for leather equipment. Being placed in a situation where one could either accept their demands or go without this most important element of military service, I thought it better consent to such their demands under such circumstances. I also managed to arrive at such a decision by convincing myself that having discussed the matter with the regiments, most of them were having the same

Martinet presents this sergeant in full dress. The plume was in theory abolished in 1810.

> problems with their own suppliers. I have therefore agreed that the regiments could, if it was impossible to do otherwise, agree prices that were ten per cent higher than those outlined within the general rates.[6]

At the end of his letter, Comte de Cessac mentions that this increase would only be applicable to *gibernes* and other leather accoutrements; while drums, trumpets and *cornets* were part of the same equipment category, they were not as vulnerable to price increases due to the lower quantities needed.[7]

To address the first point, Comte de Cessac wrote to line and light infantry colonels on 21 April 1813, to press into service old articles:

> Within many military stores, there are leather accoutrements that while not new are still considered to be in good condition. It is my intention to allow those infantry *dépôt*s that, by their geographic location or their distance from supply lines, are experiencing difficulties in providing new equipment to the conscripts of the last six levies to make use of them …[8]

About three weeks later, on 10 May 1813, the War Administration wrote to the commissary inspectors, sub-inspectors and the regiments of all branches of service to inform them that:

> You are aware that I am only responsible for supplying fabrics and that I have not been able to provide, nor am I responsible for providing, articles that the units are supposed to acquire for themselves. In any event, I have used all means at my disposal to aid those units most in need. I have therefore agreed to purchase a certain quantity of leather accoutrements, as well as *havresacs*, to be delivered to the stores in Paris in May and June […] Those units in need of such articles may send requests, validated by a Commissioner for War, to my attention … Regiments are to leave only the minimum number of articles in their stores to carry out their duties and replace them as and when it is possible to do so. I expect the strictest and promptest execution of these measures but, at the same time, I will also hold those responsible that by negligence compromise or disrupt military duties.[9]

Thus, regiments were authorised to empty out their store rooms of whatever clothing remained, so men would be clothed in brand-new Bardin clothing and a mix of old pattern items.

Even with the measures of making sure that whatever buff and leather equipment could be pressed into service, even if it had been in a *dépôt* for years, the army still demanded more than supply could meet. By spring 1813, the French state, like in the 1790s, was never going to be able to provide enough buff leather to meet the needs of the army. Thus, on 22 June 1813, Comte de Cessac wrote to the commissary inspectors, sub-inspectors and regimental colonels:

Fourrier in full dress wearing an approximation of Bardin regulation. The plume, knee-length black gaiters and breeches were all abolished, but archive documents show this hybrid appearance was incredibly common until the last days of the Empire.

The Regiments' Administrative Councils are to let me know on a daily basis the difficulties that they are experiencing to get hold of leather accoutrements destined to equip their conscripts. These difficulties are notably problematic in southern France and Italy. After taking into account the different reports detailing why such difficulties were persevering, I have come to the conclusion that they are due only to the scarcity of buff leather, that was already being felt last year, as a consequence of the high demand of this product over the last two years. Since buff leather can be replaced by black cowhide to manufacture cartridge boxes, musket slings, cartridge box belts and drum belts, I have sanctioned, with the agreement of the Minister of War, the following:

1° The light infantry regiments, *chasseurs à cheval*, hussars, artillery train battalions, engineer and equipment train, irregular troops, veteran battalions, coast-guards and national guards that, as a result of my decision, are to buy leather accoutrements are permitted to use black cowhide in lieu of buff leather;
2° Line infantry regiments, *carabiniers*, *cuirassiers*, *dragons*, *chevaux-légers*, foot and horse artillery are exempted from the above decision and will continue to use buff leather;
3° The prices allocated to these objects are as follows:

Cartridge box belt in black cowhide	3fr 25 cents.
Musket sling in black cowhide	0fr 70 cents.
Leather belt in black cowhide	3fr 50 cents.
Drum belt in black cowhide	3fr 50 cents.

4° The ten per cent increase, granted on the general tariffs for leather goods, is not applicable to articles in black cowhide;
5° The lifespan of black cowhide articles is set for six years;
6° Those units permitted to use cowhide in lieu of buff leather will, as much as possible, not distribute these articles to the men in the *dépôt*s and the battalions serving inside imperial borders.

His Excellency the Minister of War and me believe that these arrangements will allow greater latitude for the different units to acquire, in a timely manner, all the leather equipment they are lacking. On the one hand, the permission given to light infantry regiments, irregular troops and other units designated by article 1 to use black cowhide will increase the buff leather available for the line infantry and other troops described in article 2 and, on the other hand, it will allow the units designated in article 1 to have access to more abundant material sources. Should the units authorised to use black cowhide in lieu of buff leather find themselves unable to get hold of articles in black cowhide, they are to acquire the necessary materials and direct their regimental workmen to make cartridge boxes and belts.[10]

A fusilier of the 100e *de Ligne*. The sun ray plate is unexpected.

The cost of the new black leather work was fixed with a ministerial decision of 12 August 1813, and was now extended to cover the line infantry.[11]

We note that the War Ministry had decreed that no old-pattern clothing was to be issued after 8 June 1813, assuming any remained to be issued.[12] Issuing old uniforms was logical and sensible, but perhaps the War Ministry overlooked an inherent weakness in this plan. It assumed the transport existed to transport the clothing and equipment to where it was needed; it assumed that the regulation stockpile had been generated in 1812 as ordered; and moreover assumed that sufficient equipment and clothing existed. On 2 July, Marshal Oudinot informed the War Ministry that his corps needed muskets, and added most grenadiers had no sabres, and lacked shoes and uniforms. In the 131[e] *de Ligne*, he noted that the regiment had no campaign equipment, and instead used earthenware bowls commandeered locally. He had 1,561 men sick in hospital due to scabies: uniforms taken from stores were contaminated with lice, and were already worn out by the time they were issued, Oudinot noted. Due to chronic shortages. items had been taken from men who had been hospitalised due to illness and put into store: the uniforms were not fit for purpose and lice ridden. Furthermore, Oudinot noted that for immediate needs, the 32e *Légère* needed 330 complete uniforms, the 36e *Légère* needed 247 *habits*, 300 *gilets manches*, 301 pairs of *pantalons*, 19 *capotes* and 900 pairs of shoes. The 131e *de Ligne* needed 270 *habits* and new *schako* plates, the 132e needed 300 *habits*, 933 *gilets manches*, 969 *capotes*, 939 pairs of *culottes*, 630 *schakos*, and 271 sabres; the 133[e] *Ligne* had not yet been issued an eagle, as well as needing 15 *habits*, 75 *gilets manches*, 120 pairs of *culottes* and 20 *capotes*. The War Ministry replied that if the men had a *gilet* and *capote*, a *habit* was not essential, nor *culottes* if they had *pantalons de route*.[13]

Despite the impossibility of being able to clothe, equip, arm and above all else feed, the men already under arms, on 27 September 1813, Napoleon signed a *senatus-consulte* calling up 280,000 conscripts: 160,000 from the 1815 class and 120,000 reservists from the 1805 to 1814 classes. On 15 November 1813, another *senatus-consulte* levied another 300,000 men from the classes between 1802 and 1803 to 1814. Half would be called up immediately, while the rest would be held in reserve and would only be called out in the event of an enemy invasion of the eastern borders. The decree of 20 November 1813 increased the levy to 160,000 men. How these men were to be clothed is anyone's guess.

Because of the ongoing shortages of buff leather, from 17 November 1813, black leather work was to be used universally by the conscripts of the class of 1814 called up under the 15 and 20 November Levy.[14] On 25 November 1813, Napoleon signed a decree allowing black cowhide to be used for the conscripts called up by the *senatus-consulte* who were to serve in the Midi and Italian reserve corps.[15]

On 5 December 1813 the War Ministry decreed that due to shortages of beige broadcloth, beige tricot was allowed to be used along with *blanc picque de bleu* broadcloth, which was traditionally used for cavalry cloaks, for infantry *capotes*.[16] At the end of the year, the War Ministry ordered that men were to be mobilised as long as a soldier had two good pair of shoes, a pair of gaiters, *pantalons de route* made from strong linen, a *gilet manches*, a *capote*, a *schako* with cover, a *bonnet de police*, and leather equipment.[17] The last

Grenadier wearing full dress. Again, it is an approximation of the Bardin regulation as he has a fusilier's *schako*: we know from archive documents that this is the most common appearance of a grenadier, as very few grenadier *schakos* were ever made.

Fusilier wearing Bardin regulation, but we notice the cuff has no flap, perhaps a regimental tradition?

major change to the dress of the *ligne* came on 8 January 1814 when the War Ministry allowed that *capotes* were to be made from green, chestnut brown, white, grey and blue broadcloth and tricot.[18]

The 1814 Collation

By spring 1814, after three campaigns, the army was exhausted. Bardin regulation had evolved, with many aspects not being implemented due to lack of time and lack of funds. The most visible impact of the changes to Bardin were the black cross belts, nut brown *capotes* rather than grey, and tricot *gilets manches*! Time and lack of funds, as well as the hugely displaced deployment of the army meant Bardin was not in universal use, nor was every regulation fully implemented by the time the Emperor rode away from Fontainebleau. The King was back on his throne and the *fleur-de-lys* was once more the symbol of France. One of the first acts of the restored monarchy was a 'major rebranding' exercise for the army. White cockades were formally brought into use with the decree of 17 April 1814.[19]

The War Ministry *circulaire* of 22 April 1814 stated that the decree of 19 January and 7 February 1812 for the dress of the army was to be enforced rigorously. Any clothing not made to these regulations was to be removed from use. To assess the clothing needs for the army, every regiment was given a shake-down inspection that summer. The War Ministry, as part of the 'rebranding' exercise, made the following amendments to the Bardin regulations, the fifth such major change:

> On the retroussis of the *habits* the crowned N will be removed and replaced by a *fleur-de-lys*, 70mm tall (2 pouces ½ or thereabouts) and of proportionate width.
>
> The crowned N will be removed from the *schako* plates
>
> The crowned N will be removed from the *gibernes*
>
> The crowned N will be removed from sabretaches
>
> The crowned N will be removed from the buttons of the gendarme
>
> The drummers, trumpeters and musicians will abandon the colour green and will use *bleu de Roi* in its place for *habits* and will use the Livery of the Royal Household.
>
> All other aspects will be in strict conformity to the two decrees.[20]

At the same time, a second circular from the War Ministry ordered that all the codicils that made up the Bardin collation of orders generated from January 1812 through to June 1813 were to be deleted:

1. Black leather work was to be replaced with whitened buff
2. *Pokalems* were undress headgear
3. All *gilets* were to be made from broadcloth

4. Grenadiers had scarlet epaulettes, *aigrettes* and elite company *schakos*. Bearskins were abolished for all but *sapeurs*
5. Voltigeurs were allowed yellow *aigrettes* and yellow epaulettes were tolerated
6. All capotes were to be beige
7. All pre-Bardin clothing to be taken out of service

In essence, all non-standard clothing and equipment was to be replaced. This was the first time that the War Ministry had the chance to impose the Bardin regulation on the armed forces, and vast sums of money were allocated to the task of remaking the Imperial Army in the Royalist mould.

In order to ensure uniformity across the army, the War Ministry, rather than relying on *circulaires*, drew up a detailed set of new regulations for the army. Thus, the 1814 collation of orders was codified into dress regulations of 8 February 1815, or the sixth variance on Bardin.

The regulations were framed on the Bardin regulation of 1812. It was the first time that the army had had a chance to be totally re-equipped with new-pattern clothing and equipment, although some regiments clung on to the old-style habits, and other idiosyncrasies. A huge reclothing programme began in spring 1815. These thousands of uniforms were all delivered to the reactivated Napoleonic state. For the line infantry the dress regulations of 8 February decreed that the clothing and equipment was to be:[21]

Linen for lining 104cm wide	1fr 40
Linen for *pantalons* and *caleçons*, 89cm wide	1fr 65
Large buttons	40 centimes a dozen
Small buttons	24 centimes a dozen
Labour costs:	
Habit	2fr 45
Drummer's *habit*	8fr 52
Gilet manches	1fr 15
Pantalons	1fr
Capote	1fr 50
Bonnet de police	60 centimes
Caleçon	40 centimes
Lace:	
Gold for *sous-officier*	8fr 50
In yellow wool for corporals	55 centimes
In red wool for chevrons	55 centimes
Silver for drum major and musicians	5fr 60
Livery for drummers No. 1	90 centimes
Livery for drummers No. 2	90 centimes

Epaulettes	
Scarlet wool for grenadiers	3fr 40
For adjutants	25fr
Aigrettes:	
Scarlet for grenadiers	3fr 50
Yellow for *voltigeurs*	2fr 50
Houpettes for fusiliers	60 centimes
Hooks and eyes	10 centimes
Braces for *pantalons*	60 centimes
Schakos with no neck cover for grenadiers, cavalry model, garnished with scarlet wool lace of *Cul de De* type 22mm wide and 40mm wide, plate bearing Arms of France and regimental number, and chinscales	10fr 40
Schako without neck covers for fusiliers and *voltigeurs* with plate and chinscales	8fr 60
Schako plates of the new model	55 centimes
Chinscales	75 centimes
Chinscale bosses	25 centimes

For equipment the regulations stated:[22]

Giberne for *sous-officier* with no plate
Giberne for soldier
Entwined LL cypher with crown for *giberne* of fusiliers
Grenade plate for grenadiers
Hunting horn plate for *voltigeurs*
Porte-giberne with no bayonet frog for *sous-officier*
Porte-giberne with bayonet frog for grenadiers, *voltigeurs* and fusiliers
Musket sling
Baudrier, 62mm wide for *sous-officier*
Drum, drum sling, drummers' apron in sheep hide or lacquered buff.
Sapeur's axe, axe case, gauntlets, apron
Horn for *voltigeurs*

Petty equipment was to comprise:

Pair of shoes	5fr
Shirt	4fr 75
Half gaiters in black twill with flat copper buttons	3fr 15 a pair
Half gaiters in grey linen	1fr 85
A pair of ankle socks in wool or cotton	90 centimes

Black stock	40 centimes
Pantalons du toile after the regulation of 19 January 1812	3fr 16
Sac à distribution	3fr 70
Havresac	8fr 30
Cockade	15 centimes
Musket worm	30 centimes
Epinglette	10 centimes

This document is very informative. It is clear that only grenadiers in 1815 had the taller cavalry-style *schako* with red lace. *Voltigeurs* wore the same *schako* as fusiliers, but were allowed a yellow horse hair *aigrette*. Only grenadiers were allowed fringed epaulettes, while *voltigeurs* had shoulder straps like the fusiliers. It was now in spring 1815 that Bardin's ambitious plans as laid out in January and February 1812 were taken off the drawing board and put into production en mass to reclothe the army. Imperial Livery was substituted for Royalist, and the entwined double L cypher of Louis replaced the eagle, while the *fleur-de-lys* replaced the grenade and N cyphers. The return of the exiled Emperor derailed these plans.

The 100 Days' Collations

In new year 1815 Napoleon returned to Paris. He inherited an army that had been largely reclothed and organised over the previous nine months. The army had been mobilised over the Saxon Crisis of new year 1815. As Napoleon took back up the reins of power, men were flooding back to the army from leave, which they had been on since the previous summer. Realising he had to face a war on several fronts, Napoleon began preparations to massively expand the small peacetime army of the Bourbons.

The army Napoleon inherited was decked out in new Royalist uniforms and symbols. It was to be restyled in the Imperial image. At the start of the 100 Days, yet another collation of dress regulations appeared. According to the decree of 28 March 1815, the two decrees of 19 January and 7 February 1812 were to be reinstated: drummers and trumpeters were to wear green with Imperial Livery, the Royal Cypher and *fleur-de-lys* were abolished in favour of the crowned 'N'.[23] Under the Bourbon regime, 6,550,224fr worth of clothing had been made and issued but largely not paid for. Of this massive debt, Marshal Davout agreed to pay 4.7 million fr to manufacturers and suppliers.[24] Due to a lack of funds, the Emperor was forced to raise 30 million fr in credit alone for the service of clothing, and the Administration of War estimated that it would be necessary to increase it to 51 million fr in the course of the year.[25] Work was pursued actively in the regimental *dépôts* by the regimental tailors, using what stocks of cloth could be purchased locally.[26] However, due to non-payment of bills for clothing produced in 1813 and 1814, the contractors demanded that their debts be paid before they would start work on new government contracts.

Martinet gives us front and back views of the new-regulation clothing, adopted from winter 1812 onwards.

Napoleon had inherited an army dressed in almost brand-new clothing, and massive debts. The total cost of clothing the army to date stood in May 1815 at an estimated at 30 million fr with a further 21 million fr needed to clothe the new entrants to the army in the course of the year. In order to produce uniforms, Davout centralised manufacturing in the Paris region. With soldiers on hand to oversee operations, it was hoped that the cobblers would manufacture 1,800 pairs of shoes per day. However, they required to be paid in cash before starting work, for which the money was released totalling 13 million fr for the production of clothing and equipment. The workshops were in theory able to supply 1,250 *habits* per day.[27] Work was pursued actively in the regimental dépôts by the regimental tailors, using what stocks of cloth that could be purchased locally or was already to hand.[28] However, due to non-payment of bills for clothing produced in 1813 and 1814, cloth suppliers and tailoring companies demanded that their debts be paid before they would start work on new government contracts. The accumulated debt owed was around 14 million fr. The bills were submitted at the start of the 100 Days and were simply ignored by Napoleon: this was an issue for the old government and not his, he argued. Yet, without clearing the debts, production of clothing could not begin. In order to begin production and restore credit, Davout proposed an advance of 4,728,782fr to be made to manufacturers and suppliers.[29] Also in short supply were serviceable saddles and harness, which were of vital importance if the cavalry was to field as many horses, and therefore troopers, as possible.[30]

Napoléon budgeted to grant 13 million fr for the production of uniforms, shoes and saddles: yet when the government came to raise the credit in the form of loans from the Bank of France, it succeeded in only unlocking 2 million fr.[31] This left a debt of 4million fr and more money was needed to buy additional uniforms and equipment. The amount of credit available to the French state had collapsed in the autumn of 1813, and it had had serious implications. Due to the lack of credit the army could not purchase sufficient numbers of horses for the cavalry and artillery trains, neither could it clothe, equip, feed and pay the army. The non-payment of debts and lack of credit would frustrate Napoléon's ambitions in 1815.[32]

Another issue, just as it had been since 1812, was the supply of cloth. Comte Daru, in charge of the army's intendance, once more noted that:

> There is concern that there is insufficient blue cloth to clothe the army. It is proposed to increase its production, which requires considerable time. Could we not, until the necessary blue cloth has been produced, clothe the soldiers with a good *capote*, *pantalons de route, gilet* and gaiters? In the last campaign, the majority of Allied troops were dressed that way.[33]

Many hundreds of men marched to Waterloo and other campaign theatres dressed in this manner. When we look at inspection returns, we find that in addition to beige *capotes*, we find them made from white, *blanc picque de bleu*, grey tricot and a wide array of colours out of necessity. Furthermore, through a circular issued by the office of clothing in the

Grenadier wearing a greatcoat. The Bardin issue was double-breasted, but thousands of the earlier single-breasted design were in use until the end of the Empire in 1815.

Ministry of War, Davout made known to all sectors of government, civil and military, that the Emperor accepted the prices set by manufacturers, even though they were often 10 to 15 per cent higher than the War Ministry allowed. Through pressure from the ministry, manufacturers were forced, albeit reluctantly, to provide all the equipment, clothing and materials the army required. Davout knew they would only be paid when state finances permitted it, and that if the war was lost, then the debts would go unpaid.[34] The manufacturers were no doubt painfully aware of this situation, hence their reluctance to work for the War Ministry.

The manufacture of shoes and boots was of paramount importance. Davout estimated that four pairs per soldier were necessary for the duration of a campaign. To get close to this figure, it was necessary to establish in Paris a reserve of 100,000 to 150,000 pairs of shoes, which were to be sent directly to the army corps that remained on the border. However, to make such a reserve, Davout required 750,000fr. Due to the chronic lack of credit available to the regime, only 100,000 pairs of shoes could be ordered, the manufacture of which could not begin until the middle weeks of May, for delivery in July. As the economy geared back up to a war footing, the huge unpaid debts incurred when Napoleon returned to power hamstrung Davout's efforts. Very quickly, problems arose. The manufacturers of Paris refused to begin work without an advance of 3.7million fr payable within twenty days so that they would be paid for the work as opposed to being issued promissory notes. These promissory notes had been the traditional Napoléonic *methode* of payment and, being realists, the manufacturers realised if the new government fell, the promissory notes were worthless. To resolve this issue Daru convened a meeting on 18 April 1815 between the manufacturers and the government. Due to Daru's superhuman efforts, a majority of the manufacturers agreed to work with the Imperial Government. But the suppliers required prompt payment.[35]

Davout and Comte Daru estimated that the reserves of shoes and clothing would only be completed by the first weeks of July 1815. In bringing forward the date for the start of the hostilities, not all regiments had yet received their uniforms before marching to Belgium on 10 June 1815, nor had all regiments been equipped with their camp effects.[36]

As well as clothes, the army needed munitions. On 1 April 150,000 muskets were in stores to be issued and a further 300,000 needed repairs. Of the muskets that needed to be repaired, by 10 June almost 150,000 had been fixed and were being distributed to the army, of which some 80,000 were destined for the National Guard. The result of this effort was that by the end of June the remaining 68,000 muskets needing to be repaired had been, and a further 20,000 new muskets were available to be issued and were hastily issued to troops in Paris for the defence of the city. Davout estimated that by 1 August 1815 a reserve of 150,000 muskets would be created. Yet, in reality, despite the acceleration in the production of firearms, the increase in production could not cope with the increased flow of men into the army, particularly between mid-May and mid-June. This resulted in a huge shortage of muskets and this only improved after 10 June. By 1 May, there were about 60 million cartridges for the infantry in stock, while there was

Grenadiers in barrack dress wearing *pokalem*, *gilet manches* – the red collar and cuff tell us these are grenadiers, before November 1812 – and *pantalons de route*.

A corporal teaching the marching pace. Oddly the men's undress jackets – *gilets manches* – are shown as blue.

about 1.4 million kg of powder for the production of another 55 million new cartridges.[37] As Napoléon's last army marched to war, it lacked clothing, muskets and cartridges. A report of 21 May 1815 tells us 1e Corps had 1,794 men in *dépôts*, of which 686 were not clothed; 2e Corps had 4,972 men in *dépôts*, but a staggering 3,741 were not clothed, and 6e Corps had 1,265 men in the *dépôts*, but 548 were not equipped. This meant that the army at Waterloo could have been reinforced by 5,520 men, but they were not clothed, equipped or in some cases armed. Out of a total of 8,623 reserves, a staggering 64 per cent lacked clothing, equipment and arms.[38] One can only imagine what an extra 5,000 or more men could have contributed to the outcome of the battle.

As in 1813, the army by April 1815 had run out of supplies of buff leather for equipment. A supplementary regulation was issued on 1 April 1815. The tariff removed from the *voltigeurs* and grenadiers the sabre and belt, and allowed for the *porte-giberne* and musket sling to be made from blackened cow hide. Whitened cow hide could be used for the manufacture of *havresacs*. Remarkably, rather than regimental buttons, all buttons were to be the model of the Imperial Guard.[39] Standardising all buttons to a single model made a lot of sense logistically! This left regimental allocation purely down to the *schako* plate.

A second decree was issued on 17 June – largely repeating that of April – to speed up the process of supplying the army and to make the process cheaper. The infantry, *légère* and foot artillery were allowed a capote, *habit-veste*, *pantalons de route*, *schako*, *giberne* with belt made from blackened cow hide, and blackened cow hide musket sling. A major change with the decree was that the *gilet manches* was officially done away with, and the artillery were authorised beige *capotes* to save blue broadcloth for uniform *habits*. As in April, no chamois broadcloth was allowed for *voltigeurs* and no epaulettes for grenadiers: every man in the infantry and *légère* wore the same *habit-veste*! Grenadiers were forbidden to carry sabres, and the *sous-officiers* were allowed blackened cow hide *baudriers* costing 3fr 50 each. It repeated that all buttons were to be '*modèle de la Garde Imperiale*'. Drummers were allocated 248m of Imperial Livery, costing 216fr, and tellingly not an inch of green broadcloth.[40] As in April, here is official sanction of drummers wearing standard infantry *habits* adorned with Imperial Livery, as no special allowance was made for a different drummer's *habit*.

Just as in 1813, blackened cross belts became regulation once more, no distinctions for elite companies were allowed, and the official abandonment of *gilets manche*s witnessed the final and eighth iteration of Bardin. This the army at Waterloo wore a medley of uniforms. With the hasty re-numbering of regiments, and transfer of men from one unit to another, as well as the mass use of eagle buttons, the use of metal detector finds from Waterloo to say what regiment was where on the field, is largely impossible.

Chapter 5
The Reality

Having reviewed the various evolutions of official dress regulations, we need to assess how these were applied to the army. To do so, we have embarked on a unique and ground-breaking study to obtain copies of the regimental paper for every regiment in the French Army from 1811 to 1815. From this, we have extracted details from inspection returns and regimental accounts to be able to say exactly what a regiment really wore, and how that related to the official utterances from the War Ministry. Due to word count constraints, the 134e to 156e regiments are described in our companion volume with the *légère* regiments.

1e *de Ligne*

Inspected on 27 September 1814. That day the regiment had 145 officers and 813 other ranks. At the end of the campaign of France the clothing was in terrible condition. For example, 428 *habits* needed total replacement as they were of the previous pattern, 116 men had no *habit*, and 66 *habits* needed repairs with just 211 in service that were considered in good condition. Furthermore, without replacing the worn-out clothing, the regiment needed to equip every man under arms with a total of 285 *vestes*, 244 pairs of *pantalons de tricot*, 714 pairs of linen *caleçons*, 198 *capotes*, 149 *schakos* and 356 *bonnets*

Officers' *schako* plate of the 1^e^ *de Ligne*. (*Photograph and collection of Bertrand Malvaux*)

de police. Equipment wise, 178 *gibernes* were needed, 148 *porte-gibernes*, 97 *baudriers*, and 265 musket slings. When we look at *petit equipment* we find that 400 pairs of black gaiters existed and 309 of grey ones: simply not enough to give each man a pair of each: as long as you had a pair of gaiters one suspects no one cared what colour they were. Some 322 pairs of *pantalons de route* were in use: again, as long as a soldier had legwear, no one really complained a great deal. We note just 433 black stocks were in use, and the bulk of the men used improvised stocks. Some 560 *sacs de peau* were in use, so we ask how half the regiment carried their belongings! Despite shortages, *dépôt* held 333 brand-new *gilets manches* – more than sufficient to make up for the shortfall! – 260 pairs of *caleçons,* 198 *capotes*, 20 *habits*, 281 *gibernes*, and 493 *porte-gibernes*. No epaulettes, no *aigrettes* or drummers' lace existed.[1]

As the senior regiment of line infantry in the French Army, the Royalist authorities were very keen to make sure the *Régiment du Roi*, the former 1e *de Ligne*, was reclothed as quickly as possible. Between 1 May and 22 August 1814 huge quantities of new items of clothing were ordered and distributed to the regiment:[2]

Habits: 898 made new, of which 718 were for fusiliers, the remainder for *voltigeur*s. In addition, 481 were repaired.
Gilets manches: 1,511 made new, 112 repaired
Pantalons: 1,673 made new, 79 repaired
Caleçons: 948 made new, 17 repaired
Capotes: 1,401 made new, 155 repaired
Schakos: 890 made new, of which 340 for grenadiers.
Bonnets de police: 1,601 made new, 39 repaired
Gibernes: 516 made new, 132 repaired
Porte-gibernes: 516 made new
Baudriers: 404 made new, 29 repaired
Drum carriages: 2 repaired
Drums: 5 repaired
Musket slings: 920 made new, 58 repaired
Sapeurs' axes: 13 made new
Sapeurs' aprons: 7 made new
Sapeurs' gauntlets: 7 made new
Grenadier *aigrettes*: 400 made new
Voltigeur aigrettes: 400 made new
Houpettes for fusiliers: 980 made new
Drummers' aprons: 30 made new
Grenadier epaulettes: 375 pairs made new
White cockades: 2,670 made new
Sapeurs' bearskins: 6 made new
Fleur-des-lys embroidered in silver: 1,600 made new

Fusiliers in undress wearing an order of dress in a form shown that only existed in the theoretical state of the Bardin regulation but never made it to reality beyond a few examples of the *pokalem* and first-model *gilet manches* being made.

The regiment had, it seems, six *sapeurs*, as their equipment was made new in summer 1814. Of comment, only grenadier and fusilier *schakos* were listed, so *voltigeurs* did not have their own pattern. No archive documents exist for the dress of the regiment in 1815, but we assume given the clothing of the regiment was nearly entirely new in 1814, that was worn in 1815.

2e *de Ligne*

Inspected on 23 August 1814, the regiment's clothing was in shocking condition:[3]

Item	In Good Repair	In Need of Repair	Need Replacing	Items due to be replaced	Items missing
Habits	97	167	178	104	285
Vestes	95	66	90	126	454
Pantalons de tricot	147	51	151	96	386
Caleçons	12	1	13	1	804
Capotes	150	56	108	99	418
Schakos	261	62	98	115	295
Bonnets de police	155	40	21	82	533

The inspector remarked that in order to clothe the men with serviceable uniforms, the regimental *dépôt* had been emptied, adding that a goodly proportion of the *habits* were not made according to the regulation of 19 January 1812.[4]

Cloth in the *dépôt* included 11m 95 white broadcloth, 5m 88 scarlet broadcloth, 0m 94 chamois broadcloth, and 367m 23 white milled serge. Purchased between 1 May 1814 and 23 August 1814 was 70m 20 white broadcloth, 40m 80 scarlet broadcloth, 6m 75 crimson broadcloth for drummers, 4m 80 chamois broadcloth, 254m 30 white serge, 4m 80 white tricot and 464m of drummers' lace, of which 440m 80 was used to make new drummers' *habits*. In the same time period 135 *capotes* were made and issued, 584 fusilier *habits*, 608 *gilets manches*, 844 pairs of *pantalons de tricot*, 132 *bonnets de police*, 613 fusilier *schakos*, 1520 *schako* covers, 286 *gibernes* and belts, 750 musket slings, 463 red plumes, 350 yellow plumes, 360 pairs of *voltigeur* epaulettes, and 410 pairs of grenadier epaulettes.[5]

Partial regimental accounts for the regiment add some details about how it was reclothed. We note that 212 *fleur-de-lys* badges for *gibernes* costing 212fr were purchased in the third quarter of 1814, and that 3,057fr was raised from the sale of band instruments on 13 October 1814.[6] The troublesome 'N' device from the *habit* tails was replaced, with a *fleur-de-lys* cut from blue broadcloth ordered to be issued. At the same time, for the *voltigeur*s on 22 August 1814, 350 feather plumes and 360 pairs of epaulettes were purchased, along with 463 grenadier plumes, and 410 pairs of grenadier epaulettes.[7] The accounts also show the purchase of materials from 23 August 1814 to 22 April 1815:[8]

70m worsted fringing at 1fr a metre, total 70fr
80m lace for *fifres* at 70 centimes a metre, total 56fr
354m white wool lace at 45 centimes a metre, total 159fr 30
740 plume covers costing 40 centimes each, total 370fr
380 pairs epaulettes for *voltigeurs* at 3fr a pair, total 1,140fr
17 bearskins for *sapeurs*, at 40fr each, total 680fr
Total: 2,475fr 30

200 *schako* covers at 15 centimes each, total 30fr
950m red wool lace at 10 centimes a metre
571m red wool lace at 45 centimes a metre
149 dozen cockades at 70 centimes each, total 104fr 30
1,796 *houpettes de fusilier* at 40 centimes each, total 718fr 40
17 *sapeurs'* aprons, total 176fr 80
17 pairs of gauntlets, total 16fr 15
17 axe cases, total 212fr 50
17 axes, total 68fr
36 drummers' aprons, total 14fr 40
Total: 1,692fr 50

Purchases in 1815 included:[9]

800 musket worms, total 320fr
[illegible] Cockades, total 123fr 55
150 *baudriers* costing 4fr 65 each and 1,472 white cockades at 15 centimes each. Total 918fr 30
560 *houpettes de fusilier* total 168fr
28 pairs of *voltigeur* epaulettes, total 84fr
30 *houpettes de grenadier*, total 27fr
20m of lace for *fifres* at 70 centimes a metre, total 14fr
[illegible] beige broadcloth and white tricot, total 16,363fr 15
40m 45 drummers' lace at 90 centimes a metre, total 36fr 85
150 *baudriers*, total 697fr 50
508 *schakos* costing 8fr 60 each, total 4,368fr 80
102 *schakos* plates costing 55 centimes each, total 56fr 10

So, the drummers had, we assume, Royalist Livery, *fifres* had their own pattern lace strictly against regulation about which we know nothing. Likewise, in direct contradiction of Bardin 1812 and the 1815 regulations, plumes were worn and not *aigrettes*, and *voltigeurs* wore fringed epaulettes. Accounts also list the purchase of 1,400 polishing sticks for *gibernes*![10] We wonder if the wearing of *voltigeur* epaulettes was an innovation of 1814 or a continuation of practice from say 1806? The table below shows broadcloth use in the period May to December 1814:[11]

Fusilier in full dress by Vernet.

<table>
<tr><th></th><th>Blue</th><th>White</th><th>Scarlet</th><th>Chamois</th><th>Crimson</th><th>Beige</th><th>Green</th><th>White serge</th><th>Drummers' lace</th><th>Crimson serge</th></tr>
<tr><td>In store 21 May 1814</td><td></td><td>1m
95</td><td>5m
88</td><td>0m
94</td><td></td><td></td><td rowspan="4">None</td><td>367m
23</td><td></td><td></td></tr>
<tr><td>Purchased since 1 August</td><td></td><td>70m
25</td><td>40m
80</td><td>4m
80</td><td>6m
75</td><td></td><td>254m
30</td><td>464m</td><td></td></tr>
<tr><td>Used up to 23 August 1814</td><td></td><td>72m
20</td><td>46m
68</td><td>5m
74</td><td>6m
75</td><td></td><td>464m
61</td><td>440m
80</td><td></td></tr>
<tr><td>Purchased since 23 August 1814</td><td>951m
64</td><td>231m
12</td><td>141m
94</td><td>nil</td><td>nil</td><td>2,448m</td><td>1,275m
53</td><td>730m</td><td>4m
80</td></tr>
</table>

Crimson – presumably used by drummers and *fifres*? The *dépôt* held 584 *habits* of the old model to be disposed, and 135 *capotes*, again old model. The drummers' livery was clearly Royalist pattern lace. We wonder what happened to any drummers' lace that may have existed pre-May 1814. The amount and type of cloth used in the 100 Days is tabulated below:[12]

<table>
<tr><th></th><th>Blue</th><th>White</th><th>Scarlet</th><th>Chamois</th><th>Crimson</th><th>Beige</th><th>Blanc Picque de Bleu</th><th>Green</th><th>White serge</th><th>Crimson serge</th></tr>
<tr><td>In Magazine 1 January 1815</td><td>Nil</td><td>3m</td><td>nil</td><td>nil</td><td>7m</td><td></td><td></td><td></td><td>312m
12</td><td rowspan="5">None</td></tr>
<tr><td>Purchased 1 January 1815 to 26 September 1815</td><td>2,315m
39</td><td>481m
50</td><td>213m
49</td><td>6m
75</td><td></td><td>3,703m
65</td><td>243m
70</td><td>18m
40</td><td>2,100m</td></tr>
<tr><td>Used up to 26 September 1815</td><td>2,309m
60</td><td>426m
94</td><td>213m
28</td><td>3m
65</td><td>6m</td><td>3,504m
45</td><td>243m
70</td><td>18m
40</td><td>1,381m</td></tr>
<tr><td>In magazine 26 September 1815</td><td>5m
79</td><td>57m
59</td><td>0m
21</td><td>3m
10</td><td>1m</td><td>199m
20</td><td>Nil</td><td>nil</td><td>1,031m
12</td></tr>
<tr><td>Sold 16 and 17 December 1815</td><td>5m
79</td><td>56m</td><td>nil</td><td>3m
10</td><td>1m</td><td>190m
22</td><td></td><td></td><td>1,012m
71</td></tr>
</table>

Clearly, as in 1814, the crimson was used as a facing colour and lining colour – for the regiment *fifre* and drummers? The green was used clearly for drummers' *habits* during the 100 Days. It also seems some *capotes* were made from cavalry cloak cloth, *blanc picque de bleu* where one in every eight white fibres was blue. The accounts furthermore list 730m of drummers' livery being purchased in 1814, of which 694m 05 was used to make new drummers' *habits*, leaving 35m 95 of Royalist livery in stores. After 22 April 1815, 1,065m of Imperial Livery was purchased, of which 345m was used, leaving 695m 95 in stores. Of this, 655m was sold, leaving 40m 95 of lace. Also, of comment, 790 pairs of grenadier epaulettes were purchased in 1814 and a further 183 during the 100 Days, all being issued. More than 1,000 pairs of epaulettes show that all ranks wore fringed epaulettes, likewise 833 scarlet *aigrettes* were purchased and issued in 1814 along with 145 more in the 100 Days, and 1,222 *voltigeur aigrettes*. This is odd as 2,150 fusilier *houpettes* were purchased in 1814, of which 2,085 were issued, and a further 947 were purchased in the 100 Days. Does this mean that each man had a *houpette* and *aigrette*? Seemingly so. In terms of clothing, in 1814 the regiment produced 1,250 new *habits*, all being issued, along with 1,574 *vestes*, 1,637 pairs of *pantalons de tricot*, and 1,155 *capotes*. In 1815 a further 1,796 *habits-vestes* were issued, along with 1,363 *vestes*, 1,932 pairs of *pantalons de tricot*, 1,927 pairs of *caleçons*, 1,447 *bonnets de police* and 1,780 *capotes*. Clearly the colonel wanted to make his regiment as well dressed as possible.[13]

The stores held on 18 December 1815:[14]

1m 59 white broadcloth, total 12fr 70
0m 21 scarlet broadcloth, total 2fr 75
8m 98 beige broadcloth, total 73fr 72
18m 41 white milled serge, total 25fr 40
0m 58 white tricot, total 2fr 13
56m 84 linen for lining, total 79fr 57
40m 45 drummers' livery, total 36fr 85
301 sets of hooks and eyes, total 30fr 10
1 *capote*, total 25fr 72
1 *bonnet de police*, total 4fr 10
7 musket slings, total 7fr 07
97 *baudriers*, total 451fr 05
Total value of *Dépôt*, 751fr 16

Clearly all the beige broadcloth had been used to produce new *capotes*, and virtually all the tricot had been used to make new *pantalons*. Just 18m 40 green broadcloth was purchased in the 100 Days and every inch was used to make new *habits*. Since January 1815, 1,040m 95 of drummers' lace was purchased and 345m used, leaving 965m 95 in *dépôt*. A huge amount of this 655m was destroyed by December, suggesting this was all Imperial Livery that had been burnt. Ergo in 1815, some drummers at least had Imperial Livery and others had Royalist Livery.

3e *de Ligne*

Inspected on 16 July 1814, the regiment mustered 1,229 other ranks. The inspector noted that at the end of eighteen months' active service, the regiment's clothing was in terrible condition. For example, 101 men were missing a *habit* and of the 1,108 in use, just 465 were in good condition, with the rest needing repairs or replacing. Also, 532 men had no *veste*, 213 no *pantalons de tricot*, 82 men had no *schako* and 98 no *capote*. The regiment had eight *sapeurs* and the regimental band comprised four clarinets in Bb, one clarinet in Eb, one flute and two horns. The flute and Eb clarinet were of no use as they were described as *hors de service*. Their uniforms were decorated with silver lace, stores holding 5m 32 of this material. The *dépôt* held 241 *aigrettes* for grenadiers, 267 *aigrettes* for *voltigeurs* and 115 *houpettes* for fusiliers. In the *dépôt* were 4 pairs of epaulettes for *adjutant-sous-officiers* and 81 pairs of grenadier epaulettes. The regiment was a total shambles, the inspector noted. He added, furthermore, that the regiment had not yet affected a full conversion to the regulation of January 1812 and had a 'mix and match approach' to clothing.[15]

We get an idea of what the regiment wore in the 100 Days' campaign when it was disbanded on 21 September 1815. Materials held in the regiment's magazine included:[16]

5m 29 chamois broadcloth
32m 70 lace '*Modèle du Roi*', i.e., Royalist Livery drummers
210m lace '*Modèle N*', i.e., Imperial Livery for drummers

The small amount of Royalist Livery strongly implies that this was all that remained from making new drummers' *habits* during the first restoration. The stock of Imperial Livery implies drummers had this lace in service at Waterloo, but we cannot be certain of the colour of the *habit*, or the appearance of the grenadiers and *voltigeurs*.

4[e] *de Ligne*

Inspected on 28 July 1814, the regiment mustered 844 other ranks, which included the seven-strong regimental band. Of the *habits* in service, 373 were in good condition, 149 needed repairs, 159 were fit only for disposal as pre-Bardin and 52 men had no *habits*. Likewise, 117 *vestes* were fit only for disposal and 89 men had none, 128 men had no *capote*, 411 men had no *caleçon*, and 244 men had no *bonnet de police*. Furthermore, 83 men had no *pantalons de tricot* and only had their linen *pantalons*, of which 557 pairs were in use. Remarkably, 114 men had no *giberne* and belt. Not an inch of green or chamois broadcloth existed, nor an inch of drummers' livery, grenadier *schakos*, *aigrettes* or pairs of epaulettes. Not a single *voltigeur aigrette* existed. Clothing in the *dépôt* included 90 new fusilier *habits-vestes*, and 31 fusilier *habits* of the 'old model' fit only for sale to the rag dealers.[17]

The regiment was disbanded on 26 September 1815. The *dépôt* at this held still held a lot of materials, which included 15m 02 of green broadcloth, 865m of white milled serge, and 1,104m of white tricot. Clothing stocks included 61 *gilets manches*, 196 pairs of *pantalons de tricot*, 69 pairs of *caleçons*, 43 *schakos*, and 95 *bonnets de police*. Carried away by the men on leaving the army were 211 *habits*, 139 *gilets*, 172 pairs of *pantalons de tricot*, 148 pairs of underwear, 177 *capotes*, 244 *schakos*, 124 *bonnets de police*, 44 *gibernes* and belts, and 45 *baudriers*.[18]

5e *de Ligne*

Inspected on 29 July 1814, the 5e *de Ligne* had an eight-strong band and three cadet drummers from a total of 1,061 other ranks. Clothing was either in good condition or needed repair and replacement. For example, of the 1,048 habits in use, 440 – 41 per cent – were in good condition, 183 needed repairs and 425 needed immediate replacement – 40 per cent – leaving 13 men with no habit. This almost 50/50 split of good or bad clothing was representative of the regiment as a whole.[19] The regiment had two *voltigeur cornets* and thirteen *sapeurs*, who despite having axes, had no aprons. The regiment's *dépôt* held among other materials 23m 12 chamois broadcloth for *voltigeurs*' distinctions, as well as 124 grenadier *aigrettes*, and 124 for *voltigeurs*. The reviewing general commented that the greater part of the regiment's *habits* were of the old model, the clothing overall being in 'deplorable' condition, and noted that only two-thirds of the regiment were fully equipped.[20]

Cloth and stores with the disbanded war battalions in September 1815, included 15m 22 green broadcloth, 14m 22 chamois broadcloth, 8m 55 of drummers' Livery of '*N et Aigles*', i.e., Imperial Livery that had been burned, 98 new fusilier *habits-vestes*, 1 new drummer's *habit de modèle*, 36 grenadier *schakos*, and 321 fusilier *schakos*, 47 pairs of grenadier epaulettes in the *dépôt* along with 104 grenadier *aigrettes* and 66 for *voltigeurs*.[21] Listed as destroyed in summer 1815 were 533 fusilier *schako* plates, 200 grenadier *schako* plates and the same number of *voltigeur schako* plates listed as '*avec aigle*'. The *dépôt* also held 709 *houpette*s for fusiliers and 50 pairs of grenadier epaulettes, as well as 164 grenades for the *gibernes* of grenadiers, and 112 hunting horns for *voltigeur gibernes*.[22]

6e *de Ligne*

The 6e *de Ligne* has a reasonably comprehensive paper archive. For example, we know from the archive that the regiment is one of the few regiments where we have proof for the use of army-issue canteens. In the first quarter of 1811, 24 *sacs à distribution*, 24 canteens (*petit bidons*), 24 water cans (*bidons*) and 48 cooking pots (*gamelles*) were purchased for the sum of 128fr. At the same time, 24m 15 of 27mm wide gold lace was purchased for 156fr 98, 1 pair of adjutant's epaulettes for 50fr, 40m of white tricot for 26fr and 31m 22 of beige broadcloth for 40fr 58.[23]

In the first quarter of 1813, four bearskins for *sapeurs*, complete with cords, plumes and chinscales for 56fr each, 45m of green broadcloth were purchased, as was 21m 86 of

Dating from 1813, this naïve image is one of the few contemporary images of a soldier wearing Bardin-regulation clothing. Note the very short gaiters and diamond *schako* plate. (*Collection KM*)

yellow broadcloth for *voltigeurs'* distinctions along with 2 *cornets*.[24] Here we have proof positive of *sapeurs* in bearskins, *voltigeurs* with clearly non-regulation yellow distinctions, and drummer and *cornets* dressed in green.

By the time of the 1814 summer inspection, not an inch of either green or yellow broadcloth remained, or any Imperial Livery. No epaulettes or *aigrettes* existed in use or in *dépôt*, and no *sapeurs'* equipment. No old-pattern clothing was in use, but a lot of the uniform in use was worn out: for example, 746 *habits* were in good condition, 44 needed repairs and 419 were beyond repair.[25]

When the regiment was wound up in August 1815, *dépôt* held among other items, 90m of drummers' lace, 1 *schako de grenadier de modèle*, 12 *aigrettes* for *voltigeurs* and grenadiers – clearly these items had been purchased post September 1814. Remarkably, the regiment had white cotton *pantalons*, some 8 pairs in *dépôt* – 7 pairs costing 6fr and 1 pair costing 5fr – and 39 pairs of white cotton gaiters, as well as 3m 68 of white cotton; presumably the regiment had bright white parade gaiters and *pantalons*! Not a single pair of *pantalons de tricot* existed, so we assume all the men had bright white *pantalons* worn along with bright white gaiters.[26]

7e *de Ligne*

The regiment was inspected on 1 September 1814, and the inspector recorded that rather than regulation linen *pantalons de route,* the ones in use were made from brown broadcloth. The regiment clearly had *sapeurs* as nine axes, nine axe cases with belts, nine aprons and nine pairs of gauntlets were in use. The *voltigeur* companies had three *cornets*. We note 265 canteens described as bottles covered in wicker were in use. Among the items in stores were noted 1m of green broadcloth, 295 worn *habits-longe* and 31 brand-new ones.[27] The inspector ordered that the regiment was to dress its drummers in blue and remove from use all pre-Bardin clothing. Indeed, he noted that the regiment had not acted upon the decree of 19 or 7 February 1812, nor the *circulaire* of 23 April, and the drummers were to have livery of the Royal Household and the green drummers' *habits* with Imperial Livery were to be burned.[28]

Disbanded on 3 August 1815, the regiment had 401 men on parade, yet had just 377 *habits* in use, 336 *vestes*, 350 pairs of *pantalons de tricot*, 348 pairs of linen *pantalons*, 211 *capotes*, 392 *schakos* and 200 *bonnets de police* in use – a motley mix of uniform. Men were clearly on parade either in *habits* or *capotes* and not enough *vestes* existed to give each man one, likewise not every man had a *capote*, *schako* or pair of linen overalls and *pantalons de tricot*. At the same time, stores held 900 brand-new pairs of *pantalons de tricot* along with 34 *schakos*, 55 *capotes*, 1,027 pompoms, 6 sets of drummers' equipment and 4 sets of *sapeur*s equipment and 71m 15 of worsted lace![29]

8e *de Ligne*

Inspected on 21 July 1814, beyond reasonable doubt the regiment had drummers in green *habits* as stores held 24m 88 of green broadcloth and 237m of drummers' livery, as well as 9m 08 of silver lace specifically identified as for musicians. No effects for grenadiers existed, likewise for *voltigeurs*, so we assume they were dressed as fusiliers. Stores also held 722 pairs of white tricot *culottes*, of which 300 pairs were new, as well as 76 *habits-longe* and 422 musket slings. Clearly the regiment was in the process of adopting Bardin regulation in the course of 1814. About the unit's dress, General Rottembourg made the following recommendations:[30]

1. To establish uniformity in clothing and equipment as quickly as possible.
2. Replace buttons and shako plates as well as drummers' uniforms.
3. Ensure all items are made to the regulations of 19 January 1812, with greater supervision of the regulation and materials used.

We assume these action points were indeed carried out.

When disbanded on 25 September 1815, the *dépôt* held cloth and materials, which included 13m green broadcloth, 7m 37 chamois broadcloth, and 210m of drummers' livery, 61 *habits-vestes*, 149 pairs of grenadier epaulettes, 447 *schako* covers, 112 *schako* plates, 125 fusilier *houpette*s, 105 *voltigeur aigrettes* and 117 grenadier *aigrettes*. Cut out but yet not sewn together were 26 *habits*, 76 *vestes*, 10 pairs of *pantalons de tricot* and 86 *bonnets de police*. We also note 13 sets of *sapeur* equipment.[31]

9e *de Ligne*

The regiment was inspected on 20 September 1814. The regiment had two *sapeurs* on parade that day and 2 *cornets* for the *voltigeur* companies, along with 13 drummers. The *dépôt* held among other items 1m 84 of chamois broadcloth and 61m 20 of drummers' lace, 14 grenadier *habits* – likely with scarlet epaulettes attached to mark them out as such – 6 *voltigeur habits*, 295 fusilier *habits*, 389 fusilier *gilets manches*, 200 fusilier *schakos*, 117 grenadier *aigrettes*, 63 *voltigeur aigrettes* and 146 pairs of grenadier epaulettes, 368 sets of shoe buckles and 140 white sword knots. To be written off was a single drummer's *habit*, and four more that needed repairs: presumably these were green with Imperial Livery. The inspector remarked that the regiment had not completely followed the regulation of 19 January 1812.[32]

When disbanded in 1815, we know the regiment's grenadiers sported *aigrettes*, as the *dépôt* held 96 of these and 69 grenadier *schakos*. Likewise, 68 *voltigeur aigrettes* were in stores. The 1814 review shows us that the grenadiers had scarlet epaulettes as 146 pairs existed in the *dépôt* waiting to be issued, and none existed in 1815, so had all been issued out, along with 14 grenadier *habits*, and 6 *voltigeur habits* that had been in store. No grenadier *schako*s existed but 117 *aigrettes* did, we presume worn in fusilier *schakos*.[33] Items purchased during the 100 Days included 1m 85 of chamois broadcloth for 16fr, 400 pairs of linen *pantalons*, 400 pairs of linen gaiters, 1,500 pairs of shoes, 6 green drummers' *habits* and four pack mules to carry the regimental ambulance.[34]

10e *de Ligne*

The regiment possessed 104 pairs of grenadier epaulettes on 1 September 1814, but no *aigrettes*, while every man had a woollen pompom. Furthermore, the inspector recorded

Sergeant of fusiliers depicted in a naïve engraving from 1813. (*Collection KM*)

the regiment used a mix of Bardin and pre-Bardin clothing. Pre-Bardin kit in stores comprised 45 grenadier *habits*, 53 *voltigeur habits* that clearly had chamois collars and shoulder straps, 298 fusilier *habits*, 2 drummers' *habits*, 68 fusilier *gilets manches*, 253 pairs of *culottes*, 167 *bonnets de police a la dragonne*, 1,310 pairs of *caleçons*, 837 sets of braces, 6 *sapeurs*' axes with case and belt, 1,687 fusilier *houpette*s, 360 pairs of grenadier epaulettes, 453 pairs of long black gaiters, 1,570 pairs of long grey gaiters. All the *schakos* in the *dépôt*, some 144 examples, had eagle *schako* plates of the old model, ergo they had not been replaced by new Royalist issue. Also lodged in stores were 253 pairs of black half gaiters, 96m of black broadcloth, 308m of black tricot and 8m of linen to line gaiters and 59m 80 of Imperial Livery.[35]

We have an incredible document from the first quarter of 1815 that details exactly where all the new clothing and equipment was issued to. We know 58 grenadier *aigrettes* and 43 pairs of epaulettes were issued to 1e battalion, 57 *aigrettes* and 60 pairs of epaulettes to 2e battalion and 37 *aigrettes* and 39 pairs of epaulettes to 3e battalion. *Voltigeurs* of 1e battalion were issued 57 *aigrettes*, 8 *voltigeur habits* and 19 *voltigeur gilets manches*. We also note 18 grenadier *gilets manches* went to 1e battalion, 13 to 2e, and 20 to 3e battalion: presumably in both cases 'more of the same' as those already in use. Uniquely, the regiment had three types of gaiters: black gaiters costing 4fr 20 a pair, grey gaiters costing 1fr 90 a pair and half gaiters costing 1fr: these must have been very low indeed and extended little above the ankle. This is the only example of such items existing. Remarkably, three *sous-officier* sword knots were issued to the grenadier companies of 1e and 3e battalion.[36]

11e *de Ligne*

Inspected on 26 July 1814, the regiment had 540m of drummers' lace of the old pattern in use i.e., Imperial Livery; which was to be totally replaced. Such a large quantity implies that every scrap of lace was to be taken off the drummers' and *cornets' habits*. The regiment had 12 *sapeurs*, as 12 sets of *sapeurs'* kit was in use, along with 2 *voltigeur cornets*. A total of 200 grenadier *aigrettes* were fit for disposal, along with 205 *voltigeur aigrettes*. Some 85 pairs of grenadier epaulettes were in use and 115 pairs were fit only for disposal. The *dépôt* held 14 brand-new *capotes*, 16 *voltigeur habits*, 3 fusilier *habits*, 18 drummers' *habits* – without shadow of a doubt green with Imperial Livery – 208 fusilier *gilets manches*, 185 fusilier *schakos* and 36 pairs of grenadier epaulettes. The stores return lists 1m 44 chamois broadcloth – further proof that the *voltigeurs* had chamois collars and shoulder straps.[37]

The regiment was disbanded on 10 September 1815 and the *dépôt* held among other items 0m 86 chamois broadcloth and 287m 40 drummers' livery. Green broadcloth was listed but none remained, presumably after making drummers' clothing. Among the items of clothing in stores we find 61 new *capotes*, 1 new drummer's *habit*, 7 *habits* for *sapeurs* needing repair, 68 pairs of grenadier epaulettes, 75 grenadier *aigrettes*, 56 *voltigeur aigrettes* and 532 fusilier *houpettes* as well as 6 pairs of *culottes* for drummers, which were presumably green like the *habit*. We also find '*effects de modèle*' for *capote*, *habit de tambour maître*, *habit pour chef de musique*, *habit de musicien*, *habit de fusilier*, *habit de tambour*, fusilier *gilet manches*, *porte-giberne*, *baudrier* and musket sling. The *dépôt* held in addition a whole range of items for *sapeurs*, namely 5 axes with cases and belts, 15 aprons, and 3 pairs of gauntlets.[38]

12e *de Ligne*

Inspected on 30 July 1814, the regiment had two *sapeurs* on parade, and the inspecting general added that ten aprons, axes, axe cases and belts were needed to bring the regiment's *sapeurs* up to strength. Just 10 pairs of grenadier epaulettes were in use and 65 pairs were needed for every grenadier to have a pair. Of note, not a single bearskin existed for them.

We must imagine therefore the grenadiers had epaulettes and no other distinctions. The men on the day of the review had had delivered to them 347 brand-new shirts, 187 pairs of *pantalons de route*, 153 pairs of shoes, 171 pairs of black gaiters and 92 pairs made from grey linen. Even so, men still lacked shoes, gaiters and *pantalons de route* and not a single pair of socks were in use or underwear.[39]

When the regiment was disbanded in 1815, the *dépôt* held 195m of drummers' lace, 241 *vestes* or *gilets manches*, 243 pairs of *pantalons de tricot*, 587 pairs of *caleçons*, 591 *houpettes* and *aigrettes*, 2 pairs of *adjutant-sous-officier* epaulettes, 145 *schako* covers, 431 *gibernes*, 521 *porte-gibernes*, oddly 2 *sapeurs*' axes with 4 axes cases and 5 *sapeurs*' aprons. Some 162 pairs of grenadier epaulettes were held as well. Not an inch of green or chamois broadcloth, or drummers lace existed in 1814, therefore the new lace was purchased sometime after October 1814 – was it Royalist Livery or Imperial? We cannot say.[40]

13e *de Ligne*

Delivered to the regiment 20 February 1812 were 490 pairs of grenadier epaulettes, 548 grenadier *houpettes*, 45 pompoms for *sous-officiers* and 1,600 pompoms for fusiliers and *voltigeurs*; delivered on 8 July 1812 were 600 *giberne* belts, 600 musket slings and 15 drums with carriages; delivered on 6 January 1813 were 97 pairs of grenadier epaulettes and on 18 October 1813, 600 brand-new *schakos* of the model of 1810 were received by the *dépôt*.[41]

Inspected in February 1813 by Inspector Francois Lhéritier, the regiment had 3,278 *habits* in use, of which 1,632 were pre-Bardin *habits-longe* and 1,646 were *habits-vestes*: an almost 50/50 split between models for every item of cloth and equipment. In addition, 2,972 pompoms were in use and 571 pairs of grenadier epaulettes. The *sapeurs* had 12 axes and cases, and 12 aprons. All the regiment's leather work was old pattern. Some 22 light cavalry *mousquetons* were in use with *voltigeur cornets* and *sapeurs*. The *voltigeurs* were armed with standard infantry muskets.[42]

The regiment was inspected on 6 October 1814. We note grenadiers and *voltigeurs* had *houpettes* rather than *aigrettes*, and 137 pairs of grenadier epaulettes were in use. The regiment had nine *sapeurs*, each equipped with an apron, axe case, axe and pair of gauntlets. The regiment also had 19 drummers and 8 *voltigeur cornets*. The *voltigeurs* were armed with 155 dragoons' muskets, the drummers and *cornets* – although not all of them – were armed with 17 light cavalry *mousquetons* and we assume also *gibernes* and belts. The *dépôt* held among other items 7m 22 chamois broadcloth, 1,092m 30 drummers lace, and 12m 64 gold and silver lace, the latter being used by the band. Clothing in the *dépôt* included 4 brand-new *voltigeur habits*, 32 brand-new fusilier *habits*, plus 29 needing repairs, and 3 new drummers' *habits* and 1 needing repairs – we can't say what colour the *habits* were or the pattern of drummers of the lace sewn on them, but potentially green with the Imperial Livery given one was damaged, implying these were not brand new – 1 *sapeur*'s axe of the '*modèle*' and 6 needing repairs, 86 brand-new pairs of grenadier epaulettes and 6 *sapeurs*' axe cases to be written off.[43]

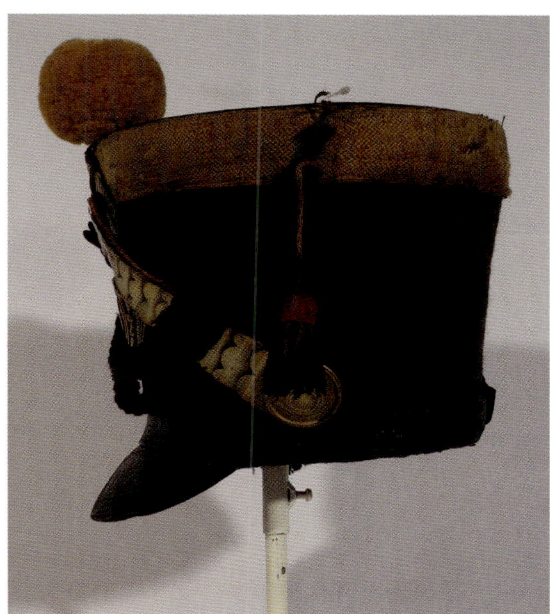

Voltigeur schako of the 3ᵉ *de Ligne*. Cords were abolished in theory in 1810, yet this 1812-pattern *schako* has cords – assuming they are original to this item – and a non-regulation yellow lace top band. (*Collection de l'Office du Tourisme de Pontarlier. Dépôt au Musée municipal de Pontarlier, France*)

Officers' *schako,* adorned with non-regulation cords, assuming they were originally fitted to this item. (*Collection de l'Office du Tourisme de Pontarlier. Dépôt au Musée municipal de Pontarlier, France*)

At the very end of the 100 Days on 28 June 1815 the regiment purchased 0m 65 of chamois broadcloth and 4m 88 of Imperial Livery and 4 fusiliers' *habits* for 395fr 23 among other items.[44] No disbandment records can be found, so we can say nothing more. Presumably the materials purchased were 'more of the same' of those already in use.

14e *de Ligne*

Inspected on 29 August 1814, we note only the grenadiers and *sous-officiers* were armed with sabres, no *sapeurs'* equipment is listed or *cornets* for *voltigeur* companies. It seems the grenadiers had no epaulettes, the sabre being their sole distinction. The *dépôt* held no stocks of cloth or materials, nor any clothing or equipment.[45]

In 1815 the *dépôt* was empty of cloth, materials and equipment, but the men of the 4e battalion were allowed to take away with them 172 *habits*, 80 *vestes*, 164 *capotes*, and 177 *schakos*, which really does not advance our knowledge of what the regiment wore at all![46]

Officers

A kit list for *sous-lieutenant* Louis Blacherot, who served in 4e battalion, has survived. It details all his kit to be auctioned off to fellow officers after his death on the field of battle:[47]

1 *surtout*
1 *redingote* in blue broadcloth
2 pairs of *pantalons* in blue broadcloth
1 pair of *pantalons* in white Casimir
1 *veste* in blue broadcloth
2 napkins
1 *veste* in white Casimir
1 *bonnet de police*
1 pair of *culottes* in nankeen
1 pair of half gaiters in nankeen
2 flannels
5 shirts
5 kerchiefs in muslin [i.e., neck cloths]
3 handkerchiefs
9 false collars for the shirt
1 pair of white silk stockings
1 epaulette and *contre-epaulette*
1 sword knot
1 pair of gloves
1 cotton night cap
1 waistcoat in stripped ticking

Bardin-regulation fusilier *schako* of the 102e *de Ligne*. (*Collection de l'Office du Tourisme de Pontarlier. Dépôt au Musée municipal de Pontarlier, France*)

Grenadiers *schako* of the 85e *de Ligne*. (*Collection de l'Office du Tourisme de Pontarlier. Dépôt au Musée municipal de Pontarlier, France*)

2 *vestes* in white polished linen
2 razors and case
1 box of shaving soap
3 pairs of socks
1 pair of boots with retroussis, old
1 sabre belt, old
1 aurore pompom
1 stock
1 gold embroidery for *schako* [does he mean *schako* cords? Or did he simply class the gold lace separate to the *schako* itself?]
1 *schako* garnished with the plate and chinscales
2 pairs of boots
1 *porte-manteaux*
1 *gilet manches* in flannel
1 pair of boot hooks
1 legion of honour
1 drill manual of 1 August 1791
1 portfolio containing assorted items.

Even *a sous-lieutenant*, the lowest-ranking commissioned officer in a regiment, had, even on campaign, an extensive wardrobe of items. Interestingly, he only had with him his *surtout*, listed as a *frac*, and a whole panoply of legwear and *vestes*. Clearly this one item served many different functions. The nankeen breeches and gaiters are something of a surprise for a line infantry officer as these are traditionally associated with the light cavalry. This auction gives us a snapshot into the amount of clothing even the most junior officers had with them even in the turbulent days of October 1813.

15ᵉ *de Ligne*

Inspected on 16 September 1814, the regiment was badly dressed. For the 1,285 other ranks, 309 had no *habit*, 647 no *veste*, 654 no *pantalons de tricot*, 515 had no *capote*, and 449 no *schako*. To make up for the lack *of pantalons de tricot*, 794 pairs of *pantalons de route* were in use. The clothing was made to the Bardin regulation, the inspector noted, but was mostly missing or needed immediate replacement. The *dépôt* held 166m 96 of red flannel – we have no idea of the use of this material – as well as 151m 94 of chamois broadcloth and items '*de modèle*' for grenadier *schako*, *aigrette* and epaulettes: the only examples it seems.[48]

The regiment was disbanded on 9 November 1815, when it held 158m 55 of blue broadcloth first quality, 958m 44 blue broadcloth second quality, 5m 53 white broadcloth, 136m 64 chamois broadcloth, 35m 85 beige broadcloth, and 35m 83 red broadcloth. Lace in the *dépôt* comprised 96m 85 gold lace, 9m 36 silver lace for the band, 68m 06 yellow worsted lace, 18m 32 red worsted lace and 50m 65 white worsted lace – this was inherited from the 140e *de Ligne* and not used.

No green cloth existed and no drummers' lace. Interestingly, 114 beige broadcloth *capotes* were in *dépôt* alongside 154 made from second-quality blue broadcloth cloth, accompanied by 173 grenadier *aigrettes* and 129 for *voltigeurs*, and lastly 241 pairs of grenadier epaulettes.[49]

16e *de Ligne*

When inspected in summer 1814 the regiment mustered 758 men and 6 *enfants de troupe*. We note the regiment had 3 *sapeurs*, who carried axes and axe cases and are likely to have been issued pistols as four pairs were in use. The *sapeur* sergeant, traditionally, did not carry an axe. The majority of the regiment's clothing was fit only for the dustbin or repair workshop, the inspector noted: of the 758 *habits,* only 122 were in good enough condition to remain in use, 204 needed repairs and 340 were fit for the rubbish heap, which were all of the old model. The *dépôt* held, among other items, 34 brand-new fusilier *habits-vestes*, 140 grenadier *aigrettes*, 140 *voltigeur aigrettes*, 89 *houpettes* and 2 *voltigeur cornets*. The inspector noted the regiment had 410 *giberne* belts and 36 musket slings made from black cow hide, and added that the unit had ignored the decrees of 19 January 1812, but noted that 60 *habits-vestes* had been drawn from government stores to clothe men in the *dépôt.*[50]

Disbanded in 1815, the *dépôt* held 84m of chamois broadcloth, 4m of linen, 33m 20 red worsted lace and 184m of drummers' lace. Clothing included 16 old *habits*, 1 new drummers' *habit*, 28 *bonnets de police*, 2 pairs of *caleçons*, 1,025 sets of braces and 165 *schako* covers. Other items included 464 black stocks, 11 pairs of shoes, 19 *sacs de peau*, 198 *sacs à distribution*, 166 cockades, 402 musket worms, 424 *epinglettes*, 240 pay books, 13 pairs of black gaiters and 170 pairs of grey gaiters. We also find in *dépôt* 380 buff musket slings and 36 in blackened cow hide, 581 *giberne* belts in buff and 79 in blackened cow hide.[51]

17e *de Ligne*

Regiment records report that on 1813 the regiment had 980 pairs of *pantalons* in beige broadcloth made for the detachments in *dépôt*. The war battalions we assume had 'more of the same' very much non-regulation items. The same document reports eight *habits* were made for the *sous-officiers* costing 2fr 75. The accounts for January to April 1814 record 792 *habits-longe* costing 2fr 65 each and 292 *habits-vestes* costing 2fr 20 were made.[52] New clothing issued on 7 July 1814 included 67 *capotes* in beige broadcloth, 303 *habits-vestes*, 698 *gilets manches*, 842 pairs of *pantalons de tricot*, 519 *bonnets de police*, 799 pairs of *caleçons*, and 1,336 *schakos de fusilier*.[53] The inspector noted that new *habits* replaced a lot of the pre-Bardin clothing that was in use.

The *dépôt* on 7 July 1814 held among other items 15m 53 of chamois broadcloth, 246 brand-new fusilier *habits*, 2 brand-new drummers' *habits* – do we assume green

Grenadiers' *schako* of the 75ᵉ *de Ligne*. The cords – if original – are non-regulation, but it seems colonels had some leeway in deciding how their regiments were dressed. Because one regiment did X, does not mean all regiments did X. What we are seeing here with non-regulation items are regimental distinctions, unique to the regiment at a certain time. (*Collection de l'Office du Tourisme de Pontarlier. Dépôt au Musée municipal de Pontarlier, France*)

Fusiliers' *schako* with the *lentille* disc pompom. (*Collection de l'Office du Tourisme de Pontarlier. Dépôt au Musée municipal de Pontarlier, France*)

with Imperial Livery? – 162 pairs of white gaiters and the same number of grenades for grenadier gibernes. In addition were 77 grenadier *aigrettes* and 77 pairs of grenadier epaulettes, as well as 77 *voltigeur aigrettes* along with 603 fusilier *houpettes*, 79 *giberne* covers, 69 pairs of shoe buckles and 4,147 *rabats du col* – the removable white piping. The inspector noted that 'many of the *banderoles* are made from blackened cow hide and need to be replaced in buff'.[54]

When the regiment was disbanded in September 1815, the *dépôt* held very little in the way of clothing: 32 *habits*, 8 *vestes*, 170 *bonnets de police* and 1 pair of *pantalons* de *tricot*. No blackened cow hide equipment was in store, so we assume this had all been replaced or was in use. Also, in *dépôt* were two cavalry trumpets for *voltigeurs*![55]

18e *de Ligne*

When inspected on 16 July 1814, the regiments clothing was in tatters. Of the 794 men on parade 40 men lacked *habits*, 124 *habits* needed to be repaired and 133 were to be written off as old pattern *habits-longe*. Likewise, 132 men lacked a *gilet manches*, 88 men had no *pantalons de tricot*, 366 men had no *caleçon*, 68 lacked a *capote*. The *dépôt* held some stocks of materials, notably 8 drummers' habits and 2m 32 chamois broadcloth, 382m serge, 1193m 88 white tricot. No items for grenadiers or *voltigeurs* were in use. The regiment also possessed five pack ponies with harness and five horses for the *vivandières*' cart.[56]

Disbanded on 25 September 1815, the regiment's *dépôt* held 191m 35 of blue broadcloth, 16m 73 of red broadcloth, 30m of white milled serge, 56m15 of white tricot and 708m 44 of linen for linings. Clothing included 88 new fusilier *habits* and 2 to be written off, 104 new *schakos*, 274 *gibernes*, 281 *porte-gibernes*, 7 *baudriers*, 10 drums and carriages, 2 *voltigeur cornets*, 313 *voltigeur* and fusilier pompoms, 86 *voltigeur* and fusilier *flammes* (pompoms or circular *lentile* pompoms with worsted tufts, I suppose.), and 250 pairs of *voltigeur* epaulettes, all of which were bought after August 1814. The returns list grenadier *habits* – presumably marked out as such with scarlet-fringed epaulettes – pompoms and *flammes*, but none were in *dépôt*, ditto drummer and *voltigeur habits* are listed but none existed in *dépôt*; had they all been issued? Alas we cannot tell.[57]

19e *de Ligne*

Inspected on 26 July 1814, the 19e *de Ligne*'s clothing was in deplorable condition. Of 729 other ranks on parade, 169 men had no *habits*, 163 *habits* needed total replacement, and 213 needed repairs, leaving just 184 in serviceable condition. The regiment had five *sapeurs* under arms with full equipment, and needed additional two axes, two axe case and belts, two aprons and two pairs of gauntlets to equip all seven men.[58]

With a chronic lack of clothing for the men under arms, it is no surprise that the *dépôt* held little in the way of brand-new clothing to issue. It had 35 *capotes*, 38 fusilier *habits*, 153 *voltigeur gilets manches*, 115 pairs of *pantalons de tricot*, 145 *bonnets de police*, 115 pairs of *caleçons*, 1,318 pairs of braces, 143 fusilier *schakos*, 4 grenadier *aigrettes*, and

Grenadiers' *schako* for the 93e *de Ligne*. It has seemingly lost its non-regulation cords. (*Collection de l'Office du Tourisme de Pontarlier. Dépôt au Musée municipal de Pontarlier, France*)

Grenadier *schako* of an unknown regiment. (*Collection de l'Office du Tourisme de Pontarlier. Dépôt au Musée municipal de Pontarlier, France*)

If the pompom is original, this is a fusiliers' *schako* used by a grenadier of the 10e *de Ligne*. Archive documents overwhelmingly tell us this item is the typical *schako* used by grenadiers in 1813–15. The regulation item is atypical, and was seldom used. (*Collection de l'Office du Tourisme de Pontarlier. Dépôt au Musée municipal de Pontarlier, France*)

2 *voltigeur aigrettes*. The *dépôt*, the inspector remarked, had taken delivery of 2,523 fusilier *houpettes*, 5 pairs of adjutants' epaulettes, 333 pairs of grenadier epaulettes and 337 grenadier *houpettes*, all brand new and waiting to be issued as none were in use. We must assume therefore that grenadiers had *houpettes* to replace the *aigrettes*. The *voltigeur gilets manches* presumably had chamois collars, for which 6m 30 chamois broadcloth was in stores. Drummers wore green with Imperial Livery as 13m 60 of green broadcloth was in stores, along with 389m 40 of Drummers' Livery No. 1 and 102m 60 of Drummers' Livery No. 2.

The regimental band, which mustered eight men on the books, possessed two drum majors' maces, four clarinets, one serpent, one harmony trumpet, one bass drum, one tenor drum, one trombone, two pairs of cymbals and two Chinese pavilions, all of which had been paid for by the officers of the corps. We note 13 instruments and 8 men, so clearly the regiment unofficially employed *gagistes*.[59]

During the First Restoration and 100 Days we know a great deal about the dress of the 19e *de Ligne*. Cloth used and purchased between August 1814 and 1 September 1815 was as follows:[60]

	Blue broadcloth		White broadcloth		Red broadcloth		Beige broadcloth		Chamois broadcloth		White milled serge		White tricot	
	Purchased	**Used**	**Purchased**	**Used**	**Purchased**	**Used**	**Purchased**	**Used**	**Purchased**	**Used**	**Purchased**	**Used**	**Purchased**	**Used**
In Magazine 1 July 1814	1138.5		1,265.4		13.59				6.07		3404.45		2211.6	
1814		641.4		167.75	66.01	59.91	180.80	48		5.36		470		1375.8
1815	1,152.72	1,313.74	117.36	1,057.68	159.81	120.24	481.60	597.6	11.03	4.82	305.41	805	543.6	1378.4
Total	2,291.10	1,954.88	1,382.70	1,225.44	239.47	186.15	662.46	645.6	18.07	10.18	3709.86	1275	2755.2	2754.3
In *Dépôt* 16 September 1815		336.22		157.25		59.26		16.8		7.88		2434.8		0.9

The cloth purchased in 1815 cost 3,786fr 49 centimes, and this was still owed to the supplier at the time of disbandment. The regiment owed at disbandment 23,196fr 65 centimes. At the time of disbandment, the *dépôt* held cloth cut out ready to make 124 *habits* and 45 *vestes*, namely 171m 40 blue broadcloth, 71m 98 white broadcloth, 16m 44 red broadcloth, and 0m73 chamois broadcloth. Sufficient cloth remained to make 50 *vestes*, and 50 *houpettes* and *schakos* were yet to be delivered to the *dépôt*. Between August 1814 and October 1815 all the green cloth had been destroyed along with the Imperial Livery in the *dépôt*. Some 22fr 40 centimes was spent mending drummers' *habits* in the second quarter of 1815.[61]

Fusiliers' *schako* with non-regulation cords of the 76e *de Ligne*. The diamond plate was the most common plate in use during 1813 as colonels used up stockpiles of plates already in existence before ordering more items to the latest regulation. (*Collection de l'Office du Tourisme de Pontarlier. Dépôt au Musée municipal de Pontarlier, France*)

The number of *habits* made between July 1814 and September 1815 were as follows:[62]

Habits-vestes								
	Grenadier		Voltigeur		Fusilier		Drummer	
	Made	Issued	Made	Issued	Made	Issued	Made	Issued
In Magazine 1 July 1814					38			
1814	58	53	73	73	292	330	26	26
1815	74	79	57	56	626	582	12	12
Total	132	132	130	129	956	912	38	38
In *Dépôt* 16 September 1815		Nil		1		44		Nil

Grenadier and fusilier *habits* were ostensibly the same garment, bar the grenadiers' items having different turn-back devices and no doubt scarlet epaulettes. In 1814, during the First Restoration, it is clear the drummers had blue coats faced in crimson with Royalist Livery, some 570m being purchased with 390m being used, and 26 new *habits* were made. In 1815 270m of drummers' livery was purchased for the production of 12 new drummers' *habits*. Not an inch of green broadcloth was purchased in the 100 Days. All 26 of the 1814 issue and all 12 of the 1815 issue were, we assume, worn side by side.

Grenadier company officers' *schako* of the 70e de Ligne. The pompom, plate and chinscale bosses all concur on this identification. The black velvet bands are non-regulation, but exceptionally common in 1814–15. (*Collection de l'Office du Tourisme de Pontarlier. Dépôt au Musée municipal de Pontarlier, France*)

Voltigeur officers' schako of the 69e *de Ligne*. The plate is a non-regulation variation of the fusilier plate. The narrow gold lace braid on the black velvet upper band perhaps denotes the rank of *sous-lieutenant*, and is again non-regulation. (*Collection de l'Office du Tourisme de Pontarlier. Dépôt au Musée municipal de Pontarlier, France*)

The stock of green cloth from July 1814, the archive tells us, had 'been entirely burnt', and no green cloth was purchased in 1814 or 1815, so we can be very confident that the drummers' *habits* were blue. The *habit* used in 1815 was either single breasted as per the Bardin regulations, or was a standard *habit*, laced with Imperial Livery, as Colonel Jolly shows.[63]

As well as producing four patterns of *habit-veste*, two types of *veste* were used:[64]

	Vestes in broadcloth						*Vestes* in tricot					
	Grenadier		Voltigeur		Fusilier and drummers		Grenadier		Voltigeur		Fusilier and drummers	
	Made	Issued	Made	Issued	Made	Issued	Made	Issued	Made	Issued	Made	Issued
In Magazine 1 July 1814					120						33	
1814					65	185					275	308
1815	46	46	33	33	858	739	18	18			189	189
Total	46	46	33	33	1,043	924	18	18	Nil		497	497
In *Dépôt* 16 September 1815		Nil		Nil		119		Nil		Nil		Nil

Battalion commander of the 85e *de Ligne*. (*Private collection, France*)

Junior officer of a grenadier company of the 17e *de Ligne*. (*Private collection, France*)

Colonel of an unknown *ligne* regiment. (*Private collection, France*)

Clearly drummers had white *gilets manches* and *pantalons*, just as Colonel Jolly shows. A total of 1,155 pairs of *pantalons de tricot* were made, of which 607 were issued in 1814 and 548 in 1815. All ranks had beige *capotes*, a total of 326 being made, 64 of which were issued in 1814 and 261 in 1815, with a single example being placed into the *dépôt*.[65] Of interest, 337 '*houpettes de grenadier*', which are likely to be pompoms with a wool tuft protruding from the top of the felt pompon, were purchased. *Voltigeurs* and fusiliers wore regulation-issue *houpettes*, and some 2,622 fusilier *houpettes* were obtained, of which 680 were issued in 1814 and 631 in 1815. The inspector noted that the regiment had not yet fully adopted the regulation of 19 January 1812, and that all new items were to match the regulation.[66]

At disbandment, the *dépôt* held 315 grenadier *houpettes* and 1,371 fusilier *houpettes*. The grenadiers had 333 pairs of epaulettes purchased for them in summer 1814, with 107 pairs being issued in 1814 and 139 issued in 1815, leaving 87 pairs in the *dépôt*. In addition, for the grenadiers 209 *aigrettes* were obtained in 1814, 51 being issued in

1814 and 158 in 1815. We assume they supplemented 'more of the same' already in use. For the *voltigeurs*, 288 *aigrettes* were purchased in 1814, 124 being issued in 1814 and 164 in 1815. Only fusilier *schakos* are listed, so seemingly all ranks wore this *schako* type. Confirming this, a single grenadier *schako de modèle* was purchased in 1814 and never issued. The regiment in 1815 had in stores 687 *schako* plates with the Imperial Eagle, and 1,285 'N' devices for *gibernes*, which had been purchased and issued during the 100 Days' campaign and hastily taken out of use and burned at the end of it with eagle *schako* plates. How one 'burns' metal items I am at a loss to understand, but clearly the adjutant felt this was the correct word to describe the destruction of these items. Both grey and black gaiters were in use, 730 pairs of black being issued in 1815 along with 829 pairs of grey. Only 84 pairs of *pantalons de toile* were made, 81 pairs being issued in 1814, presumably supplementing those already in use. The paper archive also lists the debts of the regiment for clothing and equipment purchased during the 100 Days but which arrived after Waterloo and were not paid for:[67]

Linen for linings. 798fr 02
Gold lace, worsted lace, drummers' lace. 802fr 31
Schakos. 8,788fr 50
Braces for *pantalons* and making the same. 2,908fr 60
Schako and *schako* covers. 860.fr
Fusilier *houpettes*. 60fr
Leather work and buttons. 4,110fr 73
Blue, red and white broadcloth. 3,786fr 49
Linen for lining. 733fr 61
Linen for lining. 312fr 38
Repairs to clothing. 36fr
Total: 23,196fr 65

Clearly, the drummers had more Imperial Livery ordered, but it seemingly arrived too late to be actually used. Either way, no green broadcloth existed, so we have drummers in presumably standard infantry *habits* with Royalist Livery applied and then perhaps Imperial Livery.

Almost uniquely among all the regiments studied have we found proof positive of the 2e and 3e *porte-aigle* being armed with spontoons, with two such items in *dépôt* along with two *baudriers* in varnished black leather. Arguably therefore despite the 1808 and later edicts, it simply never seems to have been put into practice until 1815. Other weapons in use included 10 light cavalry carbines for *sapeurs*, one rifle, in French *carabine rayé* issued to an officer of *voltigeurs*, and three patterns of *sabres briquet*: 345 new model, an undisclosed number of old model, all of which were taken out of service in 1814, and 195 'foreign models', possibly the Dutch infantry hanger or indeed of any other nation at the time. *Voltigeurs* were issued standard infantry muskets.[68]

Grenadier in full dress during the 100 Days. Note the non-regulation cords and plume. We remember that what is shown is a particular regiment during this period, and should not be taken as typical. (*Collection KM*)

20[e] *de Ligne*

Inspected on 16 August 1814, the inspector noted 'the majority of the *habits* are of the old model and I have passed orders for repairs to be carried out and new habits to be produced'. He added 'that when off duty the officers dressed as middle-class men, which he noted was strictly forbidden and that he would send to the regiment sealed patterns of clothing for the master tailor to copy, which was to be rigorously kept to'.[69] The grenadiers had epaulettes but no *aigrette*, and no *voltigeur aigrettes* existed either.[70] Furthermore, the 1,480 men on parade were issued 2,621 shirts, 1,943 pairs of *pantalons de route*, which every man on parade was wearing due to the shortages of *pantalons de tricot*, 1,531 black stocks, 63 pairs of linen ankle socks, 13 pairs of woollen stockings, 851 pairs of black and 332 pairs of linen gaiters. There not enough of either type of gaiter for the men to have a pair of each, but as long as a soldier had a pair of gaiters the colonel clearly was not concerned. Just 60 men had a canteen. The *dépôt* held stocks of cloth and materials, notably 217m of drummers' lace.[71]

When we look at the 1815 disbandment records, we find in the *dépôt* 16m of crimson serge – arguably used to line the tails of the drummers' *habits* when wearing the new Royalist Livery. We also find 18m 24 of green broadcloth – no doubt purchased in the 100 Days to make new drummers' *habits* – 5m 40 chamois broadcloth, 82 pairs of grenadier epaulettes, 87 pairs of *voltigeur* epaulettes accompanied by 95 grenadier *aigrettes*,111 *voltigeur aigrettes* and 141 brand-new blackened cow hide *porte-gibernes*.[72]

21[e] *de Ligne*

The 6[e] battalion was reviewed on 26 January 1813, when the men were wearing 492 *habits-vestes*, 492 *gilets manches*, 492 pairs of *pantalons de tricot*, and the same number of *schakos*, *capotes*, *bonnets de police* and *caleçons*. They were equipped with 487 muskets and bayonets and 46 sabres for drummers and *sous-officiers*.[73] Presumably the use of *habits-vestes* is reflective of the unit as a whole.

Sadly, the 1814 inspection report is missing from the regiment's archive, but the inspector's comments exist and from these we learn that the officers had been negligent in allowing innovations to the cut, dimensions and colour of the uniform *habit*. He also remarks the officers' used soldiers as servants against regulations, and the officers were to appoint and pay servants and no longer abuse their men.[74] What these comments mean in reality are hard to fathom without the inspection return proper. Perhaps the inference here is to drummers and the band rather than the rank and file?

At the time of disbandment on 20 September 1815 the 276 men under arms in the war battalions were wearing *habits-vestes*. Stocks of materials in the magazine on 20 September included 18m 24 green broadcloth, 255 Imperial Livery – drummers clearly were in green, or at least some of them – 9m 36 silver lace for the band, and 10 pairs of grenadier epaulettes: were the epaulettes in the *dépôt* all the stock the regiment had, or were these all that remained from the pairs that were issued, i.e., the surplus pairs? It is hard to tell without more research.[75]

22e *de Ligne*

Reviewed on 19 June 1814, the report informs us the men had *habits*, *vestes*, *pantalons*, and *schakos*, no mention made of *schako* covers, epaulettes, *aigrettes*, bearskins or *sapeurs*: clothing was all of Bardin regulation.[76] Only *sous-officiers* had *baudriers* and sabres, the grenadiers needed 322 *baudriers* and sabres. Some 150 *baudriers* were in use, yet we find 204 *sabres briquet* in good condition, while 31 needed repairs and 6 were to be written off. We ask how these sabres were carried as not enough *baudriers* existed! Every man on parade had a shirt, but just 474 men had a pair of linen *pantalons*. Remarkably the inspector reported that of the 1,290 men on parade, just 977 men had shoes – were men really on parade barefoot or were clogs worn? The *dépôt* held 10 drummers' *habits hors de service*: no doubt green with forbidden Imperial Livery. A single grenadier *schako* of the '*modèle*' was in *dépôt* and 87 fusilier types. No *aigrettes* or epaulettes existed; do we therefore conclude that none were in use? Possibly.[77]

By the time the regiment was disbanded in autumn 1815 the *dépôt* held 545m of drummers' lace, which we suppose was Royalist Livery. We also find in stores 187 *aigrettes* and 96 pairs of grenadier epaulettes. Cloth and materials in the *dépôt* were minimal: some 100m 80 beige broadcloth, 6m 71 white broadcloth, 2m 53 scarlet broadcloth, 10m white serge, 24m white tricot and 119m 80 of worsted lace. Clothing and equipment included 3 *habits*, 78 *gilets manches*, 101 pairs of *pantalons de tricot*, 59 fusilier *and voltigeur schakos*, 31 *bonnets de police*, 169 *gibernes*, 109 *porte-gibernes*, and 7 *baudriers*. Thus by 1815 the grenadiers and we assume *voltigeurs* had *aigrettes* and the grenadiers had fringed scarlet epaulettes. No green cloth existed in 1814 or 1815, nor chamois.[78]

23e *de Ligne*

When inspected on 24 July 1814 the regiment's clothing was missing or needed repair and replacement: of the *habits* in use, 617 were in good condition, 96 needed repairs, 104 needed replacing and 95 men lacked this garment. Furthermore, the inspector noted 237 men had no *veste*, and 118 no *capote*. We do note 57 canteens were in use, and the men had a mix and match approach to grey and black gaiters and linen or *pantalons de tricot* as not enough of either type existed for a man to have a pair of each. Cloth in stores comprised 198m 90 beige broadcloth for *capotes*, 13m 60 blue broadcloth, 73m 27 white broadcloth, 21m 81 scarlet broadcloth, 2,041m 90 white serge, 336m 36 white tricot and 554m 85 of Imperial Livery. In stores we find 17 *sapeurs*' aprons, 101 brand-new *capotes*, *effects de modèle* for grenadier and *voltigeur aigrettes* and grenadier epaulettes, 908m of silver lace for musicians and 16 pairs of culottes for musicians, which were presumably green.[79]

By disbandment in 1815 stores held 32 pairs of grenadier epaulettes, and 20 *aigrettes* for 'grenadiers or *voltigeurs*' as well as 0m 71 chamois broadcloth for *voltigeur habit* collars. Of the 908m of silver lace, just 5m 80 remained at disbandment, so clearly the band had been dressed in blue habits with copious lace, and possibly also the drummers: in total 903m of lace was used; applying 15m per habit was sufficient for 60 garments. We note

Voltigeur in full dress during the 100 Days. The *schako* and its plume are non-regulation. (*Collection KM*)

in the 100 Days some green broadcloth was used, and stores held 8m 16 and 434m 85 of drummers' lace. Assuming this was the same lace held in 1814, just about 100m had been used, sufficient for six Imperial Livery green *habits* made to the regulation, or far more if lace was applied in non-regulation manner.[80]

24e *de Ligne*

When inspected on 1 July 1814 the regiment's clothing was in tatters. Of 856 men on parade, 224 had no *habit*, 346 had no *veste*, and 369 had no *pantalons de tricot*. Some of them must have been wearing *pantalons de route*, of which only 274 pairs existed, meaning many men were on parade in whatever legwear they could have obtained on campaign. The grenadiers had 26 pairs of epaulettes in need of replacement and a further 65 pairs for every man to have one. No *aigrettes* of either type existed. The men were wearing a mix of *habits* and *habits-vestes*, the inspector remarked. Just 362 musket slings were in use, so we assume men used string or other improvised slings. A total of 133 *baudriers* and sabres were in use for the grenadier company, while the *voltigeurs* had no sabres. For the 856 men on parade, nearly 25 per cent wore clogs, as just 661 pairs of shoes were in use, accompanied by 237 pairs of black and 284 pairs of grey gaiters: as long as a man had a pair of gaiters, no one seems to have been overly concerned, but even then most men had none. Just 24 men had a canteen and 36 men a *sac a distribution*. Much to the inspector's chagrin, fusiliers and *voltigeurs* had black *giberne* belts. Furthermore, the inspector noted that the men had been dressed from whatever was in *dépôt*, which held a solitary brand-new *capote de modèle*, and 3 brand-new drummers' *habits. Dépôt* also held 460 *gibernes* with blackened cow hide *porte-gibernes*, and 4 drums with 2 carriages also made from blackened cow hide. The *dépôt* held very little in the way of materials: 18m 10 of beige broadcloth, 12m of blue broadcloth, 9m of white broadcloth, 1,954m 15 white milled serge, 208m 40 of tricot and 250m 77 of linen.[81]

The *dépôt* contents at the time of disbandment in summer 1815 included 82m 21 white broadcloth, 19m 70 red broadcloth, 18m 24 green broadcloth, 1,511m white serge, 424m 21 linen for lining, 12m 20 yellow worsted lace, and 100 dozen large buttons. Clothing and equipment included '*3 habits, vert, pour tambour*', 4 grenadier *aigrettes*, 32 *voltigeur aigrettes*, 3 grenadier *schakos*, 90 *schako* covers, and 17 fusilier pompoms. Equipment included 330 *gibernes*, 566 *porte-gibernes* made from blackened cow hide, accompanied by 632 musket slings also made from blackened cow hide, 103 *baudriers*, 4 drums and 2 drum carriages made from blackened cow hide.[82]

25e *de Ligne*

Copied from the regiment's now lost *registre d'habillement* on 19 January 1816, between 1 January 1812 and 1 August 1814 it appears that all items of clothing and equipment were of the *anciene modèle*.[83] Until the first restoration the regiment possessed not a single item made to the Bardin regulation. The regiment was given a shake-down inspection on 1 August 1814. Of the *porte-gibernes* in service, 355, or 56 per cent, were made from blackened cow hide, as were 378 musket slings, yet every one of the 1,118 *baudriers* were whitened buff leather – which must have made for an 'interesting' appearance on parade. The inspector ordered that all the men were to change their black leather work for whitened buff and that all missing items of equipment were to be obtained. Furthermore,

Fusilier in full dress during the 100 Days. We note non-regulation *schako* cords. The use of cords should NOT be taken as a standard practice across every regiment. We also note he wears his epinglette (vent pricker) across this revers rather than hung from the second button down on the right rever as per the regulations. Our fusilier from the 14^{e} also has musket (or is this a dragoon weapon?) with brass bands as for the *Garde Imperiale*. (*Collection KM*)

he ordered that the regiment was to place into effect the decree of 23 April 1814 and remove Imperial iconography, to burn its green drummers' habits, and ordered that in consequence of all clothing not being made in accordance to the decree of 19 January 1812 it was to be replaced immediately.[84]

The *dépôt* of the regiment held on 1 August 1814 0m 75 of drummers' livery – no doubt given the minimal amount, it was the 'fag end' of Imperial Livery that had been used to make drummers' clothing. Listed alongside was green serge, of which none existed, and hints at green *habits de tambour*. For the grenadiers, not a single *aigrette*, *schako*, sword knot or pair of epaulettes existed in *dépôt* or in use, but 10 grenades in copper for the *giberne* were in stores. *Dépôt* also held 388 blackened cow hide *giberne* belts, 34 habits – 2 were brand new – 79 *vestes*, 62 pairs of *pantalons de tricot* and 20 *capotes*.[85]

We know nothing more until the regiment was finally wound up in new year 1816. On 1 January 1816 the *dépôt* of the regiment held 180m of drummers' livery – was this Royalist Livery? – 147 pairs of grenadier epaulettes, 147 grenadier *aigrettes*, 151 *voltigeur aigrettes* and 489 fusilier pompoms, 64 *giberne* belts in blackened cow hide, 208 musket slings in blackened cow hide, 193 *baudriers*, 12 drums, 11 drum carriages and 2 *voltigeur cornets*.[86]

26e *de Ligne*

Reviewed on 5 August 1814, the men's clothing was either in good condition or missing: for example, 330 *capotes* were in good condition, 36 needed repairs, and 43 needed replacing, leaving a shortfall of 241. Of the *habits*, 627 were in good condition and 42 needed repairs, and they were made to the Bardin regulation. For the 726 men under arms, which included 9 musicians, 4 *sapeurs* and 4 master workmen, they were issued 1,708 shirts, 350 pairs of *pantalons de route* – not enough for every man, so clearly many men had just their *pantalons de tricot* for legwear – 642 black stocks, 150 white stocks for the *sous-officiers*, 104 pairs of linen ankle socks, 34 pairs of ankle socks, 999 pairs of shoes, 686 pairs of black gaiters and 393 pairs of grey gaiters – not enough of each existed for each man to have a pair of both. We note just 7 *sacs a distribution* were in use, and 617 *havresacs*. The *dépôt* held 1,663m 40 beige broadcloth, 1,101m 37 blue broadcloth, 113m 47 white broadcloth, 75m 51 scarlet broadcloth, 8,395m 90 white serge, 3,754m 96 white tricot, 80m 95 of linen and 15m of drummers' livery, 427 *schako* covers, 460 *houpette*s and 74 pairs of grenadier epaulettes. Therefore, we can be sure grenadiers had fringed epaulettes.[87]

Disbanded on 8 October 1815, no cloth or materials existed whatsoever in stores, so we can make no comment on the dress of drummers, *voltigeurs* and grenadiers.[88]

27e *de Ligne*

When inspected in summer 1814 the men were wearing a mix and match of Bardin and pre-Bardin clothing. The inspector noted that of the 433 *habits*, 214 of them were *habits-longe* with the same number of *vestes* in use in lieu of *gilets manches:* 50 per cent of the men were not wearing Bardin-regulation clothing, which had all recently been taken from the stores to replace the most worn-out clothing. We note 121 grenadier and *voltigeur aigrettes* were in use, with 17 more needed and the grenadiers had 58 pairs of epaulettes but needed 13 more pairs, and had 58 sword knots with 147 needed for every grenadier and *voltigeur* to have one. The regiment had a solitary *sapeur* on parade, and the 75 *voltigeurs* present had dragoon muskets. In stores, we note 90m of silver lace, and 672m 20 Imperial Livery, 91 new *capotes*, 24 new *habits-vestes*, 8 pairs of *pantalons de tricot*, and 136 new *bonnets de police*.[89]

Following the Waterloo campaign, the war battalions were disbanded on 17 September 1815. The *dépôt* on that date held 4m 93 green broadcloth, 17 pairs of grenadier epaulettes, 11 grenadier *aigrettes*, and 6 *voltigeur aigrettes*. All the clothing is reported as being of the Bardin pattern. An undetermined amount of Imperial Livery had been burned.[90]

28ᵉ *de Ligne*

In 1814 the regiment was merged with the 123ᵉ *de Ligne* and elements of the Young Guard. We note the grenadiers had no sabres, *aigrettes* and no epaulettes, and *voltigeurs* had no *aigrettes*. The men were also issued 1,863 shirts, 513 pairs of linen overalls, and just 29 pairs of socks: clearly shoes were worn over bare feet! In *dépôt* were 12 brand-new fusilier *habits-vestes*, 2 pairs of *pantalons de tricot*, 36 pairs of braces, 80 fusilier *schakos*, 19 *giberne* belts, 58 musket slings, 596 fusilier houpettes, 4 *voltigeur cornets*, 106m 30 red worsted lace and 50 *havresacs*. *Dépôt* also held eight brand-new *mousquetons* and four needing repairs: had these been issued to drummers?[91]

The paper archive of the regiment contains a wealth of material to reconstruct the appearance of the regiment as it was in 1815. Among the items in regiments *dépôt* we find:[92]

8 *voltigeur aigrettes*
306 fusilier *houpettes*
1 colpack for drum major
2 *voltigeur cornets*
10 pairs of gauntlets for *sapeurs*

The regiments *dépôt* also held 100 muskets, 10 carbines, 100 bayonets, 32 sabres, 5 *sapeurs*' axes, 1 pickaxe and 1 shovel. The carbines may have been used by *sapeurs* or more likely by officers of *voltigeur* companies as ascribed by the Bardin regulations. We note that one colpack was issued to the drum major and one was in the *dépôt*. Both colpacks had been inherited from the 123ᵉ *de Ligne* in 1814. Clearly, by the 100 Days, the *voltigeurs* had *aigrettes*, yet no reference is made for these items for grenadiers or indeed epaulettes. Therefore, were none in store because all had been issued for the grenadiers? Arguably so. The inspector in September 1815 noted 126m of Imperial Livery was burned. No green broadcloth existed, so presumably the lace was sewn on to standard *habits-vestes*.[93]

Voltigeur in full dress by Martinet. The tall green plume with a yellow tip as well as the green epaulettes are not part of Bardin regulation, but no doubt the regimental colonel kept in use these items from the previous regulation as a matter of economy before purchasing new items to the current regulation. The schako its self has dark green lace to the top band and side chevrons. The weapon may be a dragoon musket. The sabre looks to be the 1767 model. (*Collection KM*)

29[e] *de Ligne*

At the time of the August 1814 inspection, the regiment was dressed in worn-out rags: of the 757 *habits* in use, 377 were beyond repair and 195 needed repairs, leaving just 182 in useable condition. The men were also issued 1,508 shirts – two per man – 755 pairs of *pantalons de route*, 754 black stocks, 1,508 pairs of shoes – two pairs per man – 754 pairs of black and grey gaiters and *giberne* covers. The inspector noted that the regiment had begun the process to be reclothed, but added many *habits* were still of the old model. So, we must assume the regiment only changed over to Bardin regulation in summer 1814.[94] The *dépôt* held 12m 52 of chamois broadcloth, the inference being *voltigeurs* had chamois collars and shoulder straps or such garments were in the process of being made. Other materials in the *dépôt* included 255m of drummers' lace, and 64m of silver lace for the band. Grenadiers had scarlet epaulettes, some 40 new pairs being in *dépôt*, but no *aigrettes* whatsoever, all ranks having *houpettes*.[95]

By disbandment in summer 1815, grenadier *aigrettes* had been purchased, as the *dépôt* held 64 of these and 151 for *voltigeurs* along with 268 pairs of grenadier epaulettes. The band had silver lace to their uniforms. We note that in 1814 some 255m of drummers' livery was in *dépôt*, with 228m remaining at the time of disbandment in 1815. Only a very small amount of lace was used, assuming no more was purchased, so the drummers and *cornets habits* may have been standard fusilier *habits*.[96]

30e *de Ligne*

Inspected on 15 July 1814, the regiment had 1,219 men under arms. Half of the regiment's clothing was either worn out and had to be replaced or was in dire need of repair. For example, 786 *habits* were in good condition, 418 needed repairs, and 24 men had no *habit*. The inspector reported that 1,204 *habits* needed total replacement as they were of the old model – thus every man in the regiment was wearing pre-Bardin *habits*. Every single *veste manches* was of the old model, the men had breeches and not *pantalons*, some 117 pairs being in good condition, and 909 to be written off as life expired. The inspector remarked, furthermore, that everything in use had to be replaced as it was either worn out and or of old model. Despite this, men on parade had two shirts, a pair of grey linen gaiters and a pair of black twill gaiters, and a black stock. However, in order to make up for the shortage of regulation *pantalons de route,* of which 842 examples were in service, the inspector noted that *pantalons de route* made from brown broadcloth were in use. The *dépôt* held among other items 7m 82 of green broadcloth, 18 musicians *habits* and a solitary *epaulette de grenadier de modèle*.[97]

About the process of reclothing the regiment during the First Restoration we know a great deal, and it puts 'lie to the myth' that the Royalists spent no money on clothing the new army! For regimental clothing needs in 1814–15, rather than solely relying on making 'items in house' the regiment bought in from specialised contractors both materials and ready-made items:[98]

3rd Quarter 1814
Rund et Benninger, Metz
531 *schako* covers at 1fr 60 each, total 849fr 60
216 pairs of *grenadier* epaulettes at 3fr 50 a pair, total 756fr
1 pair of adjutant's epaulettes, total 25fr
Total 1,630fr 60

1st Quarter 1815
Rund et Benninger, Metz:
1,347m 99 linen for lining at 1fr 56 a metre. Total 1,819fr 78
124m linen for *caleçons*. Total 195fr 92
533 *gibernes* at 4fr 85 each. Total 2,585fr 05
533 *porte-gibernes* at 4fr 15 each. Total 2,211fr 95
533 musket slings at 1fr 01 each. Total 538fr 35
442 *baudriers* at 4fr 65 each. Total 2,055fr 30
10 drums at 43fr 10 each. Total 431fr
2 *voltigeur cornets* with cords at 25fr 78 each. Total 51fr 56
Total 9,888fr 89. Paid balance 8,497fr 29

Waiting to be delivered:
100 *gibernes*, 100 *porte-gibernes*, 100 musket slings, 84 *baudrier*s.
Total 1,391fr 60

Joannin of Strasbourg
622 *schakos* at 8fr 60 each
Total 5,349fr 20

Dalbanne Lebeouf of Troyes
409m 09 linen for lining. Total 572fr 72
999m 50 linen for *caleçons*. Total 1,649fr 17
Total 2,075fr 12

Toussaint of Metz
3m 05 gold lace at 8fr 50 a metre. Total 25fr 92
48m 95 gold lace at 8fr 50 a metre. Total 416fr 07
63m wool lace at 60 centimes a metre. Total 37fr 80
19m 80 wool lace at 53 centimes a metre. Total 10fr 89
340m Drummers' livery at 90 centimes a metre. Total 486fr
216 grenadier *aigrettes*. Total 756 fr
216 *voltigeur aigrettes*. Total 540fr
671 dozen large buttons. Total 268fr 40
3,202 dozen small buttons. Total 768fr 56
741 *houpette*s for fusiliers. Total 444fr 61
Total 3,754fr 24

M. Masson of Paris
338 dozen large buttons. Total 135fr 20
1,057 dozen small buttons. Total 253fr 76.
Total 388fr 96

Leroy, capitaine d'habillement 96e *de Ligne*
385 *houpettes*.
Total 231fr

M. Le Prefet of Mozelles
286m 64 blue broadcloth. Total 3,003fr 42
18m 75 scarlet broadcloth. Total 281fr 25
78m 08 white broadcloth. Total 702fr 72
198m 30 beige broadcloth. Total 1,784fr 70
500m white tricot. Total 2,000fr
269m linen for linings. Total 376fr 74
180m linen for *caleçons*. Total 298fr 15
Total 8,446fr 98

We also note that a considerable amount of kit was made or repaired the last quarters of 1814:[99]

75 *habits* at 2fr 45 each, total 183fr 75
2 *gilets* at 1fr 15, total 2fr 30
809 pairs of *pantalons de tricot* at 1fr, total 809fr
591 pairs of underwear at 40 centimes, total 236fr 40
196 *bonnets de police* at 60 centimes, total 117fr 60
262 *habits* repaired at 2fr 20, total 576fr 40
25 *habits* turned and remade at 2fr 45, total 61fr 25

'Turning a coat' literally meant taking it to pieces, turning it inside out and then being sewn back together with the 'clean' inside face of the cloth now on the outside. This prolonged the wear of the garments. The repairs to the *habits* were 25 centimes less than a new item, so we suppose the repairs were considerable: were *habits-longe* remade as *habit-vestes*, we wonder? In the first quarter of 1815 a further 84 *habits* were repaired for the sum of 184fr 80, 25 *habits* were 'turned' for 61fr 25, and 72 pairs of *pantalons de tricot* were made, along with 29 pairs of underwear and 196 *bonnets de police*. Clearly items were being patched and turned before funds were available to completely replace a lot of the clothing in the regiment. The master tailor produced in the first quarter of 1815:

Fusilier of the 121e *de Ligne* by Martinet. The white plume with red base is atypical and clearly a unique distinction for this regiment. We also see the white linen cover for the *giberne* and rolled *bonnet de police* under it. (*Collection KM*)

M. Collin, master tailor of the regiment
760 fusilier *habits*. Total 1,862fr
23 drummers' *habit*s at 8fr 50 each. Total 195fr 50
1241 *gilets manches*. Total 1,427fr 15
359 pairs of linen *pantalons*. Total 359fr
697 *capotes*. Total 910fr 50
1,494 *bonnets de police*. Total 896fr 40
486 pairs of underwear. Total 194fr 40
Total 5,844fr 95

A further six drummers' habits were made, again at 5fr 50 each in the weeks before the 1815 campaign began. A *habit-veste* cost 2fr 45 to make, to the increase in price clearly shows that these garments were heavily laced.[100]

The *dépôt* was totally devoid of cloth and materials when the regiment was wound up. Inventoried, but no longer present as the *dépôt* had been captured by the Prussians on 15 July 1815, were unknown numbers of *habits de grenadier*, *habits de voltigeur*, *habits de fusilier*, *habits de tambour*, and *habits de sapeur*, as well as *habits de musician de modèle*, *habits de grenadier de modèle*, *habits de fusilier de modèle*, and *habits de tambour de modèle*. The drummers and musicians' items were presumably Imperial Issue. The presence of *voltigeur* and *sapeur habits* suggests that these garments existed and were in use, as we note *sapeurs*' axes, aprons, and gauntlets being inventoried alongside *bonnets a poil* – bearskins for the *sapeurs* no doubt – and *schakos de grenadier*.

The *dépôt* reported the following items as stolen by the allies in May 1816:[101]

380 pairs of shoes, 519 shirts, 141 pairs of black gaiters, 464 pairs of grey gaiters, 1,341 pairs of linen socks, 365 pairs of linen *pantalons*, 806 white stocks, 105 cow hide *sacs de peau*, 16 painted *havresacs*, 255 long straps for *sacs de peau*, 62 *epinglettes*, 65 musket worms, 252 cockades, 246 pay books, 208 pairs of shoe buckles, 21 bearskin covers. Total 10,401fr 30

Concerning the bearskin covers: this is the only reference we have come across, other than the art work by Albrecht Adam, which proves such items existed. It also proves that the *sapeurs*, we assume of the 30e *de Ligne*, and by inference also the grenadiers, had bearskins at some stage to warrant the covers! We assume given the presence of bearskins, and bearskin covers, the *sapeurs* indeed wore bearskins in 1815.

32e *de Ligne*

The regiment is particularly well documented for the end of the Empire thanks to an almost – and unique – set of regimental accounts:[102]

M Lefebvre, lace maker, Paris
30 June 1813. 17m 40 gold lace, 48m red and yellow worsted lace, 180m drummers' lace, total 384fr 06
21 November. 500 *houpette*s, total 378fr
9 December. 630 *houpette*s, total 378fr
26 December. 1,000 *houpette*s, total 600fr.

M. Guy, hatter, Paris
21 November 1813. 500 *schako* covers, total 800fr
9 December. 630 *schako* covers, total 1,008 fr
26 December. 1,000 *schako* covers, total 1,600fr

M. Barbaud, clothier, Paris
21 November 1813. 2,300m linen for lining, 620m linen for *caleçons*, total 3,990fr
9 December. 781m linen for *caleçons*, 2,809m 80 linen for lining, total 5,027fr
26 December. 4,460m linen for lining, 1240m linen for *caleçons*, total 7,980fr

M. Baudesir, master tailor of the regiment
4th quarter of 1813. 2,130 *habits*, 2,130 *gilets manches*, 2,130 pairs *caleçons*, 2,130 *capotes*, 2,130 *bonnets de police*, total 15,123fr

M Garceau, Paris
18 December 1813. 276 *capotes*, 1,000 *sacs de peau*, 1,000 long *sacs de peau* straps, total 15,570fr

Sadly, we do not know the drummers' lace pattern purchased, but arguably given the date it was Imperial Livery. Alas, we do not have the purchase accounts for broadcloth, we can only assume the drummers' *habits* were green. The new habits were all Bardin regulation, and the numbers suggest a total re-dressing of the regiment at the end of the campaigns of 1813.

The regiment was inspected on 1 August 1814 by Inspector of Review Buchot. He commented that the regiment had been equipped from government magazines. The *habits* were described as 'in good condition, nearly all conform to the regulations, they are well cut and sewn' but the materials were sub-standard and had to be replaced. He remarked furthermore, that 93 conscripts were still waiting to have a *habit* issued. Likewise, he noted to clothe all the men on parade 360 *gilets manches* were needed, along with 378 pairs of *pantalons de tricot*, 413 pairs of *caleçons*, 341 *capotes*, 129 *schakos* and 653 *bonnets de police*. All the *schakos* were past the regulation period of usage, and thus we imagine were the 1810 model, while 171 *habits* were pre-Bardin, as were 39 *gilets manches*. He also recorded that the grenadiers and *voltigeurs* needed 289 *aigrettes* as none existed. Also needed as a matter of urgency were 291 muskets to replace those of foreign manufacture along with 298 bayonets, and 412 bayonet scabbards! The unit also needed 188 sabres,

This variation by Martinet shows a fusilier during the First Restoration: the crescent of the *schako* plate has been retained, but the offending eagle has been removed. This was perhaps a cost-effective solution until new plates could be made. The presumably, large regimental button below the cockade was sufficient to denote regimental affiliation. Perhaps this practice was common place.

as the 192 in use were of 'the old model'.[103] Yet in spite of these major issues he wrote to the Minister for War 'the weapons are all good, all new or nearly so'.[104] One feels that what Buchot told the War Ministry and what he found in the field were two different things – was he talking bribes to pass on 'fake news'? Entirely possible as he described the regiment's clothing as 'a credit to the colonel' to the War Ministry and at the same time he told the colonel to scrap everything and make new!

Indeed, to stress this point even further that Buchot was not telling the truth to the War Ministry is the fact he noted in his report to the colonel – who clearly knew this already! – that the regiment's leather work was 'grossly incomplete, old or worn out and a great number of the gibernes need repairs'. How is this a credit to the colonel, we wonder? Indeed, 273 men had no *giberne*, 274 men no *giberne* belt, 193 men had no *baudrier*, and 330 musket slings were missing. Indeed 24 drums and carriages were needed along with 12 sets of *sapeurs'* equipment, while the regiment had just 6 drummers and 6 *cornets* for the *voltigeur* companies.

Yet, given the lack of basic equipment, *dépôt* held 180 fusilier *schakos*, 379 *schako* covers, 328 *gibernes*, 349 *giberne* belts, 168 *bonnets de police*, 72 *gilets manches* and 3 *habits*, all brand new and waiting to be issued: the leather work would certainly have given those men without a *giberne* and belt the required items, so we wonder why they were not issued? *Dépôt* also held 28 old-pattern fusilier *habits-longe* as well as 107 shirts, 277 pairs of linen *pantalons de route*, 390 black stocks, 63 pairs of knee-length long black twill gaiters, 63 pairs of grey linen gaiters, 70 pairs of shoes, 34 pairs of black twill half gaiters, 161 pairs of grey linen half gaiters, 480 *sacs à distribution*, 363 *etui d'habit* – a non-regulation item – 430 *giberne* covers and 30 pairs of socks. No stocks of cloth or materials in the *dépôt* were acceptable for further use and had all to be replaced, Inspector Buchot informed the War Ministry 'the magazines have been badly kept'.[105]

Disbanded on 7 August 1815, the regiment had 18m 24 of green broadcloth in the *dépôt* and 180m of what we supposed to be Imperial Livery – was this the same stock as purchased in 1813? Perhaps, or is it pure coincidence that exactly the same amount of lace remained in *dépôt* as we know had been purchased?

Regimental records reveal 429 fusilier *habits* were made new in 1815 by the regiment, 276 were supplied by external manufacturers, and 2 were repaired. The regiment had 96 grenadier *schakos* and 360 fusilier *schakos* at time of disbandment, along with 99 pairs of grenadier epaulettes and 21 grenadier *aigrettes*. No *voltigeur schakos*, *aigrettes* or epaulettes existed, and not an inch of chamois cloth either. Therefore, did *voltigeurs* wear fusilier *habits*, or were these garments part of the consignment of 'bought in items'? It seems very likely that they were 'bought in' but this is a guess and not fact. We also find in *dépôt* 330 shirts, 753 pairs of shoes, 340 *sacs de peau*, 596 *sacs à distribution*, 414 black stocks, 64 pairs of long black twill gaiters and 414 pairs of short black gaiters, accompanied by 63 pairs of long grey linen gaiters and 671 pairs of short grey linen gaiters. Also, in *dépôt* were 42 *etuis d'habit* – far fewer than in 1814 suggesting some had been issued – accompanied by two qualities of *schako* covers, 171 examples valued at 1fr, and 12 valued at 1fr 60, 347 pairs of linen *pantalons de route* and 160 linen *giberne* covers.[106] We suppose a mix of Bardin and pre-Bardin clothing was worn in 1814 and the items in *dépôt* were the leftovers from taking these items out of service. We know little about the drummers, other than supposing materials were in hand to make new Imperial Livery clothing and that none was made as exactly the same amount of green broadcloth is found in several other regiment's stores lists, suggesting this amount of cloth was a 'standard unit of purchase'.

The regiment was renumbered at the restoration as 31ᵉ. Remarkably an officer's *habit* of a grenadier company exists from the nine-month period when the regiment had been renumbered 31ᵉ *de Ligne*. The *habit* is in the ex Fichtner collection at Fontainebleau and is remarkable that the *revers* are piped white not red, and the cuff facings are blue with white piping! The tails carry gold embroidered flaming grenades with five flames backed on to scarlet cloth. The tails themselves are faced in superfine white broadcloth, piped and lined in white superfine broadcloth. Did all members of the regiment have blue cuff facings and white piping to the *revers*? Alas we cannot tell. The garment is very high cut in front, the base of the *revers* being well above the natural line of the waist.

We also note than an extant officer's regimental artillery *habit* buttoned as 31ᵉ *de Ligne* exists in the collection JN in France. It is a Bardin-regulation *habit-veste*: the cuffs are pointed and piped red. The tail facings and lining are likewise blue with red piping. It is accompanied by a white *veste*, *chapeau* and *manteau*. Quite clearly the regiment had attached artillery in the First Restoration, which is the only time the 31ᵉ *de Ligne* existed. The chaotic nature of the 1814 paperwork renders any further comment impossible.

33ᵉ *de Ligne*

Reviewed in summer 1814, the regiment's clothing was fairly shambolic. The inspector noted that he had issued contracts for the production of 350 *habits-vestes*, 1,424 *gilets manches en drap*, 201 pairs of *pantalons de tricot*, and 127 *capotes*. *Dépôt* held 1,740m of broadcloth of differing colours – we do not have the amounts of each colour sadly –

Opposite: This variation of the Martinet plate gives this fusilier white gaiters. Some regiments did indeed have these items. An idea of who a soldier was who was issued his kit can be found in the personal papers of Jean Louis Fourniol of the 16e *de Ligne* in the author's collection. Born on 4 June 1792, he is recorded as standing 1m 61cm. He joined his regiment as MAT. No. 8409 on 5 April 1812, and was admitted to the *voltigeur* company in 2e battalion on 1 August 1812. He served in Spain in 1812–13 and thence the campaign of France, being promoted *fourrier* on 1 January 1814 in 2e company. He left the army on 1 September 1815. On the day he joined the regiment at Toulon, he was issued his *giberne* and belt, bayonet, musket, and *sac de peau*, and received the same day his *habit*, *gilet*, *schako* and *capote*, and his linen and footwear comprising two shirts, one black stock, one pair of *pantalons de route* and one pair of grey gaiters. He was issued a pair of *pantalons de tricot* on 1 April 1813, and finally a *bonnet de police* on 1 October 1814: we assume the delay was due to chronic shortages of clothing. He is recorded as buying a new pair of black gaiters for 3fr on 27 August 1814, taken directly from his pay of 6fr 60. Issued on 1 October 1814 were: three shirts, one black stock, two white stocks, two pairs of cotton socks, one pair of wool stockings, two pairs of shoes, two pairs of grey gaiters, one pair of black gaiters, two pairs of white gaiters, one *sac de peau*, two pairs of *pantalons de route* made from bleached white cotton canvas and a box of grease. On 1 April 1815, he had these items reissued, but received just two shirts and one pair of cotton socks. These bleached white *pantalons* and gaiters were an innovation of the February 1815 dress regulations, and should not be used to give credence to the use of these items before 1815.

139 brand-new *capotes*, 142 *habits-vestes*, 32 *gilets manches en tricot blanc*, 615 *bonnets de police* and 1,526 pairs of underwear, which had all been recently made by the regimental workmen. The inspector lamented that there was a great indiscipline about the dress of the regiment, and that modifications had been made without regulation.[107] Sadly we are ignorant as to those changes, but it may include the blue collar patches piped or edged white Bucqouy suggests the regiment had.

At the time of disbandment in summer 1815, the regiment possessed 3m 27 of chamois broadcloth, 18m 24 of green broadcloth and 32m 87 of drummers' livery. It is likely therefore that *voltigeurs* had chamois collars to their *habits*. The green broadcloth suggests Imperial Livery was used.[108]

34[e] *de Ligne*

Drawn up for inspection on 29 July 1814 by Inspector of Review Chaalon, the regiment had a huge shortfall in clothing, needing 478 *habits*, 502 *gilets manches*, 540 pairs of *pantalons de tricot*, 524 *capotes*, 605 *schakos*, and 792 *schako* covers. We also note 66 men were dressed in pre-Bardin uniforms.

No materials were in *dépôt* but it did hold 3 white *habits*, a master musicians' *habit de modèle* and also a musician's *habit* '*de modèle*' and 16 drummers' *habits*, as well as a '*habit de tambour de modèle*'. We also note that insufficient gaiters existed to give every man a pair, let alone a pair of each: just 218 pair of black and 130 pairs of grey gaiters were in use alongside 120 pairs of *pantalons de route*, 220 black stocks, 54 pairs of linen socks, 1,053 shirts, 817 pairs of shoes and just 6 canteens. We note a solitary *aigrette de modèle de grenadier* and a similar example for *voltigeurs* were in store: we assume more were in use, likewise we find one *schako de modèle pour grenadier*.[109] An inventory of the regiment's *dépôt* was compiled on 19 June 1815:

Materials
7m 08 scarlet broadcloth, 650m 77 white serge, 433.2 dozen large buttons, 2,634.1 dozen small buttons

Clothing
217 *vestes*, 17 *bonnets de police*, 70 *schakos*

Equipment
18 *baudriers*, 614 *porte-gibernes*, 48 musket slings, 9 drum carriages, 9 drummers' aprons and waistbelts, 4 *sapeurs*' axes, 7 axe cases with belt, 2 pairs of gauntlets for *sapeurs*, 9 bayonet scabbards.

Petit Equipment
313 shirts, 104 black stocks, 499 pairs of shoes, 505 pairs of black gaiters, 125 pairs of grey gaiters, 103 *sacs de peau*, 430 *epinglettes*, 7 large straps for *sacs de peau*, 19 small straps for *sacs de peau*, 142 *giberne* covers, 1 grenadier *aigrette* '*de modèle*', 1 *voltigeur aigrette* '*de modèle*'

Martinet presents this sergeant of *voltigeurs*. The green epaulettes and plume were regulation since 1807, and seemingly were carried over in use for economic reasons. The yellow lace trim with tassels to the gaiters is whole unexpected and shown in no other print: clearly unique to who ever Martinet witnessed wearing this uniform. We note, again contrary to expectations, the cuff flaps are scarlet piped white, with three points to the leading edge.

> Armament
> 9 muskets and bayonets
>
> Comment.
> The corps has made orders for the clothing of 433 men. The corps will take delivery on the 20 of this month 923m 61 blue broadcloth for replacement clothing for the year 1815. For the replacement clothing the following material has been ordered:
>
> 982m 42 white broadcloth
> 83m 76 red broadcloth
> 2,361m beige broadcloth
> 9m 63 chamois broadcloth
> 2,702m white tricot
>
> M. Mastier, clothier of Lodeve, has been charged to supply these items to the regiment by the director of clothing.
> The regiment has received 317 muskets and 35 sabres. In the *dépôt* are 9 defective muskets with bayonets.[110]

The document is interesting on several accounts. From the cloth breakdown, it is clear the regiment had red, presumably garance, facings in lieu of the more expensive scarlet, and that *voltigeurs* had, according to regulations, chamois collars.[111]

The *dépôt* at the time of disbandment held, among other items, 33 grenadier *aigrettes*, 169 *voltigeur aigrettes*, 554 fusilier *houpettes*, 372 cockades, 601 *schako* covers, 96 pairs of grenadier epaulettes, 11 axe cases and belts for *sapeurs*, 9 *sapeurs'* aprons, 9 *sapeurs'* aprons, 11 pairs of *sapeurs'* gauntlets and 4 *sapeurs'* axes. Also, in stores were '*4 habits selon non reglementaire*', i.e *habits-longe* that may well have been white with violet facings.[112]

35ᵉ *de Ligne*

The inspection report dated 16 July 1814 reveals that 99 *aigrettes,* sword knots and epaulettes were used by grenadiers, and 115 *aigrettes* were used by the *voltigeurs*, who needed 48 sword knots. Furthermore, the inspector noted that:

> He would like to draw the regiment's Council of Administration to obtain copies of, and to thoroughly understand, the following indispensable decrees ... The decree of 19 January and 7 February 1812 and the *circulaire* from the War Minister of 23 April 1814 for the clothing of the soldiers.[113]

Reading between the lines here, it seems that the Bardin regulations had not yet been fully acted upon and clearly Imperial iconography was in use. The *dépôt* was modestly well stocked with cloth and clothing, which included 10m 69 chamois broadcloth, 50m 50 of drummers' livery, the latter being we assume all that remained from making green

Imperial Livery *habits*. The report furthermore lists 548 grenadier *schakos*, 489 fusilier *schakos*, 17 grenadier *aigrettes* and 12 *aigrettes* for *voltigeurs*. We also note 762 stock buckles as well as 956 *giberne* covers.[114] From these reports, we can see that the regiment was in the process of fully changing over to Bardin regulation that summer. The huge number of grenadier *schakos* suggests these were waiting to be issued and none were in use.

On 3 August 1815, among other items the *dépôt* held 18m 24 green broadcloth and 230m 50 drummers' lace, 2 pairs of adjutant's epaulettes, 61 pairs of grenadier epaulettes and 1,596 pompoms in various colours.[115] When the 1e battalion was wound up on 1 November 1815, the stores held 1m chamois broadcloth and 1m 50 of lace. Also, in store were 92 *schakos*, 92 pairs each of grenadier and voltigeur epaulettes, 92 grenadier *aigrettes*, 74 *voltigeur aigrettes*, 76 pompoms as well as 8 s*apeurs*' axe cases and aprons along with 5 pairs of gauntlets and 6 axes.[116]

36e *de Ligne*

The regiment's paperwork for 1812 to 1815 is remarkable as it is totally complete, which allows us unrivalled detail in reconstructing its dress. The tailor's accounts were as follows for 1812:[117]

765 *habits* costing 2fr 20 each
700 *habits* costing 2fr 45 each
49 *habits de tambour* in blue cloth costing 8fr 95 each
1,095 *vestes* costing 1fr each
500 *vestes* costing 1fr 15 each
15 *gilet sans manches* costing 50 centimes each
1,052 pairs of *culottes de tricot* costing 90 centimes each
1,184 *bonnets de police* costing 40 centimes each
700 *bonnets de police* costing 60 centimes each
500 pairs of *pantalons de tricot* costing 1fr each
300 *capotes* costing 1fr each
700 *capotes* costing 1fr 50 each
500 pairs of *caleçons* costing 40 centimes each
15 pairs of *pantalons* costing 75 centimes each

We are ignorant at the difference between the two *habit* types: one clearly needed more labour than the other. We also see that the regiment was wearing two types of sleeved *veste* and the adjutants had white sleeveless *vestes* and blue *pantalons*. The 49 drummers' *habits* clearly had lace sewn to blue *habits*. The lace is very likely to be Imperial Livery and an incredibly early adoption; some 736fr 50 worth was purchased on 11 August 1812 from M. Bouquet, military supplier of Paris, costing 1fr 15 a metre. We also see two patterns of *capote* and *bonnet de police*. The regiment used both army specification

Martinet gives us this drum major in dark blue with silver embellishments, which we know from archive sources was a typical costume during the First Restoration.

Lodeve cloth and due to shortages had no option than to use lower-quality broadcloths. Among other items purchased were 484 *houpettes de grenadier*, 489 *houpettes de voltigeur* and 1,740 *houpettes de fusiliers*, along with 5 pairs of epaulettes for adjutants and 290 pairs of epaulettes for grenadiers.

Clothing produced in 1813 was as follows.[118]

415 *habits fait en veste*, costing 2fr 95 each
1,474 *habits* costing 2fr 45 each
12 *habits de tambour* costing 8fr 95 each
2,385 pairs *pantalons de tricot* costing 1fr each
2,800 pairs of underwear costing 40 centimes each
1,948 *vestes* or *gilets* costing 1fr 15
235 *gilets* costing 1fr 75
248 *capotes* costing 1fr 65
952 *capotes* costing 1fr 50
1,391 *bonnets de police* costing 60 centimes.

For the drummers' habits, just 6m 30 of green broadcloth was purchased on 10 March, and a further 702m of lace was purchased on 4 April. All the green broadcloth was used to make drummers' clothing: given a *habit* needed over 2m of broadcloth, only three such garments could be made, we assume for the drum major and the two drum masters, the other *habits* being blue with Imperial Livery: assuming the green broadcloth was not facings to blue coats! *Voltigeurs* had chamois collars and shoulder straps, as some 8m 55 of chamois broadcloth was used for this purpose and had just 200 *aigrettes* purchased to adorn their *schakos* and 150 hunting horns in copper for the *giberne*. Grenadiers had 250 copper grenades to decorate their *gibernes* and 211 *aigrettes*. Fusiliers had 250 crowned Ns purchased on 18 June 1813 – this is one of the few documentary sources to show these items actually existed beyond the written page! We also find 100 Ns and 50 crowns obtained, showing the regiment used two different types of *giberne* ornaments for fusiliers. These were the only *giberne* ornaments the regiment ever obtained, which we assume went to 1e battalion. Sixteen sets of *sapeurs*' equipment were also purchased. The *habits fait en veste* must surely be *habits-vestes*. In 1814 70 *habits-vestes*, 330 *habits*, 500 *gilets fait en veste* – surely the Bardin type – 100 vestes, 400 *capote en vestes* – i.e., double breasted and without shadow of a doubt the Bardin type – 900 pairs of *pantalons de tricot*, 956 pairs of underwear and 400 *bonnets de police* were made.

Inspected on 1 September 1814, the regiment had 124 officers and 1,156 others ranks, as well as 11 *enfants de troupe*. As one would expect at the end of the campaign of France, the clothing was either worn out, non-existent or in good condition. For example, some 332 *habits* were in serviceable condition, 92 needed repairs, 277 needed total replacement and 177 men had no *habit* at all! Likewise of 1,156 men, 329 had no *gilet*s *manches*, 359 no *pantalons de tricot*, 751 men had no *caleçon*, 269 no *capote*, 165 no *schako* and 519 no *bonnet de police*. Furthermore, 152 men had no *giberne*, 155 no *porte-giberne*, so at least 3 men had a *giberne* suspended on string or some other form of belt. The regiment had 287 grenadiers, of which no man had a sabre and belt and 745 men had no musket slings: we guess string or another ad hoc sling was used. Cloth in the *dépôt* comprised 0m 74 beige broadcloth, 51m 30 white broadcloth, 9m 49 chamois broadcloth, 1,964m white serge, 1m 63 white tricot, 240m 50 linen for linings, 79m 08 violet broadcloth – dating from 1806 when the regiment adopted white *habits* with violet distinctions – 9m 08 silver lace, 2m 80 red worsted lace. Clothing in the *dépôt* included 199 *capotes*, 538 fusilier *habits*, 355 fusilier *gilets manches*, 487 pairs of *pantalons de tricot*, 347 *bonnets de police*, 1,008 pairs of *caleçons*, 817 fusilier *schakos*, and 52 grenadier bearskins, all noted as brand new. *Dépôt* also held 16 new *sapeurs*' axes, 86 grenadier *aigrettes*, 75 *voltigeur aigrettes*, 1,788 fusilier *houpettes* and 188 pairs of grenadier epaulettes. So, we must imagine the grenadiers had bearskins and fringed epaulettes at least in the 1e battalion at some stage, while *voltigeurs* had chamois collars and *aigrettes*. The regiment was armed with a motley collection of firearms: 670 muskets existed, 224 were dragoon model for *voltigeurs* and 116 were foreign models.[119] The inspector noted that the men's clothing was not in accordance to the decree of 19 January 1812 and that 300 *habits* were needed to replace non-Bardin types along with 700 *vestes* and 700 pairs of *pantalons de tricot*, adding that the regiment needed new muskets.[120]

The paper archive for the regiment is remarkably complete for the First Restoration:[121]

	Blue broadcloth	White broadcloth	Red broadcloth	Beige broadcloth	Chamois broadcloth	White serge	White tricot	Linen	Drummers' livery
In stores 1 September 1814	113m 64	62m 66	5m 25	0m 74	9m 49	1,964m	1m 63	4,455m 23	
Obtained third and fourth Quarter 1814									
Used	11m 80	4m 96	3m 25			9m		14m 23	
Remaining 1 January 1815	101m 24	57m 70	2m 40	0m 74	9m 49	1,955m	1m 63	4,441m	
Made or purchased by the regiment	171m 40	71m 50	15m 55	231m 70		83m 73	74m 17	1,377m 18	570m
Supplied by the state	169m 20	117m 30	15m 60	1,410m 46		855m 73	193m		
Total obtained	448m 44	246m 50	33m 55	1,648m 90	9m 49	2,896m 44	268m 8	6,813m 18	570m
Total used	349m 88	149m 37	33m 55	1,641m 60	6m 35	232m	267m 5	1,514m 22	
Remaining in *dépôt* 26 August 1815	93m 22	97m 13		1m 30	3m 44	2,664m 46	1m 26	5,306m 30	570m

Martinet gives a variation of the drum major, dressed in sky blue and silver. Taking this light shade of blue as *Bleu de Roi* this uniform was, as far as can be judged regulation issue.

None of the Royalist-issue drummers' livery was ever used, ergo the drummers' *habits* were likely to be standard infantry *habits*. Clothing made in the same period was:

	Fusilier *Habits*		*Vestes*			*Pantalons*		*Capotes*		Drumm *habi*
	New	Previously Issued	Broadcloth	tricot	Previously Issued	New in tricot	Previously Issued	New	Previously Issued	Nev
In stores 1 September 1814	382	49	1	355	25	488	38	200	79	1
Purchased or made										
Issued	382	49	0	355	25	483	36	199	79	0
Remaining 1 January 1815			1			5	2	1		1
Issued from government magazines	211	349			548	319	11			
Obtained locally								300		
Made by the regiment	232			107		133		684	42	
Supplied by the state		15				14	7		2	
Total Obtained	443	364	1	107	548	471	20	985	44	1
Total Issued	411	364	0	104	510	469	17	980	44	0
Remaining in *dépôt* 26 August 1815	32	0	1	3	38	8	3	5	0	1

Huge amounts of clothing were 'second hand' taken from government stockpiles. The single drummer's *habit* and veste was inherited from the 144e *de Ligne* and never issued. Drummers clearly wore infantry *habits* in 1814–15. The paper archive shows that by January 1815, 50 bearskins were in store, and that 149 pairs of grenadier epaulettes, 86 grenadier *aigrettes* and 73 *voltigeur aigrettes* had been issued. Grenadiers wore fusilier *schakos*. *Voltigeurs* also had chamois collars and shoulder straps. Interestingly, the regiment had 389 French muskets in use, 344 'foreign' muskets, 4 light cavalry carbines for *sapeurs* and 3 rifles were issued to *voltigeur sous-officiers*.[122]

A self-portrait by Jean Baptiste Thysbeart in the archive of Lucien Rousselot can shed more light on the dress of *voltigeurs*:

This copy of a naïve period sketch presents a grenadier observed during June 1814. This is the only period depiction of a small fanion carried in a musket barrel. No archive documents attest to their use.

> MAT No. 10081 Jean Baptiste Thysbeart was born 8 August 1794 in Brussels, he was a conscript of the class of 1814. His mother's maiden name was Vauhaubeyeck, father not known. He stood 1m 57, had an oval face, grey eyes and brown hair. By profession he was a wagon painter. He was conscripted to the 36ᵉ *de Ligne* on 18 April 1813 and admitted to the *voltigeur* company of 3ᵉ battalion. Clearly literate, he was made corporal 30 April 1813. PoW 12 November 1813.[123]

In his portrait attached to a letter he sent from Calais, he is dressed as a *voltigeur* and has corporal's stripes. What is unusual is that the *habit* has a blue collar, the *schako* has a yellow *aigrette* with green base over a green pompom, yellow epaulettes with green crescents, and has short light infantry-style black gaiters![124] From the paper archive we know only a small amount of chamois cloth was obtained – ergo a blue collar is fully expected if the regiment restricted chamois distinctions to the 1ᵉ and 2ᵉ battalions alone. We wonder if in the 36ᵉ *de Ligne* therefore that scarlet collars were the reserve of grenadiers, and fusiliers and *voltigeurs* had blue collars? Arguably so. Yet the archive makes no mention at all of *voltigeur* epaulettes! Is Thysbeart mistaken? His letter is from Calais, where the regiment was in barracks, and he was a real man, so we have no reason to doubt what he shows. We wonder if the *voltigeur* epaulettes dated from pre-1812 and were issued en masse? Further, did just 1ᵉ and 2ᵉ battalions have chamois collars? Arguably so if we believe this image.

The regiment had 16 sets of *sapeurs'* equipment in stores in January 1815. During the 100 Days a bearskin was issued to the corporal *sapeur* and 14 grenadier *schakos* were issued to the *sapeurs* with cords and plume, scarlet-fringed epaulettes, apron, axe case and belt, gauntlets. Line infantry *briquet* were used.[125]

37ᵉ *de Ligne*

The only document we can locate that gives us a detailed snapshot of the regiment is the inspection report of 4 August 1814. As could be predicted, the clothing was either recently issued, worn out or missing. For example, of the *habits* in use, 544 were new *habits-vestes*, 102 *habits* needed repairs, 80 needed replacement and 232 men had no *habit*. Likewise, 307 had no *veste*, 314 no capote and 288 no *schako*. The regiment only armed sergeants, *fourriers* and sergeant majors with sabres: 42 *baudriers* were issued and remarkably 165 sabres, so we ask how these were carried. Further, two *cornets* were in use. Not a single pair of *pantalons de route* was issued and instead overalls made from 'rough broadcloth and tricot of various colours' were in use: seemingly adopted in 1813 and 1814 out of necessity and practicality in the depths of winter. Likewise, using *habits-longe* and *habits-vestes* side by side was a 'common sense' approach. Remarkably, every man had a pair of shoes – 981 pairs being issued – along with 760 pairs of black gaiters and 230 pairs of grey – clearly as long as a soldier had a pair of gaiters, no one really commented – but every man did have a black stock and two shirts. Among the items in the *dépôt* were 8 brand-new drummers' *habits*, 101 pairs of *culottes*, 14 grenadier *aigrettes*, 157 pairs of grenadier epaulettes and 645 fusilier *houpettes*. We also find stored away 9 stock buckles, 4 pairs of knee buckles, 131 giberne covers, and 77 pairs of *schako* cords.[126]

Disbanded in September 1815, the *dépôt* held 16 *habits-longe,* 101 pairs of *culottes* – exactly the same number as 1814, which shows that despite shortages of clothing these non-regulation items were not pressed back into service – 169 *vestes*, 37 pairs of *caleçons*, 169 *schakos*, 76 *bonnets de police*, 161 grenadier *aigrettes*. No drummers' lace and no green cloth existed, so we assume they wore fusilier *habits* in the 100 Days. No chamois cloth existed either for voltigeurs, but 42 *aigrettes* did.[127]

39ᵉ *de Ligne*

The regiment was reviewed on 11 August 1814, when it mustered 94 officers, 978 other ranks and 10 *enfants de troupe*. We note 353 men had no *habit*, 383 *habits* needed repair and 248 were little more than rags. Likewise, 373 men had no *gilets manches*, 573 no *pantalons de tricot*, 395 had no *capote* and 327 no *schako*. The equipment was in a similarly poor state, with 267 men having no *giberne* and belt, 16 drummers had no drum, the 6 *voltigeur cornets* had no instruments, and the 215 grenadiers had no sabres: these were issued just to *sous-officiers*. The men were also issued 2,143 shirts, 772 pairs of linen *pantalons de route*, 850 black stocks with 769 buckles – clearly some were tied with a tape and therefore Bardin regulation and other men were wearing the older pattern with buckle closure – 1,323 white stocks, 558 pairs of linen socks, 1,685 pairs of shoes, 653 pairs of black gaiters, 1,048 pairs of great gaiters, 309 *sacs à distribution*, 963 *havresacs* and 745 *giberne* covers. The *dépôt* held very little in the way of cloth: 0m 07 blue broadcloth, 1,654m 07 white serge, 0m 16 white tricot and 193m 50 drummers' lace. No clothing was held in the dépôt.[128] The lace was presumably left over from making Imperial Livery habits.

Regimental accounts record that 30 gold embroidered *fleur-de-lys* costing 30fr, 28 copper grenades costing 28fr and 100 hunting horns costing 75fr – presumably 'more of the same' – were purchased on 24 September 1814, and the regimental tailors were paid 72fr 65 sewing grenades, *fleur-de-lys* or hunting horns to *habit* tails.[129]

Disbanded on 21 September 1815, the *dépôt* held little in the way of materials: 1m 24 blue broadcloth, 9m 30 white broadcloth, 48m 53 scarlet broadcloth, 1m green broadcloth, 0m 53 white tricot, 1750m 56 white serge, 154m 82 linen, 47m 25 gold lace, 1m 60 silver lace –exactly this amount was inherited from the 133ᵉ *de Ligne* so was never used – 1m 30 drummers' lace – was this all that remained from the lace in 1814? – 231m 40 yellow worsted lace, and 1,375m 09 red worsted lace. Also, in stores were 14 grenadier *aigrettes*, 33 *voltigeur aigrettes*, 15 grenades in copper for *gibernes*, 11 copper hunting horns for *gibernes* and 6 *fleur-de-lys* in copper for fusilier *gibernes* . Presumably the items in store represented the items actually in use, and these were spares. We also find three *sapeurs*' axes, seven pairs of *sapeur*s gauntlets and two aprons.[130]

This grenadier, witnessed in summer 1813 around Dresden, is typical of many grenadiers who were so dressed as late as summer 1814, according to archive research, complete with bearskin. (*Collection KM*)

40e *de Ligne*

Inspected on 16 August 1814, the regiment's clothing was either new or in need of total replacement and repair. For example, of the 1,050 men on parade, 485 were wearing *habits* in good condition, 185 men had *habits* that needed repairs, and 98 habits needed replacing as they were *habits-longe* and 282 men had no *habit* and were on parade in *capotes*. Likewise, 540 men had no *veste*, 342 no *pantalons de tricot*, 342 no *caleçon*, 281 had no *capote*, 250 no *schako*, 478 no *bonnet de police*, and 128 had no *giberne* and belt. Despite having 47 good sabre belts in use, just 25 sabres existed: the regiment was a total shambles, with *pantalons* made from tricot and broadcloth of various colours in use to make up for the lack of legwear, the inspector noted. The regiment had sufficient harness and tack for five pack horses. The men were issued 1,675 shirts, 325 pairs of linen *pantalons de route*, 747 black stocks, 1,172 pairs of shoes, 685 pairs of black gaiters, 727 pairs of grey gaiters, 83 *sacs à distribution*, and 740 *sacs de peau*. Cloth in the *dépôt* included 6m of drummers' lace – this was we assume all that remained of a stock of Imperial Livery – a well as '*de modèle*' examples of a *capote*, fusilier *habit* and *gilet manches*, *pantalons de tricot*, a *giberne* and belt, musket sling, *baudrier*, *sapeur*'s axe case, and *sapeur*'s apron. The inspector further noted the many men in the ranks had no effects at all and wore civilians.[131]

To reclothe the regiment the inspector ordered 338 *habits*, 611 *vestes*, 507 pairs of *pantalons de tricot*, and the same number of pairs of underwear, and that 383 *capotes*, *bonnets de police* and *schakos* be made to conform to the regulation of 19 January 1812 and 23 April 1814: therefore we assume *voltigeurs* had chamois collars and *aigrettes*, and grenadiers had scarlet *aigrettes*, epaulettes and grenadier *schakos*. Drummers would be in Royalist Livery.[132] A report produced on 18 to 20 June 1815 gives us some information about how the regiment was dressed:

Men of the 3e and 4e battalions, present and available for service	291
Men of the 5e and 6e battalions present	123
Men present	414
Men absent	161
Effective	975

Clothing
The town of Senlis and its environs offers little in terms of resources for the workmen to make new items, they have only been able to make ten complete uniforms.
800 metres of white tricot for *vestes* has been purchased. The Administrative Council is employing its money for the purchase of broadcloth and other items of clothing and equipment.

The corps has available the following new items on 18 June:

192 *habits*
248 *vestes*
280 *pantalons de tricot*
160 *capotes*
660 *caleçons*
767 *schakos*
344 *gibernes*
344 *porte-gibernes*
996 braces for *pantalons*

There is in the magazine 74 muskets and the same number of sabres. A request for more arms has been submitted for the men arriving, in the last days 100 muskets have been received.[133]

Alas, no disbandment paperwork can be found in the regiment's archive to state what was worn at the end of its existence. The lack of archive sources detailing distinctive items for elite troops and drummers means we can say nothing for fact about how these men were dressed that would not be speculation, other than assuming the inspectors' orders were put into action.

42e *de Ligne*

The regiment was inspected on 17 August 1814, when the inspector noted that the bulk of the unit's clothing was missing or worn out: 374 *habits* needed repairs, 224 needed total replacement and 83 men lacked one. Indeed, of the 1,279 men on parade, 746 had no *pantalons de tricot*, 591 no *veste*, 366 no *capote*, 688 no *bonnet de police* and 105 no *schako*. In items of *petit equipment*, in use were 1,973 shirts, 857 pairs of linen *pantalons de route,* 699 black stocks, 1,598 pairs of shoes, 467 pairs of black gaiters, 479 pairs of grey gaiters, 6 *sacs à distribution,* and 1,110 *sacs de peau.* The inspector noted that the *dépôt* was devoid of materials to make new clothing. Little wonder we suppose as the *dépôt* held brand-new clothing ready to be issued, which included 236 *capotes*, 2 *voltigeur habits*, 97 fusilier *habits*, 108 fusilier *gilets manches*, 361 pairs of *pantalons de tricot*, 248 pairs of *caleçons*, and 288 fusilier *schakos* with 328 covers. Equipment in the *dépôt* included 328 *gibernes* with 389 belts, 268 musket slings, 19 drums and carriages, 264 grenadier *aigrettes*, 185 *voltigeur aigrettes*, 807 *houpettes*, and 1 drummers' apron. We assume the *habits* of grenadiers had epaulettes. The musket slings and *porte-gibernes* were made from blackened cow hide. No cloth or materials whatsoever were in *dépôt*. *Petit equipment* in *dépôt* included 604 shirts, 37 pairs of *pantalons de toile*, 665 black stocks, 986 pairs of shoes, 39 pairs of long black gaiters, 27 pairs of long grey gaiters, 84 *sacs de peau*, and 92 *epinglettes*.[134]

This grenadier, witnessed in summer 1813 around Dresden, is typical of many grenadiers who were so dressed as late as summer 1814, according to archive research. (*Collection KM*)

At the time of disbandment, we can be sure that the regiment's drummers had Imperial Livery; *dépôt* held 2m 73 of green broadcloth and 863m 80 of drummers' lace – such a huge amount perhaps represents a mix of Royalist and Imperial Livery, possibly left over from making garments. Other materials in the *dépôt* also included 14m 59 chamois broadcloth, and 980m 20 blue tricot it seems left over from making *pantalons* for the regimental artillery in 1813 and 1814. *Dépôt* held 13 pairs of grenadier epaulettes, and none were in use unless counted on the grenadiers' *habits*, and likewise no *aigrettes* existed in *dépôt* or in use, unless counted on the *schako* as they certainly existed a year earlier?[135]

43e *de Ligne*

Reviewed on 16 July 1814, the regiment was reduced to 334 men: half of the clothing and equipment was either missing, needed total replacement or needed repairs. The *dépôt* held 125m of drummers' lace, and 2 *voltigeur aigrettes*, among a myriad array of other items.[136] Arguably, if *voltigeurs* had *aigrettes*, we can assume grenadiers had them, and likewise epaulettes: but this is not fact, and nothing more than bare-faced speculation. During the First Restoration the regiment became the 40e *de Ligne* and to mark this change, the tails of the *habits* were decorated with cut out numerals to read '40'. These were changed to 43 on 28 April 1815.[137]

The *dépôt* in 1815 held very little at the time of disbandment, '*vert dragon*' is listed in the broadcloth returns, but none was recorded as present – had it all been used to make new drummers' *habits*? Possibly. Equipment in *dépôt* comprised 1,060 *gibernes*, 536 *giberne* belts, 728 musket slings, 646 *baudriers*, 21 drums, 21 drum carriages, and 21 drummers' aprons. For *sapeurs* the *dépôt* held eight axes, eight aprons, eight axe cases and eight pairs of gauntlets. Weapons included 464 muskets, 464 bayonets, and 409 sabres. *Dépôt* also held 369 pairs of black twill gaiters, 198 pairs of grey linen gaiters, 583 pairs of socks, 1,329 pairs of shoes, 301 *havresacs*, 235 black stocks, 287 cockades, 768 *epinglettes*, 332 *tournvis*, 468 *sacs a campagne*, and 170 *sacs de peau*. The *sac a campagne* has no clear parallels, the *sac de peau* is the period term for what we understand as the back pack, which is also recorded as *havresac*.[138] Are we dealing with another name for the *sac à distribution*? Possibly. But it seems three distinct items are listed here: is this a reference to the use of a shoulder bag like the British used? Possibly.

44e *de Ligne*

When inspected in October 1814, the inspection report reveals that the regiment's drummers had Imperial Livery. The inspector notes that the *dépôt* held '… 250m of drummers lace of the old model as are the buttons', the lace being burned. New clothing in the *dépôt* included 57 *capotes*, 219 fusilier *habits* of the old model, 520 pairs of *pantalons de tricot*, 7 *bonnets de police*, 171 pairs of underwear, and 289 sets of braces. Of interest, *dépôt* also held 300 pairs of brand-new *culottes en tricot* and a further 300 needing repairs. When we look at the inspection report, we find that the regiment had a mix and match approach to clothing. Some 1,545 *sous-officiers* and men were on parade, of which 538 men had no *pantalons de tricot* – more than a third of all men were wearing linen *pantalons*. We note that 458 men had a *habit* in good condition, 94 men had *habits* that needed repairs and 456 men *habits* needing replacement as pre-Bardin *habits-longe*. A whopping 535 men had no *habit* and were on parade wearing their *veste* or *capote*! Indeed, we note that 208 men had no *veste* and 206 *vestes* needed total replacement. Equipment in the *dépôt* included 10 *schako* covers, 521 *gibernes*, 658 *porte-gibernes* – of which 274 were made from blackened cow hide – 1,026 musket slings – of which 431 were made from blackened cow hide – 28 *baudriers*, 24 drums, 12 drum carriages, 2 *sapeurs'* axes, 4 *sapeurs'* aprons, 1,100 *houpettes* and 2 pairs of adjutant's epaulettes. No mention is made at all of *aigrettes* or epaulettes for grenadiers: did these items not exist? Perhaps so. *Petit equipment* in stores included 206 shirts, 16 pairs of *pantalons de toile*, 14 black stocks, 336 pairs of linen socks, 1 pair of black gaiters *de modèle*, 58 pairs of grey linen gaiters, 6 *sacs à distribution*, 401 handkerchiefs, 7 *sacs de peau*, and 297 *epinglettes*.[139] No disbandment paperwork for the regiment can be located, so we can say nothing else.

45e *de Ligne*

Inspected on 1 August 1814, the 611 men of the regiment were mostly wearing clothing that was past its best: 5 men had no *habit*, 228 needed repairs, and 272 needed replacement, leaving just 116 in good condition for examples. The 13 *sapeurs* had no equipment issued, but we note grenadiers and *sous-officiers* carried sabres. Of the *pantalons de tricot*, 446 pairs were totally worn out and to make up some of the shortfall 392 pairs of linen *pantalons* were in use. This still left 100 men wearing non-regulation legwear. Brand-new clothing in the *dépôt* included 45 *capotes*, 7 grenadier *habits* that needed repairs accompanied by 6 grenadier *gilets manches* also needing repairs – we assume, however, the grenadier *habits* had epaulettes with them. The grenadier *gilets manches* no doubt had red collar and cuffs or the grenade badge on the upper arm as described under the Bardin regulations. *Petit equipment* in stores included 92 pairs of *pantalons de route*, 798 pairs of linen socks, 49 *sacs à distribution* and 400 tricolour cockades.[140]

The inspecting general commented that the regiment still wore a majority of *habits-longe* and not *habits-vestes*. Furthermore, he commented that only two thirds of the men were fully equipped, and even the officers' clothing was considered merely passable rather than in good condition. He added that in addition to the officers being badly dressed, the *sous-officiers* and men's clothing lacked any regularity, and the *habits* and *pantalons* were made from poor-quality materials. All the equipment needed replacing or repairing. He added that the decree of 23 April 1814 to remove Imperial iconography had not been carried out, so we assume eagles still adorned *schako* plates and drummers were likely in green with Imperial Livery. Clearly the regiment in summer 1814 was wearing what clothing had survived the 1813 and 1814 campaigns and it was in deplorable condition.[141]

Rear view of a fusilier wearing Bardin-regulation clothing in summer 1813. Of note, he carries a sabre, which had been non-regulation since the 1770s. Again the *schako* cords are non-regulation. (*Collection KM*)

The regiment's disbandment paperwork is sparse. Clothing in the *dépôt* at disbandment comprised:[142]

22 *habits*
80 *vestes*
11 *pantalons de tricot*
7 *caleçons*
246 *schakos*
1150 *schako* plates
84 *houpettes*

The *dépôt* had minimum amounts of materials, namely 88m 26 blue broadcloth, 1,545m 93 linen for lining *habits*, 425m 18 linen for *caleçons*, 437 dozen large buttons and 3,340 dozen small buttons.[143]

We assume the regiment adopted *habit-vestes* in 1815, assuming some men were not wearing some already, and drummers took up Royalist Livery. Denis Dighton shows a *voltigeur* of the 45e wearing an approximation of Bardin kit, with a white *schako* cockade, green-fringed epaulettes with yellow crescents and green houpette.[144] We note 26 *voltigeur houpettes* did exist, which suggests some credibility to the image.[145]

46e *de Ligne*

Drawn up for inspection on 1 August 1814, the regiment's clothing either needed total replacement, was missing or needed repairs. For example, of the 675 men on parade, 113 had no *habit*, and of those in use, 191 needed total replacement, 157 needed repairs with 214 in good condition. Just 37 sabres were in use with 68 belts with the *sous-officiers* and the regiment needed an additional 215 *baudriers*, and likewise 205 *gibernes* and belts. The stand-out feature from the men on parade is that the grenadier company was wearing 183 bearskins and that only *habits-longe* were in use along with tricot *culottes* and long gaiters. The regiment had two *sapeurs* on parade who were issued aprons, axes with cases and were armed with two light cavalry *mousquetons*. The regimental band had eight clarinets, one bassoon, one serpent, two horns, one pair of cymbals, and one tenor drum, all of which were the property of the regiment's officers. We are ignorant as to how the band was dressed.

Stocks of clothing comprised 42 brand-new *capotes*, 1 new fusilier *habit*, 13 new drummers' *habits* – which we assume were green based on the inspector's comments – 78 brand-new pairs of *pantalons de tricot*, 536 pairs of *caleçons*, 82 fusilier *schakos*, 280 pairs of *culottes de peau*, 11 worn-out bearskins and lastly 6 drum carriages in blackened cow hide.[146] The dress of the regiment was a point of concern to the inspector:

> The state of the clothing of the regiment is particularly bad ... the colonel it appears from this review in particular has not acted upon the dispositions described in the regulation of 19 January 1812, and there are no indications he has acted on

> the circular of 23 April to remove Imperial symbols and change the dress of the drummers from green … there must be executed changes to the cut, to the colour, and dimensions of all parts of the clothing and equipment of the regiment … the bearskins that have been conserved in use with the companies of grenadiers, the War Minister charges that they are to be replaced in the newly formed regiment by *schakos*. The grand equipment is complete, except the *gibernes* and *porte-giberne*, it is ordered that the regiment will no longer use black equipment, and along with the drum carriages in the *dépôt,* these items are to be considered *hors de service* … the non-French muskets in use are to be swopped for the French model and sabres and belts are to be drawn of the required number.[147]

The inspector commented further that it would be a waste of materials to repair the clothing as it was non-regulation and funds were needed to reclothe the regiment. The War Ministry were to supply the regulations, sealed patterns and tariffs for the Bardin regulation to the regiment.[148]

A report produced 18 to 20 June 1815 gives us some information about what the regiment was actually dressed like at the start of the 100 Days' campaign. The review reads as follows:

46e regiment of Line Infantry

The number of effectives in the *dépôt* is 969 men and 68 officers to complete the 3e, 4e, 5e, and 6e battalions, of these 266 men are available for service and are fully armed, clothed and equipped.

The corps is to receive under the decree of 28 March 433 men, of which 343 have arrived, 90 men are missing. Of the 343 men who have joined the regiment, 70 have deserted. These men are from the Department of the Nord and of Pas de Calais, their spirit is not good.

The equipment available comprises:

> 93 *schakos*
> 433 *schako* covers
> 433 *gibernes*
> 433 *porte-gibernes*
> 433 musket slings
> 10 drums.
>
> The armament in the *dépôt* for the men available for service comprises 208 muskets and bayonets.
>
> Furthermore, a request has been made to provide for the men remaining in the *dépôt* which are fully clothed and equipped, for the provision of an additional 194 muskets and bayonets.[149]

At the time of the disbandment the *dépôt* held among other items 11m 94 green broadcloth and 15m of drummers' livery, 731 *houpettes de fusilier*, 64 pairs of grenadier epaulettes, 2 sets of *sapeurs*' equipment comprising an axe with a pair of gauntlets, 60 bearskins, 150 garnitures for *habits*, 408 tricolour cockades, 22 grenadier *aigrettes* and 6 *voltigeur aigrettes.*[150] Presumably the drummers had green *habits* with Imperial Livery, perhaps also the band.

Officers

Unique for most regiments of the line, we have a 'snapshot' of officers' clothing on campaign. The regiment fought at the Battle of Kulm on 29 and 30 August 1813 under the orders of General Vandamme. The regiment's baggage train was captured. From an inventory taken of kit lost by 30 officers we extract the following data:[151]

Chef du Bataillon Peychaud: 2 *porte-manteaux*, 1 blue *redingote* – fitted double-breasted overcoat, 1 blue broadcloth *frac* – a single-breasted *surtout* with no false pockets on the back – 1 pair of epaulettes, 2 pairs of blue broadcloth *pantalons*, 6 new shirts, 6 cravats, 10 handkerchiefs, 1 blue waistcoat with gold embroidery, 3 white gilets, 3 pairs of boots.

Chef du Bataillon Ponsonmaille: 2 *porte-manteaux,* 1 blue *redingote* with shoulder cape, 2 pairs of blue broadcloth *pantalons,* 1 pair of epaulettes, 8 shirts, 8 cravats, 8 handkerchiefs, 4 blue waistcoats, 3 pairs of *pantalons* made from nankeen, 1 pair of gilded spurs, 1 length of blue broadcloth.

Adjutant-Major Guenon: 1 *porte-manteau*, 1 blue *redingote*, 1 blue *frac*, 5 shirts, 8 handkerchiefs, 4 cravats, 3 white *gilets*, 1 blue *gilet* with gold edging, 2 pairs of boots.

Officier Payeur Bintin: 2 *porte-manteaux*, 1 blue *capote* with cape, 1 blue *frac*, 2 pairs of epaulettes, 1 epée and sword knot, 8 shirts, 10 handkerchiefs, 6 cravats, 4 white *gilet*s, 1 blue *gilet* with gold edging, 2 pairs of boots.

Capitaine Lecoq: 2 *porte-manteaux*, 1 blue *capote* with shoulder cape, 1 *levrit*, 2 pairs of boots, 2 pairs of blue Casimir *pantalons*, 2 pairs of white Casimir *pantalons*, 3 pairs of nankeen *pantalons*, 6 shirts, 4 *gilets*, 2 pairs of epaulettes, 1 sabre.

Captaine Lacretelle: 1 *porte-manteau*, 6 shirts, 7 cravats, 6 handkerchiefs, 1 blue broadcloth *frac*, 1 blue broadcloth *gilet,* 1 blue broadcloth *capote*, 1 pair of blue broadcloth *pantalons*, 1 pair linen *pantalons de route*, 2 pairs of boots.

Captaine Benaud: 1 *porte-manteau,* 1 *habit,* 4 shirts, 1 pair of blue *pantalon*, 2 pairs of nankeen *pantalons*, 1 pair of epaulettes, 1 sabre knot, 4 cravats, 6 handkerchiefs, 2 pairs of boots.

Lieutenant Baril: 1 *porte-manteau*, 1 blue broadcloth *frac*, 1 blue broadcloth *levrit*, 1 pair of epaulettes, 1 sabre knot, 1 pair blue *pantalons*, 6 shirts, 6 cravats, 6 handkerchiefs, 2 *gilets*, 2 pairs of boots.

Sous-Lieutenant Nasse: 1 *porte-manteau,* 1 blue *frac*, 1 pair blue *pantalons*, 1 pair of epaulettes, 1 sabre knot, 2 *gilets*, 6 cravats, 6 handkerchiefs, 5 shirts, 2 pairs of boots.

Sous-Lieutenant Boutin: 1 *porte-manteau*, 1 *habit*, 4 pairs of *pantalons*, 1 pair of epaulettes, 4 shirts, 1 blue *capote*, 4 cravats, 4 handkerchiefs.

Sous-Lieutenant Gallier: 1 *porte-manteau*, 2 pairs of blue *pantalons*, 1 pair of white Casimir *culottes*, 5 shirts, 1 *gilet*, 6 cravats, 7 handkerchiefs, 2 pairs of boots, 1 pair of epaulettes.

Sous-Lieutenant Decampron: 1 *porte-manteau*, 2 pairs blue *pantalons*, 3 *gilets*, 6 new shirts, 6 cravats, 8 handkerchiefs, 1 shoulder cape, 1 pair of boots.

Aide-Major Joellier: 1 *porte-manteau*, 1 uniform *habit*, 2 pairs of blue *pantalons*, 4 *gilets*, 6 shirts, 5 cravats, 7 handkerchiefs, 2 pairs of boots.

Aide-Major Belletier: 1 *porte-manteau*, 1 uniform *habit*, 1 pair of blue *pantalons*, 3 blue *gilets*, 6 shirts, 8 cravats, 6 handkerchiefs, 1 *chapeau*, 1 *trousse*, 2 sets of surgeon's instruments.

Officers, it seems, had both a *habit* and a single-breasted *frac*, and they wore predominantly blue *gilets* and blue *pantalons*. Some officers had linen *pantalons de route*. Officers wore a mix of a sleeved cavalry *manteau-capote*, a shapeless infantry *capote,* a more fitted *redingote*, shoulder capes – *rotondes* – and almost floor-length riding coats with one or two shoulder capes, which were called *a levrit*, for cold and wet weather gear! Some officers clearly could afford Casimir *culottes* or ones made from nankeen. Hardly suitable wear for campaign use, but no doubt very useful for looking smart at a soiree to attract the ladies! What we are not seeing is what the officers were actually wearing!

47e *de Ligne*

Reviewed on 1 October 1814, the regiment was wearing a mix of newly issued items, as well as clothing and equipment long past its best, if you were lucky have any. For example, we see that 307 men had no habit, 509 no *veste*, 537 no *pantalons de tricot*, 968 no *capote* and 528 no *schako*. Of the *habits* in use, 717 were *habits-vestes* in good condition, 172 items needed repairs and 197 *habits-longe* needed replacing. In terms of *petit equipment*, the men had 2,979 shirts, 879 linen *pantalons de route*, 1,085 black stocks, 1,903 pairs of shoes, 941 pairs of black gaiters, 654 pairs of grey gaiters, 54 *sacs à distribution*, 1,072 *sacs de peau*, 480 *epinglettes,* 420 screwdrivers, and 1,348 pay books. *Petit equipment* in store included 2 black stocks, 400 pairs of linen socks, 3 pairs of shoes, 8 pairs black gaiters, 330 pairs of grey linen gaiters, 970 *sacs à distribution*, 169 *sacs de peau*, and 225 *epinglettes*. We also note 12 pairs of long black gaiters, 10 pairs of long grey gaiters, 14 fatigue smocks, 248 pairs of shoe buckles, 72 pairs of knee buckles of breeches and 48 pairs of breeches back buckles all recently taken from service, which shows some men had until recently worn long gaiters and breeches.

Grenadier officer, observed around Dresden in summer 1813. (*Collection KM*)

The regiment was armed with a motley collection of firearms: 564 muskets model of 1777, 186 dragoon muskets, 134 foreign muskets, 26 artillery muskets, 4 *carabines* and lodged in the *dépôt* were a further 8 *carabines Raye* specifically recorded as 'for *sous-officier* of *voltigeurs*'. The *dépôt* held among other items, 78m of drummers' lace 2 brand-new drummers' *habits* and 4 to be written off – arguably green with Imperial Livery – 156 copper grenades for the *gibernes* of grenadiers, and 156 hunting horns, again in copper for *gibernes* of *voltigeurs* and 109 crowned 'N' for fusilier *gibernes*! The regiment had two pack horses that carried the surgeon's equipment in the field.[152]

In a second report, the inspector added that great irregularities existed in the dress of the regiment, and the colonel was ordered, where possible, to replace all non-regulation clothing and equipment as many men had black cross belts and were wearing breeches and old-style *habits*. The inspector ordered furthermore that the officers and *sous-officiers* were to no longer dress as middle-class men in civilians when off duty and in barracks, and a school was to be established to teach them their required knowledge of theoretical and practical drill and duties as officers and *sous-officiers*.[153]

No disbandment paperwork can be located at the time of writing, therefore we can say nothing more about the dress of this regiment.

48e *de Ligne*

Inspected on 20 September 1814, the regiment mustered 131 officers and 1,444 other ranks whose clothing was little more than rags for the most part as 300 *habits*, 1,200 *vestes*, every single pair of *pantalons de tricot*, and every *bonnets de police* needed replacing, and 138 men had none of these items. If men had clothing it was all in good condition except the *capotes*, of which 406 needed repairs and 900 total replacement.[154]

To make new clothing the *dépôt* held 48m 95 of white broadcloth, a paltry 4m 69 of scarlet broadcloth, and some 1,316m 05 of white tricot for making new *pantalons* and *gilets manches*. The *dépôt* held brand new, ready to be issued, 1 *voltigeur gilet manches*, 214 fusilier *gilets manches*, 130 pairs of *pantalons de tricot*, and 89 pairs of *caleçons*. Some 50 pairs of grenadier epaulettes were in *dépôt*, along with 186 fusilier *habits* needing repair as well as 4 *sapeurs*' axes, 3 aprons and 3 pairs of gauntlets for *sapeurs*. The inspector also noted there were 3 '*conducteurs de chevaux des bat*', i.e., men who led and controlled the officers' pack horses, and 34 non-regulation drummers' *habits* had been dumped in stores awaiting destruction.[155] However, as the regiment had 36 drummers, plus the 2 corporal drummers, drum major and 7 bandsmen, a shortfall of garments existed. We wonder if the drum major was dressed in a different manner to his drummers? This was the case later.

The paper archive of the regiment shows that the regiment ordered between 1 January 1815 and 1 May 1815 the following items to complete its clothing:[156]

624 *schakos*
11m 40 silver lace for drum major
14m 3 silver lace for drum major

1 *cornet* for *voltigeurs*
100 red pompoms for grenadiers
100 yellow pompoms for *voltigeurs*
450 *houpettes* for fusiliers
379 *habits*
39 drummers' *habits* costing 17fr 55 each
400 musket slings
55 *schako* plates
80 large straps for *sacs de peau*
8m 90 gold lace
8 cords for *cornets* costing 2fr 50 each
4 tassels for *cornets*
Yellow and gold lace 85fr 20
1 cover for the *drapeau* and covers for the two spontoons, 42fr 25
45m scarlet broadcloth at 15fr a metre
121m white serge at 1fr 36 a metre

The huge cost of the production of drummers' *habits* implies they were profusely decorated with lace: we are alas, ignorant of the type of lace or colour of the garments. However, of huge interest is the presence of a cover for the flag and also the spontoons for the colour party – we can only assume these were the spontoons introduced in 1809. Yet we find no reference to helmets or pistols! We also note that 6,411fr 60 was spent on buying epaulettes – based on one pair costing 3fr 50 and that more than 1,000 pairs were obtained, arguably sufficient for grenadiers and *voltigeurs* – and 4,323fr 80 was spent on making clothing. The accounts also list that in 1814, 65m of '*galon double*' in silver costing 1fr 80 a metre and 60m of silver fringing was destined for the musicians' uniforms. Clearly these uniforms were profusely embellished: Charlet shows such a uniform in his drawings made at the very end of the Empire into the Second Restoration.

The disbandment tells us nothing alas about how the regiment was dressed in the 1815 campaign.[157]

50e *de Ligne*

Inspected on 28 September 1814, the regiment had 769 rank and file and 3 *enfants de troupe*. Clothing and equipment was missing or in terrible condition and a mix of Bardin and pre-Bardin types: 389 had Bardin kit and equipment and 241 *habits-longe* and *culottes* if you were lucky to have any clothing at all. We note 283 *habits*, 350 *vestes manches*, 630 pairs of *pantalons de tricot*, 357 *capotes* and 173 *schakos* were needed to clothe every man, before the hundreds of worn-out items were replaced.

Of the *petit equipment* in use, we note 1,124 shirts were worn, 519 pairs of linen *pantalons de route*, 569 black stocks, 12 pairs of linen socks, 12 pairs of woollen stockings, 849 pairs of shoes, 433 pairs of black gaiters, 283 pairs of grey linen gaiters, 13 *sacs à distribution*, 474 *sacs de peau*, 434 *epinglette*s and 409 screwdrivers. In stores among more shirts and gaiters were 69 queue pins and 1 smock. Did the regiment have long hair? Perhaps. Stores also held 271m 80 of drummers' lace, 12 drummers' *habits*, 439 pairs of grenadier epaulettes and model examples of grenadier and *voltigeur aigrettes*, 17 for grenadier pompoms and 21 for *voltigeurs*. The inspector noted that of the 368 *habits* in the *dépôt*, some 287 were *habit-longs* accompanied by 342 pairs of brand-new *culottes*.[158] It seems likely that by September 1814 the regiment was restocking to totally change over to Bardin regulation.

The *dépôt* held at disbandment on 7 August 1815, among other items, 39m 20 green broadcloth, 3m 43 chamois broadcloth, and 383m 80 drummers' livery. In 1814 when the regiment was re-formed as the 46ᵉ, it possessed 383m 80 Imperial Livery inherited from the 50ᵉ and 144ᵉ *de Ligne*, with 39m 20 green broadcloth that clearly remained unused. Certainly, some drummers' kit in blue with we assume Royalist Livery was made, as clothing in *dépôt* included 117 *capotes*, 14 *habits-vestes*, 3 drummers' *habits*, 748 pairs of either *culottes* or *pantalons*, 98 *gilets manches*, 12 fusilier *schakos*, 683 pairs of *caleçons*, 216 pairs of grenadier epaulettes, 394 *houpettes* and 8 *voltigeur aigrettes*. We assume grenadiers had *aigrettes* and they were counted with the *schako* and all had been issued. The *dépôt* also held 2 pairs of white gaiters, 97 *sacs de peau*, 21 *chapeau* cockades, 4 pairs of *pantalons* in bleached white linen – no doubt for adjutants – 868 stock buckles – exactly the same number as in 1814 – 31 sword knots for grenadiers, 70 pompoms, 109 pairs of *pantalons* in grey linen, 50 pairs of long grey gaiters, 315 pairs of half grey gaiters, 37 pairs of black gaiters and 42lb of wax for *gibernes*. As the regiment had *culottes* in use in 1814, we assume the long gaiters were directly associated with these, and were those items taken from use in summer 1814 and bundled into the back corner of the storeroom. The white gaiters pose a quandary as they were abolished officially in 1805: were they really a decade old or were they new for parades in the restoration along with the white linen *pantalons*?

All the *habits* in *dépôt* were clearly *habits-vestes*. The two qualities of linen *pantalons* are interesting – bleached white for adjutants and *sous-officiers* and grey for other ranks, which we assume were worn with the grey gaiters. In addition, ten *sapeurs*' aprons were in *dépôt* – arguably those in *dépôt* in 1814. The absence of axes, axe cases and gauntlets imply the regiment had no *sapeurs* in 1813 to 1815. We also note four pairs of '*charivai en coutil*', or cavalry stables trousers, no doubt worn by the men assigned to lead the officers pack horses.[159]

51ᵉ *de Ligne*

Inspected in September 1814, the inspector noted that the regiment was remarkable for the lack of uniformity in its clothing, which accorded to several regulations: clearly a mix and match approach of pre-Bardin and Bardin had been resorted to to clothe the unit. We note the *dépôt* held 48 pairs of grenadier epaulettes, 250 fusilier *houpettes*, 18 fusilier *habits*, 14m 30 chamois broadcloth, 13 *giberne* covers, 697 black stocks, 42 pairs of blue

Fusilier officer observed around Dresden in summer 1813. (*Collection KM*)

broadcloth pantalons, 868 pairs of linen *pantalons de route* and 7 sets of clothing for the prisoners facing execution.[160]

The regiment's paperwork offers some snippets of details about the process of converting a regiment from Imperial iconography to Royalist. Some 540m of new-pattern drummers' lace costing 1fr 15 per metre was obtained, at a total cost of 135fr. In addition, cut out cloth *fleur-des-lys* were purchased for the decoration of the *habit* tails of sergeants at a cost of 15fr.[161]

Scrolling on a year, the *dépôt* held among other items, 4m 36 chamois broadcloth and 45m of lace for drummers, which suggests that 495m of the 540m of new Royalist Livery had been used to deck out the drummers out in new *habits* in spring 1815. The *dépôt* also held 137 grenadier *aigrettes* and 96 *voltigeur aigrettes*, and no epaulettes – we assume grenadiers had epaulettes attached to their *habits*.[162]

52e *de Ligne*

Reviewed on 4 August 1814, the regiment mustered just 440 men, who were lucky to have a uniform, and what they had was falling to bits. We note, for example, 70 men had no *habit*, 112 were in good condition, 131 needed repairs, and the remainder total replacement. The inspector noted that since 23 April, to make up the shortfall in clothing since the end of the recent campaign, the *dépôt* had issued 43 *habits*, 38 *capotes*, 190 *gilets manches* and 349 pairs of *pantalons*, but many more items were needed.[163] The *dépôt* held no stocks of cloth or materials as it had all been used to clothe the men. Furthermore, the inspector noted:

> We recommended to the new administrative council, to put into execution the decrees of 19 January and 7 February 1812 for the clothing of the soldiers and furthermore to make themselves aware of the modifications which have taken place with the *circulaire* of 23 April Instant.
>
> I furthermore remark, that the system of replacements and ordering of clothing and equipment is not as prescribed with the instruction of 25 7bre 1812 nor that of the 8 June 1813.[164]

By the time of the regiment's disbandment in September 1815, we assume that the clothing shortages had been made up, but it is unlikely if the regiment had been entirely re-dressed in Bardin regulation by this date. The drummers certainly had Imperial Livery as the *dépôt* held 2m 70 of green broadcloth: none had existed in 1814. Also, in *dépôt* was 3m 91 chamois broadcloth, 40 *habits*, 1 *capote*, 104 *schakos* – of which 78 were new and 26 were to be written off – 256 *aigrettes* for grenadiers and *voltigeurs*, 317 fusilier *houpettes*, 15 pairs of grenadier epaulettes, 228 *schako* covers, 64 sets of braces, 433 *gibernes*, 176 *porte-gibernes*, 196 *baudriers*, 133 musket slings, 10 drums, 7 drum carriages and 2 drummers' aprons.[165]

53e *de Ligne*

On 21 August 1814 the regiment mustered 576 men and 2 *enfants de troupe*: the men were dressed in old-pattern habits and breeches: *dépôt* held 99 *habits-longe* and 176 pairs of *culottes*, and was in the process of making 1,297 *habits-vestes* and 1,755 pairs of *pantalons de tricot* to totally re-dress the regiment. We understand why this great 'restocking' was necessary when we look at the inspection report dated 20 August 1814. As with all regiments at the end of the campaign of France, the clothing either needed repairs, total replacement or was totally missing: virtually nothing was in good enough condition to remain in use. The *dépôt* held 43 *habits-vestes*, 95 fusilier *habits* and 1 drummer's *habit de modèle* accompanied by 378m 95 of drummers' livery.[166]

We are fortunate that we have a breakdown of cloth, materials, clothing and equipment used between 1812 and 1815. Below is a summary of this important document:[167]

Chamois broadcloth: 10m was purchased between 1 January 1812 and 21 August 1814, all being entirely used, presumably more of the same. None was bought from 21 August 14 to 21 September 1815. *Voltigeurs* had no distinctive *habits* as those in use in summer 1814 were all replaced by fusilier-model garments.

Green broadcloth: not an inch was purchased from 1 January 1812 to 21 September 1815. Therefore, drummers and *cornets* always wore blue.

Drummers' lace: some 1,134m 20 of lace was purchased before 21 August 1814, of which 755m 25 was used – arguably this was all Imperial Livery, to make 50 *habits*: arguably for the band, drummers and *cornets*. This left 378m 95 in *dépôt*. During the First Restoration 540m of Royalist Livery was obtained, and entirely used to make 36 *habits*. In the 100 Days 348m of Imperial Livery was used to make 23 new drummers' *habits*.

Silver lace: during the First Restoration 8m 80 of silver laced was purchased and never used. Exactly the same amount had been used between 1812 and 1814. This is sufficient to lace the collar and cuffs of 8 *habits*.

Epaulettes: issued once, and only once, in January 1812. Grenadiers outside 1e battalion never had epaulettes and no grenadier had epaulettes by 1814.

Aigrettes: no *aigrettes* for grenadiers or *voltigeurs* existed between 1812 and 1815.

As we noted earlier, the regiment only adopted Bardin-regulation clothing in the First Restoration.

The *voltigeurs* were armed with 205 dragoon muskets. Further, just a single *voltigeur cornet* was purchased and never issued – ergo *voltigeur* companies had drummers rather than *cornets*. The *dépôt* on 20 September 1815 held 730m 80 blue broadcloth, 178m 80 white broadcloth, 84m 10 red broadcloth, 1,325m 41 white serge, 8m 80 silver lace, 234m 40 lace for chevrons, and 30m 50 drummers' lace. Also, in *dépôt* were 125 *habits*, 55 *vestes*, 165 pairs of *pantalons de tricot*, 49 *schakos*, 22 *schako* covers, and 89 *capotes*.[168]

Grenadier observed around Dresden in the summer of 1813. (*Collection KM*)

54e *de Ligne*

Reviewed on 21 July 1814, the regiment had 757 rank and file and 4 *enfants de troupe*. On parade, once the sick and lame had been sent home, were just 367 men, whose clothing was either in good condition or missing entirely: to clothe every man 79 *habits*, 86 *vestes manches*, 74 pairs of *pantalons de tricot*, 367 pairs of underwear, 66 *capotes*, 55 *schakos* and 288 *bonnets de police* were needed. Despite lacking uniforms, the men had 567 shirts, 88 pairs of *pantalons de route*, 298 black stocks, 496 pairs of shoes, 209 pairs of black gaiters, 184 pairs grey gaiters, 25 *sacs à distribution*, 222 *sacs de peau*, 178 *epinglettes*, 174 screwdrivers, and 367 pay books. The *dépôt* held 488 *capotes*, 171 fusilier *habits*, 205 *gilets manches*, 204 pairs of *pantalons de tricot*, 223 *bonnets de police*, and 334 pairs of *caleçons* – in short sufficient clothing existed to make up for missing clothing, and yet had not been issued to the men! No distinctions for grenadiers, drummers or *voltigeur*s existed in use in the *dépôt*. Likewise, nothing existed for *sapeurs*.[169]

Very little paperwork exists for the dress of the regiment during the 100 Days. At the time of disbandment in October 1815 the *dépôt* held 1m 90 silver lace, 29 pairs of grenadier epaulettes and little else that informs us about the dress of the unit.[170]

55e *de Ligne*

Inspected on 1 August 1814, the regiment mustered 895 men. The grenadiers had 73 pairs of epaulettes, 871 *houpettes* and *aigrettes* were in service. *Petit equipment* in use by these men included 1,919 shirts, 516 pairs *of pantalons de route*, 899 black stocks, 1,382 pairs of shoes, 730 pairs of black gaiters, 499 pairs of linen gaiters, 288 *sacs à distribution*, and 895 *sacs de peau*. In stores were 49 pairs of *pantalons de route*, 68 black stocks, 377 pairs of shoes, 58 pairs of black gaiters, and 220 pairs grey gaiters among other items. The *dépôt* held virtually no stocks of materials, 1,770m 83 white serge, and 3,950m linen. Clothing and equipment in *dépôt* comprised 174 pairs of *pantalons de tricot*, 263 pairs of *caleçons*, 680 sets of braces, 388 *schako* covers, 173 *gibernes* and belts, 415 musket slings, 4 drums with carriages and apron, 629 *houpette*s and 32 grenadier sword knots.[171]

When the *dépôt* of the regiment was disbanded on 30 September 1815 it contained among other items white tricot dyed grey for *capotes*. The regiment's major reported that this had been necessary due to the impossibility of obtaining beige broadcloth. Also in store was 180m drummers' livery and 122 *giberne* covers: this is one of the few references to these being used in the 1e Empire. They were clearly not in universal use.[172] The war battalions were disbanded the day before. We note that of the 122 men present, each man had a *habit-veste*, only 25 had a veste, 16 were wearing *pantalons de tricot*, the rest were wearing linen *pantalons*, just 101 had a *capote*, and only 3 *bonnets de police* existed. Of the 122 men, 119 had *gibernes*, and 57 *baudriers* were issued for 56 sabres. Indeed, 121 men had a musket, which included it seems the drummers. We note four drummers were on parade, and arguably each man had a musket.[173]

56e *de Ligne*

The regiment's 1814 inspection review dated 31 August 1814 stated it had no distinctions for grenadiers or *voltigeurs*. The *dépôt* held 0m 20 beige broadcloth, 397m 60 white broadcloth, 19m 49 chamois broadcloth, 4,619m white serge, 308m 47 white tricot, 62m 69 linen and 18m 85 red worsted lace. Also in stores was 1 *schako pour grenadier de modèle* – which was it seems never copied – 102 fusilier *schakos*, 1,108 *schako* covers – we note none were in use, so these were clearly all the regiment's stock of these items. Also in *dépôt* were 1 *giberne* and 1 drum carriage *'de modèle'*, 61 *porte-gibernes*, and 166 *baudriers*.[174]

The 1e battalion was wound up on 1 October 1815, when the staff mustered 23 officers and men and 529 other ranks. The battalion was issued 213 muskets in good condition, 16 needing repairs and 61 to be written off, 54 dragoon muskets in good condition and 8 needing repairs issued to *voltigeurs*, while 7 light cavalry carbines were issued to *sapeurs*.[175]

The regimental *dépôt* held, among other items, 12m 30 chamois broadcloth, and several items *de modèle*, notably, 1 *habit*, 1 veste, 1 pair of *pantalons de tricot*, 1 *capote*, and 1 *bonnet de police*. Presumably, these were issued so the regiment could adopt Bardin regulation during the First Restoration. Uniquely almost, we find two pairs of pistols in cases – these may have been for *sapeurs* or the eagle guard and had been in store since 1814.[176]

57^e^ *de Ligne*

Inspected on 16 July 1814, the regiment had 938 other ranks on parade, 7 *enfants de troupe* and 113 officers. The clothing was mostly in good condition: no grenadier or *voltigeur* had an *aigrette* or seemingly pair of epaulettes. Just 138 baudrier and sabres were issued – the regiment had 108 drummers, *cornets* and *sous-officiers* and 55 grenadiers, ergo *voltigeurs* did not have sabres and not all grenadiers. The men were wearing 1,807 shirts, 539 pairs of *pantalons de route* – not enough for every man to have a pair –, 1,496 black stocks, 1,171 pairs of shoes, 732 pairs of black gaiters, 681 pairs of grey gaiters and had 878 *sacs de peau*. The *dépôt* held a cross spectrum of cloth and materials, notably 16m beige broadcloth for *capotes*, 60m 85 blue broadcloth, 13m 05 white broadcloth, 2m 75 scarlet broadcloth, 4,910m white serge, 1,745m 40 white tricot, and 1,144m 50 linen for lining. We find the *dépôt* had 71 new *capotes*, 69 needing repairs and 70 awaiting sale to the rag merchants. Likewise, the *dépôt* had 157 new fusilier *habits*, 66 needing repairs and 80 to be written off, accompanied by 2 new drummers' *habits*, 1 that needed repair and 4 to be sold on to the rag merchant.[177] The inspector added that the officers needed to pay better attention to the regulations of January 1812 for the dress of the men.[178]

Items made during the First Restoration included 263 pairs of *pantalons de route*, 4 pairs of white gaiters – the inspector noted that these were totally forbidden items of uniform – 80fr 64 was paid out for 14m 40 of silver lace for the drum major's uniform, and a further 8fr 95 to sew the lace to the *habit* was paid out. The regiment also paid out 180fr 45 to buy three sets of *sapeurs'* equipment. On 20 March 1815, 1,400 pairs of *pantalons de route*, 1,200 black stocks, and 1,200 *schako* plates bearing '53', the regiment's new designation, arrived with the regiment.[179]

At disbandment in September 1815, the *dépôt* held 6m 05 chamois broadcloth, 180m 13 drummers' lace, 10 grenadier *habits*, 25 *voltigeur habits*, 64 fusilier *habits* and 2 drummers' *habits* – which are likely to have been adorned with Royalist livery to complement the drum major – 173 grenadier *aigrettes*, 37 pairs of grenadier epaulettes, and 307 *voltigeur* aigrettes.[180] We also note the existence of 292 *petit-bidons*, i.e., white metal canteens authorised under Bardin when 3e battalion was wound up,[181] and 1e and 2e battalions possessed 1,028 *petit-bidons* and 1028 *porte-bidons* made from leather: proof these were not carried off a length of string. The war battalions had 7 *sapeurs* under arms, and we note 10 light cavalry carbines were issued – 6 to *sapeurs*, the remainder to *cornets*, who were issued 4 cavalry trumpets.[182]

58e *de Ligne*

Reviewed on 16 August 1814, the regiment mustered 1,191 men. The *dépôt* held little in the way of cloth, but did hold 240m of drummers' lace, as well as 10 new *capotes*, 39 new *gilets manches*, 52 grenadier *aigrettes*, 48 *voltigeur aigrettes*, 940 fusilier *houpettes*, and 44 pairs of grenadier epaulettes. Also lodged in stores were 115 *schako* covers as well as 562 *habit* covers.[183]

The paperwork of the regiment, despite being incomplete, offers us many surprises. The *dépôt* on 25 September 1815 held 5 grenadier *habits*, likely having scarlet-ringed epaulettes attached to them; as well as 10 *sapeur habits*, likely with crossed axe arm badges and scarlet-fringed epaulettes attached; no *voltigeur habits*; and 90 fusilier *habits*, all of which were brand new. Clothing in need of repairs were 2 fusilier *habits*, 590 *gilets manches* and 6 drummers' *habits* that needed repairs. We also find in *dépôt* 8 *giberne* covers, 39 pairs of *brodequins* – laced boots – 7 pairs of grenadier epaulettes along with 1 grenadier *schako* '*de modèle*', which was, it seems, was never copied, and 11 grenadier *aigrettes* and 5 for *voltigeurs*, presumably the residue of those purchased and not issued.[184]

A second review dated 29 September states that cloth in the *dépôt* included 96m 63 red broadcloth, 0m 68 chamois broadcloth, and 235m 30 grey tricot for *capotes*. Clothing in *dépôt* included the following items described as '*de modèle*': one *capote*, one fusilier *habit*, one drummers' *habit*, one pair of *pantalons de tricot*, one pair of *caleçons*, one set of braces, 1 one *pokalem*, one example each of grenadier and *voltigeur aigrettes* and a fusilier *schako*. No grenadier *schako* or epaulettes are listed under either category, but a model example of a *sapeur*'s apron, axe, axe case and gauntlets did exist.[185] The regiment's archive shows that some 300m of drummers' livery was purchased between 1 January 1814 and 16 August 1814, of which 60m was applied to blue drummers' *habits*.[186] Some 60m of lace was sufficient to make just 4 *habits* laced like a Bardin example. The remaining lace was burned. Six drummers' habits certainly existed in 1815, but of their form and colour we know nothing. However, we have considerable detail on the *sapeurs*' dress. During the First Restoration a lot of regimental funds was spent on the *sapeurs*: as well as having their own *habits*, had lodged in the *dépôt* 13 colpacks, 12 axes, 13 axe cases and 2 aprons were purchased, 10 aprons were in store already.[187]

59e *de Ligne*

The regiment was inspected on 16 August 1814. That day the regiment had 97 officers and 980 other ranks. The grenadiers had 94 *schakos*, of which 54 were non-regulation, and lacked 97 *aigrettes*, none being in use. Fifteen pairs of epaulettes were in service but 82 pairs were needed. The *voltigeurs* needed 91 *aigrettes*, as again none were in use, and 23 drummers' *habits* were needed. The regiment had 5 *sapeurs* with full equipment of apron, axe with case and belt, carbine and gauntlets on parade, the *voltigeur* company had no *cornets* at all, and 7 of the 23 drummers had no drum, drum carriage and not one drummer had an apron! The muskets in use included 707 captured foreign muskets in need of immediate replacement. The *dépôt* held 1 new *capote*, 102 fusilier *habits*, 112 pairs of *pantalons de tricot*, 1 *bonnet de police*, 242 pairs of underwear, 1 grenadier *schako de modèle*, 1 fusilier *schako de modèle*, and 340 *schako* covers. Importantly, the inspecting officer noted that the four new drummers' *habits* were in the *dépôt* accompanied by a further seven needing repairs: all were green adorned with Imperial Livery, listed as to be burned.[188]

When the regiment was disbanded in August 1815, the *dépôt* held 96m 63 red broadcloth, 0m 68 chamois broadcloth, 0m 40 beige broadcloth, 235m 30 grey tricot *for capotes*, and 45m of drummers' lace. No epaulettes for grenadiers or adjutants were in stores, but we do find 476 fusilier *schakos* with 165 covers and 142 pompoms. *Dépôt* also held one *bonnet de police de modelé*, one grenadier '*aigrette de modèle*', and one '*aigrette de voltigeur de modèle*'.[189]

60e *de Ligne*

Inspected on 1 September 1814, the inspector noted that virtually every *habit* in use needed replacement as they were *habits-longe,* some 1,374 examples. The regiment had 30 drummers adorned with Imperial Livery, 6 *voltigeur cornets* and 12 *sapeur*s – each of these men having an axe, an axe case with belt, apron and pair of gauntlets, and their headdress was a *schako*. For the 1,494 men under arms, every man had a pair of *pantalons de route*, a white and black stock, a pair of grey gaiters, a pair of shoes and two shirts. Not a single pair of socks or black gaiters were in use.

The officers of the regiment possessed 19 horses, 2 for the colonel, 6 for the staff and 11 for battalion commanders, and needed 52 horses to bring numbers up to full strength. Remarkably, the regiment had had regimental artillery in 1814, possessing some 19 driving horses and 5 officers of artillery. The guns, harness comprising 9 saddles, 8 bridles, 14 driving collars and harness, the horses and officers were sent to the line artillery.[190] The *dépôt* held some stocks of cloth, materials and clothing, which included, 889m of drummers' lace, 113 *capotes*, 100 *voltigeur habits* – arguably these had chamois collars and shoulder straps – 504 fusilier *habits*, 268 fusilier *gilets manches* and 495 pairs of grenadier epaulettes.[191]

A report of 26 August 1815 gives us the contents of the *dépôt*, which held 299m 57 of blue broadcloth, 86m 79 white broadcloth, 51m scarlet broadcloth and 8m 04 of green

This *voltigeur* was drawn in 1816. The yellow cuffs to the habit are atypical. We remember that what is shown is a particular regiment and should not be taken as typical. (*Collection KM*)

broadcloth.[192] Delivered to the *dépôt* after the review was 422m 94 of blue broadcloth, 86m 58 white broadcloth, 12m 65 scarlet broadcloth, 295m 10 beige broadcloth, 9m 02 chamois broadcloth and 13m 20 of green broadcloth. The *dépôt* held 16 grenadier *habits*, 1 *voltigeur habit de modèle*, 45 fusilier *habits*, 2 drummers' *habits*, 53 *bonnets de police*, 243 pairs of *pantalons de tricot*, 63 pairs of underwear, 350 pairs of grenadier epaulettes, 1,277 *houpette*s, as well as 22 sets of drummers' equipment, 22 sets of *sapeurs'* equipment and 5 *voltigeur cornets*.[193]

61e *de Ligne*

On 21 June 1813 the 1e et 2e *bataillon provisoire de la Citadelle de Magdeburg* was disbanded. Marshal Berthier ordered that the men in this unit that had been drawn from the 61e were to be returned their *dépôt*. The 138 men returned to the 1e battalion of the 61e were all wearing pre-Bardin clothing. The inspection return offers a unique glimpse into how the 61e were dressed in 1812 and earlier. The men had between them 400 pairs of shoes, 414 shirts, 138 pairs of black twill gaiters, 138 pairs white cotton gaiters – totally non-regulation as abolished way back in April 1806! – 138 black stocks, 276 white stocks, and not a single pair of stockings, underwear or *pantalons de route*. The men were also issued with 138 *sacs à distribution*, 138 *habits* brushes, shoe brushes and button brushes, 8 *marmites*, 8 *grand bidons*, 111 *petit bidons*. Of the *habits*, 26 had been made in 1810, along with 5 *vestes manches*, 8 pairs of breeches, 25 *capotes* and 6 *schakos*. These men in summer 1813 was seemingly adorned in pre-Bardin clothing with white gaiters![194]

The summer 1814 inspection return is missing, but in January 1815 *dépôt* held, among other items, 298 capotes, 1 *habit de fusilier de modèle*, 2 *habits de tambour*, 215 *vestes de fusilier*, 20 *bonnets de police*, 4 *schakos de fusilier*, 44 *schako* covers, 6 red plumes, 1,156 white stocks, 124 pairs of grey gaiters, 1,069 pairs white gaiters, 108 pairs of linen *pantalons de route*, and 15 pairs of grey broadcloth *pantalons* for *sous-officers* and adjutants. Cloth included 1m 90 green broadcloth, 11m 77 chamois broadcloth, 843m 53 of red and white serge, 23m 58 of white tricot, and 97m 04 drummers' lace. The inference here is that the red serge of unknown quantity was used to face the tails of the *habits* of the grenadiers.[195]

The incredibly complete paper archive tells us that in 1815 1,000 shirts were made or obtained along with 2,903 pairs of shoes, 1,026 black stocks, 500 pairs of linen socks, 1,224 pairs of black half gaiters, 410 pairs of grey gaiters, 410 *sacs de peau*, 890 tricolour cockades, 595 pairs of *pantalons de route* in white linen, of which 448 pairs were issued, 595 pairs of white cotton gaiters with 448 pairs issued, 2 pairs of adjutants epaulettes costing 17fr 40, 11 pairs of *voltigeur* epaulettes costing 4fr80 each, 51 pairs of *voltigeur* epaulettes costing 4fr each, and 7 yellow *aigrette*s. Cloth used January to September 1815 included 1,001m 95 beige broadcloth, 1,177m 13 blue broadcloth, 837m 84 white broadcloth, 108m 84 scarlet broadcloth, 17m 64 green broadcloth, 11m 77 chamois broadcloth, 845m red and white milled serge, 1,723m 42 white tricot and 750m 01 of drummers' lace. Clothing made in the same period was 656 capotes, 175 grenadier *habits*, 159 *voltigeur habits*, 562 fusilier habits, 50 drummers' *habits*, 133 grenadier *gilets*, 139 *voltigeur gilets,* 761 fusilier *gilets*, 1,105 pairs of *pantalons de tricot*, and 831 *bonnets de police*. Also made were 264 grenadier *schakos*, accompanied by 312 *aigrette*s, 1,354 fusilier *schakos*, accompanied by 1,180 *houpettes* and 216 *voltigeur aigrettes*. In addition, 216 pairs of grenadier epaulettes were made, along with 834 *gibernes* and belts, 439 musket slings, 536 *baudriers* – sufficient for grenadiers and voltigeurs! –, 17 drums, 15 drum carriages, 3 *sapeurs*' axes, 3 axe cases, 2 *sapeurs*' aprons, 7 *cornets*' cords, 10 drummers' aprons and 3 *cornets*.

Clothing and equipment remaining in *dépôt* at the time of disbandment included 148 Fusilier *habits*, 707 fusilier *schakos*, 793 *houpette*s, 163 *gilets manches*, 502 pairs of *pantalons de route*, 837 *schako* covers, 315 *bonnets de police*, 362 pairs of *caleçons*, 30 sets of *schako* cords, 81 black stocks, 1,156 white stocks, 436 pairs of socks, 653 pairs of black gaiters, 68 pairs of grey linen gaiters, 1,069 pairs of white gaiters, 136 pairs linen *pantalons*, 214 pairs of shoe buckles, 24 pairs of knee buckles, and 94 stock buckles. Like the white gaiters, the *schako* cords should not have existed, but clearly they did, four years after they had been abolished. We also find in store:[196]

Grenadiers
59 grenadier *habits*, 47 grenadier *schakos*, 118 scarlet *aigrettes*, 12 pairs scarlet-fringed epaulettes, 78 *baudriers* and sabres

***Voltigeur*s**
52 *voltigeur habits*, 12 yellow *aigrettes*, 3 pairs of *voltigeur*s epaulettes costing 4fr 80 each, 25 pairs *voltigeur* epaulettes costing 4 fr each, 1 *voltigeur cornet* with cords

Adjutants
6 pairs of grey wool *pantalons*, 6 pairs grey wool gaiters, 3 red feather plumes

Drummers
1 drummer's *habit*, 8 drums, 6 drum carriages, 12 aprons for drummers

For drummers, 2 green *habits* with we assume Imperial Livery were in the *dépôt* in 1814 and 50 *habits* were made in January to November 1815. Some 97m of what we assume to have been Imperial Livery for drummers was in *dépôt* in 1814, and between January and November 1815 659m of Livery was purchased. Of the lace that existed, some 750m, it was all used, i.e., all the stock that existed in January 1815 and purchased since, but we are ignorant of the pattern. The *dépôt* had held in January 1815 1m 90 green broadcloth, a further 18m 24 was purchased in the 100 Days, making 20m 14 of green broadcloth. Of this, 17m 64 was used to make 17 drummers' *habits*.[197] Thus, of the 50 *habits* made, 33 were blue with Royalist Livery and 17 in green with all that remained of the Imperial Livery applied to them. The regiment had five *sapeurs* in the field. They are likely to have worn grenadier *schakos* and *aigrettes*, grenadier *habits* with epaulettes, axe cases and belts, aprons and we assume gauntlets, and were armed with light cavalry carbines. *Voltigeurs* were armed with dragoon muskets, and had yellow *aigrettes* and epaulettes worn on the regulation *habit*.

62e *de Ligne*

The regiment that was created in the First Restoration owed very little to the 62e that had existed since the 1790s. Reviewed on 21 September 1814, it mustered 1,053 other ranks drawn from the 41e *de Ligne* (104 men), 94e *de Ligne* (59 men), 27e *de Ligne* (48 men), 119e *de Ligne* (26 men), 62e *de Ligne* (237 men), 35e *de Ligne* (143 men), 8e *Légère* (35 men), 34e *Légère* (49 men), 3e Colonial Battalion (247 men) and the 3e battalion of Colonial Pioneers (48 men). The new regiment was dressed as follows:[198]

Battalion	Company	*Habits*		*Vestes*	*Pantalons de tricot*	*Schakos*	*Capotes*	*Caleçons*	*Bonnets de police*	Bearskins	Shirts	shoes	Gaiters		Linen *Pantalons*	*Sacs de peau*	Black stock	Stockings
		Missing	To be Replaced										Black	Grey				
Etat Major		8		9	9	9	9		9		25	84	9	9	9	9	9	19
1e	Grenadier	20	38	64	64	55	49	69	57	72	120	180	56	83	140	25	33	
	1e	21	42	68	68	43	64	70	48		143	188	59	39	112	30		73
	2e	37	20	63	55	30	39	75	70		132	163	39	41	142	14	77	77
	3e	46	10	61	66	37	49	71	40		95	131	45	84	107	9	20	74
	Voltigeur	12	53	69	73	39	48	52	50		76	75	42	37	79	10	16	67
2e	Grenadier	16	25	53	55	31	46	53	38	72	106	144	35	35	80	24	19	56
	1e	24	43	71	65	60	53	69	52		165	188	60	106	107	80	41	
	2e	33	34	63	61	58	63	63	52		143	179	55	47	101	23	80	61
	3e	40	23	64	64	56	54	66	49		119	143	48	42	92	19	32	66
	Voltigeur	8	32	60	62	14	64	69	34		143	169	66	32	103	33	22	65
3e	Grenadier	48	12	45	57	44	48	56	43	72	86	121	44	38	77	57	16	55
	1e	20	27	54	66	27	42	67	47		119	162	41	30	74	18	23	71
	2e	26	33	59	64	40	52	63	52		103	138	55	58	102	20	27	67
	3e	29	35	64	66	46	56	64	60		124	112	59	53	69	31	47	66
	Voltigeur	39	16	57	65	28	56	58	54		100	145	40	54	90	14	13	69

What is clear, is that no man in the regiment had his regulation allocation of clothing. Not a single *habit* was in good condition and were all worn out and, we suppose, Bardin and Pre-Bardin was used side by side. The stand-out feature in the report is that the 1e battalion had 76 bearskins in use, 2e and 3e battalion both had 72. Grenadier epaulettes were clearly counted with the *habits*. Seven pairs of epaulettes are recorded in use accompanied by seven waistbelts epees for the *adjutant-sous-officier*. The regiment needed 427 *habits* of the new model to replace old-pattern kit just taken out of use, and 433 as replacements for those in use. The *dépôt* held 140m of broadcloth, 5,383m of serge, 720m of linen, 242 *capotes*, 61 *habits*, 196 *gilets manches*, 171 *bonnets de police* and 400m of white tricot.[199]

Alas, we do not have a stores inspection for 1814, and in fact due to the vagaries of history, we know nothing more about the regiment until disbanded on 7 August 1815, when the *dépôt* held among other items 5m 22 chamois broadcloth, 18m 24 green broadcloth, 90m drummers' lace, 64 *capote* covers – this one of the very few references to these existing outside the Garde Impériale and in no way indicates these items were in common use – and 174 *giberne* covers. Even in 1815 the regiment had a mix of weaponry: 62 1777 pattern muskets, 36 1763 pattern muskets and 3 foreign muskets. Sabres included 6 new model and 10 old model.[200]

63e *de Ligne*

No archive paperwork exists between 1808 and 1815 that mentions the regiment's dress.

When disbanded on 25 September 1815 the *dépôt* held 13 *capotes* that were cut out and not yet sewn together and 78 *habits* cut out but not yet made up. Brand-new clothing ready to be issued included 201 *capotes*, 92 fusilier *habits*, 156 *gilets manches*, 249 pairs of *pantalons de tricot*, 128 pairs of *caleçons*, 589 pairs of black gaiters, 175 pairs of grey gaiters, 21 *schakos* and 7 grenadier *aigrettes*. In store were 198 *capotes*, 221 *habits*, 458 *gilets manches*, 748 pairs of *pantalons de tricot*, 536 pairs of *caleçons*, 748 sets of braces, 143 *schakos*, 400 *schako* covers, 355 *bonnets de police*, 896 shirts, 989 pairs of shoes, 147 black stocks, 593 pairs of grey linen gaiters, 481 pairs of black gaiters, 109 *sacs de peau* and 30 *sacs à distribution*. Regimental accounts report that a new mace for the drum major was purchased in the 100 Days for 70fr, lace, braid and epaulettes purchased came to 413fr 94, new buff equipment cost 3,167fr 55, 78 shirts accompanied by 78 pairs of shoes cost 760fr 50, and 2,194fr was spent on 589 pairs of black gaiters and 175 pairs of grey. No cloth or materials existed in *dépôt*, and only fusilier *schakos*. We have no data at all about the clothing of the drummers. *Voltigeurs* were armed with dragoon muskets, 21 remaining in the *dépôt* at time of disbandment.[201]

64e *de Ligne*

The 1814 inspection return is missing from the relevant box at the French Army Archives at the time of writing. However, the review inspector did comment on 16 August 1814 that the clothing was passable but in pitiable condition; the cloth used to make the *vestes* was not very good at all; the clothing lacking uniformity and was incomplete. Many conscripts taken into *dépôt* had not been equipped or clothed and still wore civilian garments.[202]

Disbanded on 21 September 1815, the *dépôt* held 66m 70 beige broadcloth, 91m 73 blue broadcloth, 4m 69 white broadcloth, 68m 30 scarlet broadcloth, 22m 16 chamois broadcloth, 1,958m 95 white milled serge, 256m 29 white tricot, 23m 10 yellow worsted lace and 39m 18 '*galons de tambour none uniforme*', i.e., of non-regulation pattern, which in summer 1815 surely means this was Imperial Livery. No *aigrettes* or epaulettes were in *dépôt*, but we do find 523 *houpettes* and 7 old *habits*.[203]

Officier of fusiliers drawn in 1816 showing First Empire uniforms still in service. (*Collection KM*)

Presumably *voltigeurs* had chamois collar and shoulder straps to the *habit*. We know nothing of the grenadiers. Drummers we assume wore Imperial Livery on a blue or green *habit*.

65e *de Ligne*

The regiment's clothing archive is sparse. Reviewed at Bayeaux on 1 August 1814, the inspector remarked that the dress of the regiment was good but far from uniform. The bulk of the men were wearing *habits*, *vestes*, *culottes* and *capotes*, but blue broadcloth had been ordered so that in four months the regiment's clothing would be complete and conform exactly to the prescribed uniform, i.e., Bardin regulations. The colonel was ordered to ensure that the regiment was dressed strictly according to the regulation of 19 January 1812, and that the clothing of the men that had been illegally modified by the men was replaced, with the officers to be more thorough in their inspections. Damning words indeed.[204]

A second report reveals that the pay chest had been used to buy effects in 1814:[205]

6fr 30. 7 pompoms for the staff
58fr50. 13 '*galons en laine rouge*' to decorate the bearskins of *sapeurs*.[206]
90fr to buy 28m 39 blue broadcloth
1,940fr 27 was employed in the production of 781 *habits*, 250 *vestes*, 211 pairs of *pantalons de tricot*, 200 *capotes* and 300 *bonnets de police* as well as the purchase of 1,798m 3 of linen for linings

A huge number of *habits* were replaced – arguably those noted as pre-Bardin or that had been modified by the men. Alas, we have no detail for what was purchased in the 100 Days and no disbandment paperwork to say how the regiment was dressed. Clearly the *sapeurs* wore bearskins, the cords being strictly non-regulation. However, the lack of data means we can say nothing about the elite companies or drummers. We can suggest they were dressed as per the 8 February 1815 decree, but we cannot prove that: any suggestions of what was worn would be blatant guesswork and not facts.

66e *de Ligne*

At the time of writing, no archive paperwork for the dress of the regiment has come to light concerning Bardin-regulation clothing. Reviewed at Blaye on 21 July 1814, the inspector remarked that the regiment was well dressed, and that the *dépôt* held sufficient resources to repair existing clothing and make up for men lacking clothing. The *dépôt* held no scarlet broadcloth and no linen but did hold 1,370m blue broadcloth, 353m white broadcloth, 398m white milled serge and 1,835m white tricot. The colonel was ordered to ensure that all future items of clothing were to conform strictly to the decree of 19 January 1812 and also the circular from the War Ministry dated 23 April 1814.[207]

From this comment, we assume the regiment was wearing either entirely pre-Bardin clothing or was dressed in a mix and match of Bardin and pre-Bardin.

The lack of data means we can say nothing about the elite companies or drummers, or indeed say how the regiment was dressed.

67e *de Ligne*

The paperwork for the regiment is grossly incomplete. Nothing exists in the archives between February 1808 and the disbandment of the regiment on 25 September 1815. On this date the regimental stores held a whole cross section of '*effects de modèle*':[208]

2 *capotes*
2 *habits de tambour*
2 *habits* de fusilier
2 *gilets manches*
2 *pantalons de tricot*
2 pairs of *caleçons*
1 *bonnet de police*
1 *giberne*
3 *porte-giberne* in buff
1 *porte-giberne* in blacked cow hide
1 *baudrier* in blackened cow hide
1 set of braces
3 musket slings – 1 in blackened cow hide
2 drum carriages – 1 in blackened cow hide
1 shirt
1 pair of shoes
2 *pantalons de toile*
3 pairs of grey gaiters
3 pairs black gaiters
1 black stock
1 *giberne* cover
1 pair of socks
1 *sac de peau*
1 box of cloth samples

In essence here was the Bardin-regulation start-up kit, including cloth to provide colour swatches!

From this list we can learn several important points about the regiment:

1. The regiment from summer 1813 had black leatherwork and the War Ministry issued sealed pattern examples to copy.

2. Two sealed pattern drummers' *habits* suggest two different lace options here, ergo Royalist and Imperial. Indeed, the inspector noted that since 23 April 1814, drummers had adopted blue *habits* with Royalist Livery, as had musicians, and that Imperial symbols had been swapped with the *fleur-de-lys*.[209]
3. Rather than hoping regiments would adopt the correct colour broadcloth, serge etc for uniforms, the War Ministry clearly supplied cloth samples to regiments to mandate exactly what colours were used.

When we look in detail at other items in the report, we find that cloth and materials in the *dépôt* included 592m 90 beige broadcloth, 27m 40 blue serge, 572m 70 white tricot, 50m red worsted lace, and 260m drummers' lace. Brand-new clothing included 64 *habits*, 2 drummers' *habits*, 498 pairs of *pantalons de tricot*, 25 *capotes*, 19 pairs of grenadier epaulettes, 8 new grenadier *schakos*, 1 new fusilier *schako* and 180 old, 373 fusilier *houpettes*, and 716 white cockades. The inspector noted that drummers' lace had been lost when the magazine at Gênes had been captured on 17 April 1814. This was undoubtedly Imperial Livery at this date. The *dépôt* also held 5 *sapeurs'* axes, 2 pairs of *sapeurs'* gauntlets, 3 axe cases and 2 aprons. Also, in *dépôt* were 114 *giberne* covers, 149 black stocks, 25 white stocks and 1,600 dozen small copper buttons for black gaiters.[210] We suppose therefore that the regiment was dressed as per Bardin regulations. The blue serge had one purpose, to line *habit* tails or *vestes*, and was clearly used to line the tails of the *habits* of the regimental artillery company formed on 1 March 1813 for the 1e and 2e battalions serving in the Army of Catalogne.

The revue inspector commented that the regiment had in *dépôt* since 1814 300 *habits*, 300 *vestes*, 300 pairs of *pantalons de tricot*, and 300 pairs of *caleçons*, all of the old model, as well as cloth of diverse colours, *Schakos* of different dimensions garnished with plates of different types were all inherited from the 119e *de Ligne*. The regiment also possessed 328 old-pattern light infantry *habits*!

69e *de Ligne*

Reviewed on 6 September 1814, the regiment's clothing was mostly fit only for replacement. Of the 957 men on parade, 364 men had *habits* in need of replacement and 78 men had no *habit*. Likewise, 358 men lacked a *gilet manches*, 479 had no *pantalons de tricot*, 509 no *caleçon*, 188 no *capote*, 330 no *schako* and 378 no *bonnet de police*. Despite the clothing being in shreds, each man had 3 shirts and 2 pairs of shoes. However, 849 pairs of *pantalons de route* were issued, 790 black stocks, 439 white stocks, 4 pairs of socks, 395 pairs of black and 700 pairs of grey gaiters: not enough for a man to have a full allocation of clothing. Ironically given the acute shortages, the *dépôt* had 115 brand-new fusilier *habits* as well as 101 old-pattern *habits-longe*, which had been taken out of service on 23 April 1814. We have no clue as to the distinctions worn by grenadiers or *voltigeurs*, although the chamois cloth implies *voltigeurs* had chamois *habit* collars. We are totally ignorant of the dress of drummers.[211] It is clear that the regiment was wearing a mix of Bardin and pre-Bardin as the Empire fell.

Disbanded on 25 September 1815, the regiment had two types of drummers' lace, the *dépôt* had 52m of '*Galons Anciene government*', i.e., Imperial Livery, and 132m 70 '*Galons du Roi*' i.e., Royalist Livery. By 1815, seemingly grenadiers had *aigrettes* and epaulettes as 69 pairs of scarlet epaulettes were in *dépôt* and 69 *aigrettes*, as well as 74 *voltigeur aigrettes*. The inspection listed grenadier *habits* and *schakos*, of which none existed; but does this mean they did indeed exist on the men? Perhaps so. Likewise, *habits* for *voltigeurs* and drummers are listed but none were in stores.[212]

70e *de Ligne*

Inspected on 16 September 1814, the regiment had 149 officers and 925 other ranks and 13 *enfants de troupe*. The inspecting officer reported that '713 habits are mediocre, have been in service longer than regulated, 180 are made from cloth captured from the English which is very mediocre'.[213] The inference here is that the *habits* were pre-Bardin model, and had been made on campaign in Spain from, as the inspector reports, captured English cloth. Indeed, the inspector remarked:

> the corps does not possess a single uniform habit in good condition, the sabres likewise … the totality of effects of clothing, equipment and armament in use and in the magazine needs to be totally replaced.

further noting:

> a great disparity in the clothing and equipment reigns, there is very little uniformity, the Colonel needs to be stricter in this regard, and the dress does not accord to the regulation, and in this regard many innovations have been tolerated, especially for the dress of the officers: it is strictly forbidden for them to wear the dress of the bourgeois when in barracks, around town and off duty.[214]

We must imagine the officers were wearing 'civvies' for most of the time: one can sympathise as, back in barracks after living in squalid conditions on campaign, the desire to get back to being an officer and gentleman must have been overwhelming. Cloth in the *dépôt* included 121m 13 English blue broadcloth, which the inspecting officer recommended was best used for making new *bonnets de police*. No *aigrettes* or epaulettes existed for grenadiers or *voltigeurs*, and as no chamois broadcloth existed, we assume these men were dressed as fusiliers.[215]

Disbanded on 21 September 1815, the *dépôt* held cloth and materials to make new items of clothing, which was 570m *Galon de Tambour (nouveau modèle)*, which is very likely to be Royalist Lace. Tellingly, the *dépôt* held 136 blackened cow hide *porte-gibernes* issued in 1813, accompanied by 139 brand-new blackened cow hide musket slings and

213 old examples, again made from blackened cow hide. No mention is made of grenadier *aigrettes*, epaulettes or *aigrettes*, so we assume grenadiers were dressed as fusiliers, along with *voltigeurs*.[216] The grenadier epaulettes could be counted with the *habits*, ditto the *aigrettes* with *schakos*, but that is not demonstrable fact.

72[e] de Ligne

Regimental accounts report than in 1811 worsted *houpettes* for *bonnets de police* were used: these tassels according to regulation were cut from strips of cloth and not worsted fringing. The inspector refused to sanction government funds be spent on these, or *schako* cords, grenades and hunting horns in copper for *gibernes*, chinscale bosses and *schako* plates as they were all non-regulation when they arrived with the regiment.[217] The 2e battalion was reviewed on 14 March 1813. The cadre comprised 21 officers and 65 *sous-officiers* and men and was filled out with 645 conscripts. The cadre were well dressed, the inspector noted, but added that 'in order to complete the conscripts received into the *dépôt,* the *sous-officiers* and soldiers that have been received into the army have been clothed entirely in effects that are *hors de service*'. The battalion needed every single habit replacing, 500 pairs of *pantalons de tricot* and the same number of capotes. The broadcloth and tricot used was totally substandard, as were all the *gibernes* and belt.[218] It seems from this that the *dépôt* had basically been emptied of any clothing and equipment that remained, regardless of condition, in the haste to get men into the field.

In the midst of the Armistice of 1813, to make up for men killed in action, or who had died of wounds or deserted, the 1e battalion received a draft of men from the 4[e] battalions of the 27[e], 28[e], 29[e], 30[e] *de Ligne* as replacements on 30 August 1813: a total of 4 staff officers, 29 company officers and 1,061 other ranks. The major of the 72[e] was incredulous that the newly arrived men were missing 214 *habits*, 115 *vestes de tricot*, 176 pairs *pantalons de tricot*, 182 pairs *caleçons*, 39 *capotes*, 20 *schakos*, 116 *bonnets de police*, 12 muskets, 86 sabres with belts, 174 musket slings, 10 *gibernes* and belts, 3 drums, 2 drum carriages, 6 *voltigeur cornets*, 421 pairs *of pantalons de route*, 213 pairs of black gaiters, 508 pairs of grey gaiters, 711 shirts, 388 black stocks, 1,094 pairs of shoes, 107 *sacs de peau*, 42 *sacs à distribution*, 231 *aigrettes*, 135 pairs of grenadier and *voltigeur* epaulettes, 326 *giberne* covers, 88 grenadier sword knots, 6 *sapeurs' habits*, and 2 *sapeurs'* aprons![219] Active service clearly wore down the regiment's clothing and equipment or these men never had these items issued. What this does show, however, is that *voltigeurs* used epaulettes in 1813 and *sapeurs' habits* also existed.

The 1[e] battalion was reviewed again 10 November 1813 and mustered just 25 officers and 229 men, and was to receive a draft of 8 officers and 264 conscripts. The inspector noted that:

> The clothing of the men in the companies is generally in bad condition, particularly the capotes which have deteriorated to the point of being considered *hors de service* due to the effects of bivouacking and marching continually virtually nonstop; to

Drum major drawn in 1816. (*Collection KM*)

enable the corps to commence campaigning it needs 33 *gibernes* and belts, 83 musket slings, 53 *baudriers*, 3 drummers' aprons, 52 muskets, 57 bayonets and 55 sabres to replace those lost in the affairs the corps has taken part. The linen and footwear is in bad condition, numerous soldiers have lost their *sacs de peau*, they don't have two pairs of shoes or two shirts.[220]

We know nothing more until the regiment was reviewed on 12 August 1814. The inspecting officer noted that the 842 other ranks on parade were wearing:[221]

Item	In Good Repair	In Need of Repair	Need Replacing	Items due to be replaced	Items missing
Habits	383	189	47	223	
Vestes	365	95	69	254	58
Pantalons de tricot	241		191	411	
Caleçons	203		251	224	164
Capotes	301	217	75	191	58
Fusilier *schakos*	591	119	38	94	
Bonnets de police	391		66	48	337
Braces	241		190	411	
Schako covers					842
Fusilier *houpettes*	842				
Adjutant's epaulettes	9				
Grenadier epaulettes	160				
Voltigeur epaulettes	178				

The men were also wearing or had issued 1,245 shirts, 651 pairs of *pantalons de route*, 682 black stocks, 24 pairs of linen socks, 4 pairs of woollen stockings, 930 pairs of shoes, 726 pairs of black gaiters, 656 pairs of grey gaiters – insufficient pairs of either type existed for every man to have a pair of each – and 732 *sacs de peau*. The *dépôt* held some cloth and materials, notably 1,860m of beige broadcloth, 9,771m 61 blue broadcloth, 419m 79 white broadcloth, 90m 34 scarlet broadcloth, 714m 17 white milled serge, 2,111m 31 white tricot, 3m 70 of gold lace, 1m 72 silver lace for musicians, 15m of worsted lace and 30m 60 of drummers' lace. The *dépôt* held a considerable quantity of new clothing: 40 *capotes*, 29 fusilier *habits*, 242 *gilets manches*, 473 pairs of *pantalons de tricot*, 42 *bonnets de police*, 154 fusilier *schakos*, 137 grenadier *aigrettes*, 134 *voltigeur aigrettes*, 457 fusilier *houpettes* and 19 pairs of grenadier epaulettes. Alas we do not know the pattern of drummers' lace in use. We also find in stores 72 shirts, 249 pairs of *pantalons de route*, 593 black stocks, 55 pairs of linen socks, 48 corporals' sword knots, 45 sergeants' sword knots, 541 pairs of black gaiters, 16 pairs of grey gaiters, 819 *sacs à distribution,* 623 screwdrivers, 70 cockades and 229 *epinglettes.*[222] The sergeants' sword knots, presumably red and gold, are just one of two examples we have found in the entire army out of 137 regiments of line, the other being the 10e *de Ligne*. Fewer than 1 per cent of all regiments had these items, which shows that they were not in common use!

When disbanded on 11 August 1815 the regiment's *dépôt* held the following items of clothing:[223]

277 *habits*
173 *vestes*
350 pairs of *pantalons*
627 pairs of *caleçons*
212 *capotes*
451 *schakos*
162 *bonnets de police*
484 *schako* covers
89 pairs of grenadier epaulettes
581 *houpettes*
65 grenadier *aigrettes*
106 *voltigeur aigrettes*
60 pairs of black gaiters
446 pairs grey gaiters
775 *sacs à distribution*
349 *sacs de peau*
614 *epinglettes*
619 screwdrivers
794 tricolour cockades
75 *giberne* covers
93 sword knots
884 pay books
188 long straps for the *sacs de peau*
104 short straps for the *sacs de peau*
108 musket worms
603 black stocks
800 white stocks

The *capotes* were made from beige broadcloth as per regulation. The grenadiers had epaulettes and *aigrettes*. Stocks of cloth included 484m 03 blue broadcloth, 8m 16 of green broadcloth, 10m 03 chamois broadcloth, 22m 54 red broadcloth, 455m 40 beige broadcloth, 121m 09 white broadcloth, 938m 10 white tricot, and 1,030m 27 white milled serge. Clearly, *voltigeur*s may have had chamois collars as well as *aigrettes*, drummers had green *habits* but we are ignorant of any lace applied to them – no green broadcloth existed in 1814 so clearly this was an innovation of the 100 Days.[224]

The *sapeurs* had their own-pattern *habit* but none existed by summer 1814, when the *dépôt* held 16 axes, 4 axe cases and belts at disbandment but no aprons or gauntlets! We note that on 11 August 1814 three new axes and cases, along with red epaulettes were obtained for *sapeurs* costing 163fr 65.[225]

75e *de Ligne*

Inspected on 26 September 1814, the regiment mustered 599 men. The inspecting officer noted the bulk of the regiment's clothing was either in need of repair, replacement or the men simply lacked most items: 340 *vestes* were needed, 357 pairs of *pantalons de tricot*, 112 *capotes* and 58 *habits* among other items.[226] The *dépôt* held very little stocks of cloth, just 0m 60 of beige broadcloth, 0m 13 of blue broadcloth, as well as 120m of drummers' livery. The *dépôt* also held 242 pairs of *pantalons de tricot*, 100 *bonnets de police* and 380 *porte-gibernes* in blacked cow hide. Found lurking in the *dépôt* were 2,223 old-model white stocks for parades and 289 pairs of knee buckles.[227]

Disbanded on 14 September 1815, the *dépôt* held among other items, 6 new pairs of *pantalons de tricot*, 452 pairs of *pantalons de tricot* that had been recut as *culottes* and 10 pairs of *culottes* – quite remarkable that breeches were still being made in 1815! Also, in the *dépôt* was 300m *livrée de tambours ancien modèle* and 45m *livrée de tambours nouveau modèle*: the latter being – presumably – Royalist Livery, and shows that blue *habits* were made in the restoration. Stocks of materials included 3m 20 of chamois broadcloth.[228] One of the stand-out items from the regimental accounts is a receipt for 15fr for making a wooden leg: the leg was made for a fusilier of the regiment and an entry requirement for men into Les Invalides who were amputees was that they needed to provide their own prosthetic. The regiment provided the leg out of an act of 'humanity'.[229]

76e *de Ligne*

Reviewed on 16 August 1814, the regiment mustered 869 other ranks, which included 13 *sapeurs*, though only 7 were equipped, only 48 grenadiers out of 216 had epaulettes, and none had an *aigrette* or sabre. The *voltigeurs* likewise had no *aigrettes* and needed 216, and the inspector noted just two of the six *cornets* had horns.[230] The *dépôt* held some stocks of cloth and other materials, notably 187m 80 drummers' lace. The *dépôt* held no clothing, but it did hold 797 *schako* covers, 16 *gibernes*, and 330 fusilier *houpettes*.[231]

A document prepared on 16 August 1814 adds more details. The regiment from 1809 to 1814 never purchased green broadcloth, therefore the drummers always had blue *habits*. Indeed, the accounts show that in 1811 25m 30 of drummers lace was used and a further 214m 50 in 1812. A further 199m 20 was obtained after September 1812, which no doubt was Imperial Livery, with just 25m used in 1813 and 21m 40 in 1814. In 1814 172m of Royalist Livery was purchased. The same document reports that grenadiers up to 1814 were dressed as fusiliers, wearing a fusilier *schako* with *houpette*: the regiment only issued 22 sabres in 1812 and 102 in 1813! Not even corporals had sabres! The only issue of epaulettes to grenadiers was in 1811 when 360 pairs were issued – not a single pair was issued in 1809, 1810, 1812, 1813, or 1814! Those in use in 1814 were it seems for

Drummer of *voltigeur* company of the 2e *de Ligne*. The regiment's archive tells us the drummers did have crimson facings, however the *voltigeur* companies had *cornets* and not drummers, and the lace was white. Presumably this is a grenadier drummer with colourists embellishments, which does not match the known facts for the unit. This neatly shows the dangers of relying solely on iconographic sources. (*Collection KM*)

corporals and *sous-officiers* and a few lucky individuals. We also note that drummers were issued 36 light cavalry musketoons in 1813, and were issued the corresponding number of *gibernes* and belts. The regiment's archive reveals that in 1812 83m 13 of silver lace was purchased and used to adorn the clothing of the band.[232]

A report produced on 18 to 20 June 1815 gives us some information about how the men in the *dépôt* were actually dressed:

> The *dépôt* only has 33 men available. The Major would like to note that in accordance with the minister's order of the 17th of this month, 39 men have been supplied to the squadrons of artillery train and have been sent to Vincennes.
>
> The *dépôt* possesses all the necessary resources to cloth and equipment for all the men that have arrived with the regiment [...] The cloth in the *dépôt* comprises:
>
> 667 m 81 Blue broadcloth, 866m 61 white broadcloth, 101m 84 scarlet broadcloth, 0m 73 chamois broadcloth, 1,442m 90 beige broadcloth.[233]

From this, we see the *capotes* were made from regulation beige cloth, the *voltigeurs* had the regulation chamois facings, and those of the grenadiers and fusiliers scarlet facings.

A statement of accounts reports 49,395fr 92 was spent in the 100 Days to buy:[234]

50 grenadier *habits* costing 24fr 69 each
50 *voltigeur habits* costing 24fr 65 each
159 fusilier *habits* costing 24fr 91 each
40 grenadier *gilets manches* costing 10fr 08 each
52 *voltigeur gilets manches* costing 10fr 48 each
672 pairs of *pantalons* costing 9fr 14 each
466 fusilier *gilets manches* costing 10fr each
240 *bonnets de police* costing 3fr 70
248 pairs of *caleçons* costing 8fr 26 each
43 grenadier *schakos* costing 12fr 04 each
438 fusilier and *voltigeur schakos* costing 9fr 45 each
853 *schako* covers costing 1fr 60 each
236 sets of braces costing 60 centimes each
36 pairs of grenadier epaulettes costing 3fr 50 each
69 grenadier *aigrettes* costing 4fr 60 each
49 *voltigeur aigrettes* costing 3fr 60
207 fusilier *houpettes* costing 60 centimes each
445 *capotes* costing 25fr 13 each

From this list we can fully reconstruct how the regiment was dressed in the 100 Days. The grenadier *habits*, *schakos* and epaulettes were the first and only known purchase of these garments. The accounts confirm that *voltigeurs* and fusiliers wore exactly the same *schako*. The price difference with the grenadier examples clearly shows they had no lace whatsoever.

At the time of disbandment, the *dépôt* held on 26 September, 58 chamois broadcloth, 10m 20 silver lace for the band, 165m of *livrée de l'anciene Gouvernement*, i.e., Imperial Livery, and 82m *livrée de Roi*, which is self-evident. Also, in *dépôt* were 12 *capotes*, 17 *voltigeur habits*, 231 fusilier *habits*, 72 fusilier *gilets manches*, 90 pairs of *pantalons de tricot*, 63 grenadier *schakos*, 932 fusilier *schakos*, 855 *schako* covers, 60 pairs of grenadier epaulettes, 46 grenadier *aigrettes* and 46 *voltigeur aigrettes*.[235] A mix of French and foreign muskets were in use: 1,162 French and 575 foreign.[236]

79e *de Ligne*

The paperwork for the regiment is confused, thanks to the 1814 amalgam. Thus, we find documents for the regiment spread between the boxes for the 79e *de Ligne* and the 69e *de Ligne*! Inspected on 8 August, we see that 90 per cent of the clothing was new, but the grenadiers needed 155 new pairs of epaulettes and *aigrettes* as none existed, and the *voltigeurs* needed 100 new *aigrettes*, again none existed. New clothing in the *dépôt* included 12 *capotes*, 12 fusilier *habits*, and 3 drummers' *habits* in green with Imperial Livery, as well as 96 new pairs of grenadier epaulettes. The *dépôt* also recorded chamois broadcloth but none existed, 36m 17 of green broadcloth and 210m of drummers' livery.[237] No disbandment paperwork can be found.

81e *de Ligne*

Reviewed on 18 September 1814, the regiment's uniforms were either new, a bit shabby needing repairs in the minority or missing: we note 622 *habits* were new in good condition, 72 needed repairs, 89 needed replacing and 136 men had no *habit*. The grenadiers had 110 sets of epaulettes, just one pair being in good condition. Every man had a *houpette* and just 2 men had a canteen.

The regiment also had 18 drummers, and 4 *voltigeur cornets*. For an infantry unit, shockingly 178 men had no *giberne* and belt, and 197 no musket sling: presumably some form of improvised slings and *gibernes* were in use. The *dépôt* held some stocks of cloth and materials, viz: 41m 80 beige broadcloth, 67m 20 blue broadcloth, 42m 90 white broadcloth, 2,536m 34 white serge, 33m 80 white tricot, 810m 15 linen and 34m 30 of drummers' lace – likely to be Imperial Livery. The regiment also had a single driving horse and canteen waggon.[238]

No disbandment paperwork can be located at the time of writing.

82e *de Ligne*

The regiment was reviewed on 11 August 1814, when it had 1,612 other ranks on parade, 11 *enfants de troupe* and 172 officers. Clothing in use was new or entirely missing, with for example, 234 *habits* in condition and 211 needed, 169 *vestes* in good condition but 340 needed. Likewise, the regiment had a huge shortfall in equipment: 266 men had no *giberne* and belt, for 125 *baudriers* the regiment possessed just 116 sabres: were men really on parade wearing a *baudrier* with no sabre in it? Worse still, for 575 men just 247 muskets in good condition existed! Yet despite these acute shortages, every man on parade had two shirts, 1,215 being issued, 398 men had linen *pantalons* and 375 men had a black stock – the regiment's clothing really was shambolic. Only 794 pairs of shoes existed, 289 pairs of black gaiters and 484 pairs of grey gaiters. Cloth in the *dépôt* included 1m 51 beige broadcloth, 0m 04 blue broadcloth, 72m 40 scarlet broadcloth, 11m 80 green broadcloth, 2m 48 chamois broadcloth, and quite remarkably 601m 10 of drummers' lace and 39m 25 of silver musicians' lace. Remarkably, given 314 men had no *pantalons de tricot*, 765 brand-new pairs existed in *dépôt* with 66 *capotes* and 135 *bonnets de police* as well as 160 grenadier *aigrettes*, 2,209 fusilier *houpettes*, 5 *voltigeur cornets*, 1 pair of adjutant's epaulettes, 41 pairs of grenadier epaulettes, 19 pairs of *culottes*, 21 pairs of long black gaiters, 34 pairs of long grey gaiters, 647 stock buckles, 382 pairs of knee buckles, and 1,063 buckles for buff work.[239]

Ordered during the 100 Days were 433 *schakos*, 433 *schako* covers, 241 *houpettes*, and 192 *aigrettes* for the sum of 5,373fr 89.[240] The *dépôt* contents on 24 September 1815 included 30m 04 green broadcloth, accompanied by 5m 31 of drummers' lace, 133 *habits*, 573 *gilets manches*, 364 *pantalons de tricot*, 169 pairs of *pantalons de route*, 99 *capotes*, 11 *bonnets de police*, 379 *schakos* with 588 covers, 65 grenadier *houpettes*, 341 fusilier *houpettes*, 90 grenadier *aigrettes*, 87 *voltigeur aigrettes*, 2 pairs of epaulettes with sword knots for adjutants, 108 pairs of grenadier epaulettes, 105 black stocks, 92 pairs of long grey gaiters, 21 pairs of long black gaiters, 1,007 pairs short black gaiters and 56 *sacs de peau*.[241]

84^{e} *de Ligne*

The regiment was inspected on 1 August 1814, when the inspecting officer recorded the 172 grenadiers under arms needed 39 new pairs of epaulettes to replace ones in use that were life expired. Moreover, an additional 28 pairs were needed so every man had a set. The *voltigeurs* had 72 *aigrettes* in use and needed a further 107. Five *sapeurs* were equipped, as were four *cornets*. Every man had a shirt and a pair of shoes, 372 pairs of *pantalons de route* were issued, which no doubt made up for a lack of *pantalons de tricot*. Men wore a mix of gaiters: 528 black and 307 pairs of grey were in use: every man had a pair, but not a pair of both. The *dépôt* held 8 *habits de voltigeur*, 1 *habit de tambour de modelé,* 482 *habits de fusilier*, 41 *schakos* de grenadier, 292 grenadier *aigrettes*, 39 pairs of grenadier epaulettes, and 247 *voltigeur aigrettes.* Cloth and materials included 12m 50 silver lace for the band and 262m 80 drummers' lace. The regiment also had 3 pack horses, 4 ambulances and 4 *cantinière* carts![242]

We can say nothing more about the dress of the regiment until after Waterloo, when the *dépôt* held 712m 80 drummers' livery, 110 *habits* de fusilier, 288 pairs of *caleçons*, 20 *schakos*, 669 pairs of braces, 53 grenadier *aigrettes*, 61 *voltigeur aigrettes*, 930 fusiliers *houpettes*, 826 *gibernes*, 750 *porte-gibernes*, 772 musket slings, and 260 *baudriers*.[243]

85e *de Ligne*

Inspected on 16 September 1814, the regiment's clothing was in shreds: just 80 *habits* were in good condition, 61 needed repairs, 84 needed replacing and 238 men had no *habit*. The inspector noted everything was worn out or missing bar *capotes* as most were in good condition, he noted; even so, many men had none. We note *sous-officiers* alone carried sabres, just 20 being in good condition, 40 needed repairs, and a further 72 were needed to equip corporals and grenadiers. Given the parlous state of the regiment's clothing, it is quite remarkable that the *dépôt* held 360m of drummers' livery, over 734m of beige broadcloth to make much-needed *capotes*, 1,012m 78 of blue broadcloth to make new *habits*, along with 144m 41 of white broadcloth for *habit* revers, 99m 41 of scarlet broadcloth for *habit* collars, cuffs and piping and 228m of white serge for tail lining and facing along with 1,641m of linen to line *habits* and 360m of drummers' livery. Ready to be issued brand-new clothing in the *dépôt* included 293 *capotes*, 24 new *habits*, 76 *gilets manches*, 1,186 pairs of *pantalons de tricot*, 1,133 pairs of *caleçons*, 315 *bonnets de police*, 322 fusilier *schakos*, 681 *schako* covers, 1,334 fusilier *houpettes* and 4 pairs of grenadier epaulettes. Also in store were 575 shirts, 248 pairs of *pantalons de route*, 59 black stocks, 1,349 pairs of linen socks, 1,438 pairs of shoes, 966 pairs of black gaiters, 681 pairs of grey gaiters, 548 *sacs à distribution*, 212 *sacs de peau*, and 223 *epinglettes*.[244] Stocks of clothing could have easily made up many of the shortfalls in clothing: we suppose the quartermaster was a bit of a jobsworth when it came to issuing kit. The inspecting officer adds:

> the regiment had not enacted the decree of 19 January 1812 for its clothing, which it was henceforth to adhere to, and the modifications to the dress under the circular of 23 April 1814 are to be carried out.

From this we assume that all items of clothing were henceforth to be made to the new model, i.e., Bardin 1812 pattern and drummers and *cornets* to be dressed as per the 23 April 1814 decree in blue with Royalist Livery. Clearly therefore, the regiment wore pre-Bardin clothing in 1814 and had Imperial Livery: but were the changes carried out? When disbanded in September 1815 the *dépôt* held 84 *habits*, 106 *vestes*, 475 *pantalons* de *tricot*, 311 pairs of *caleçons*, 15 *capotes*, 187 *schakos* and 490 *bonnets de police*. Other items in stores included 4m 68 chamois broadcloth and 88m 45 of white tricot that had been dyed grey for making *capotes*: the lack of supplies of beige broadcloth to make *capotes* meant that cloth destined to make *pantalons* was dyed to make *capotes* for the war battalions.[245] Alas we do not know the pattern of *habit* in use!

Rather surprisingly, the regiment's accounts report on 4 March 1815 an expense claim for the following items:[246]

12 bearskins for *sapeurs*, total 576fr
1 colpack with *flamme* for *sapeur* total 60fr
1 *schako* for drum major, total 91fr 60

Colonel of *ligne* infantry wearing his blue *redingote*. (*Collection KM*)

13 pairs of gauntlets for *sapeurs*, total 24fr 5 centimes
13 aprons for *sapeurs*, total 158fr 8 centimes
Total: 909fr 73

The corporal *sapeur* wearing a colpack is remarkable, as this is very much non-regulation. The drum major wore a *schako* that cost the huge sum of 91fr 60, the set tariff being 9fr 40! Under Bardin they were allowed to wear a colpack. The high cost of the *schako* for the drum major surely implies that it was heavily ornamented with gold lace. We can only speculate that his uniform was also highly ornate, no doubt with elaborately laced breeches in imitation of the *Garde Imperiale.*

86e *de Ligne*

At the time of its inspection on 13 August 1814 the inspector tells us the regiment had worked hard to dress the men in new-pattern clothing, but many still lacked their uniform: 335 men had no *capote*, for example, 208 no *schako*, and 391 men had no *veste*. Despite this, the bulk of the clothing was new and did not need repair. The report shows the *voltigeurs* had *cornets* and nine *sapeurs* were equipped with axes, aprons and axe cases. Of note, all bar 70 *giberne* belts were made from blackened cow hide, as were 390 musket slings, and nearly 400 men had an improvised musket sling. Remarkably, when the regiment's muskets were inspected, 82 were listed as 'foreign' and not of standard calibre! In addition, the inspector noted that the men had blue *capotes* and also beige examples. Drummers wore green with Imperial livery as 15m of drummers' lace was in *dépôt*.[247]

When disbanded in September 1815 we find in stores 10 grenadier *aigrettes*, 12 *voltigeur aigrettes* and 25 pairs of grenadier epaulettes. Cloth included 62m 80 blue broadcloth, 1m 25 scarlet broadcloth, 0m 98 chamois broadcloth, 175m white serge, 716m 72 white tricot, 5m 04 silver musicians' lace, 39m yellow worsted lace and 18m red worsted lace. Also in stores were 5 *sapeurs'* axes, 5 axe cases and belts, 1 new *sapeur*'s apron, 7 old *sapeurs'* aprons, 350 brand-new blackened cow hide *giberne* belts, 855 blackened cow hide *baudriers* and 280 blackened cow hide musket slings. Lodged in stores were 450 black leather stocks, 200 linen black stocks and 47m of black wool twill for making gaiters.[248]

88e *de Ligne*

The regiment's archive is remarkably complete from 1 January 1814 to September 1815, as the following table attests:[249]

	Habits		Vestes		Culottes		Habits-Vestes		Gilets		Pantalons		Capotes	
	Made	**Issued**	**Made**	**Issued**	**Made**	**Issued**	**Made**	**Issued**	**Made**	**Issued**	**Made**	**Issued**	**Made**	**Issued**
In Store 1 January 1814							405		777		1650		132	
1st and 2nd quarter 1814	195	67	175	69	633	67	200	410	230	909		558	117	240
In Magazine 8 July 1814	128		106		566		195		470		1092		9	
3rd and 4th Quarter 1814		33		35		22	951	1067	549	1059	742	1076	1057	990
1st and 2nd Quarter 1815		95		31		544	367	366	1126	444	573	460	485	479
Total		**195**		**106**		**633**								
In *Dépôt* 16 September 1815	0						80		707		270		18	

The report shows that in 1814 the *dépôt* was still making pre-Bardin kit and 195 men were dressed as new in these items. A further 38 *habits*, 27 *vestes* and 52 pairs of *culottes en tricot* were in store needing repairs. A huge number of men in 1815 were wearing knee breeches and consequently we assume with long gaiters. Of the *capotes* made, just 54 were made from beige broadcloth and had required 129m 70 of fabric. The remainder were produced from grey tricot.

Also, in *dépôt* in January 1814 were 572 pairs of grenadier epaulettes; 11 pairs being issued, leaving 561 pairs in *dépôt* ready to be issued. No chamois cloth existed or was purchased in the first half of 1814, which proves *voltigeurs* in 1814, if not earlier as well, wore fusilier *habits*. Yet we find 156 *voltigeur habits*, brand new in *dépôt* on 8 July 1814! Therefore, we can only assume therefore that these garments had chamois facings, using cloth already in store. One unique distinction of grenadiers in the 88e was their use of white broadcloth *gilets manches*, which in 1813 required 138m 64 of white broadcloth. According to army regulations, *gilets manches* were made from tricot due to the shortage of white broadcloth – alas the regiment's accounts don't say if the grenadier *gilets manches* had scarlet collars. Only a single *schako* type was in use prior to the First Restoration, fusilier model.

Inspected on 8 July 1814, the *dépôt* held a motley collection of materials, 470m 30 of beige broadcloth, 6m 12 white broadcloth, 9m 14 of white broadcloth, 258m 61 of white serge, 585m of linen and 349m of drummers' livery. Regiment archives report that in the first half of 1814, 378m 20 of drummers' lace was used, from a total purchase of 727m 30. Clearly drummers' kit was blue as not an inch of green broadcloth existed or was purchased, yet as *voltigeur habits* were in store, with chamois collars, clearly, chamois broadcloth had existed in 1813 and was used in 1814, so using the same logic, green broadcloth may have existed in 1813 to be used in 1814. We cannot confirm that these garments were green, and they may well have been blue. The *voltigeur habits* may not have had chamois facings: yellow is possible, or indeed simply a fusilier garment with hunting horns to the tails! The balance of probability, however, suggests yellow or chamois facings.

The *dépôt* held good stocks of brand-new clothing reading to be issued, which comprised 9 *capotes*, 150 *voltigeur habits*, 45 fusilier *habits*, 537 fusilier *gilets manches*, 1,092 pairs of *pantalons de tricot*, 388 *bonnets de police*, 1,141 pairs of *caleçons*, 7 fusilier *schakos*, 443 *schako* covers, 651 *gibernes*, 451 *porte-gibernes*, 305 fusilier *houpettes*, and a huge number of grenadier epaulettes: some 561 pairs! Stores held in addition 266 pairs of *pantalons de route*, 600 white stocks, 240 pairs of linen socks, 504 pairs of shoes, 249 pairs of black gaiters, 386 pairs of grey gaiters, 10 *sacs à distribution*, and 55 *sacs de peau*. Needing repairs were 38 old-pattern *habits-longe*, 87 *vestes* and 52 pairs of *culottes*.[250]

Regimental paperwork tells us that grenadiers used fusilier *schakos* until summer 1814, when 220 grenadier *schakos* were purchased, 147 being issued in 1814 and 53 during the 100 Days. Grenadiers had 551 pairs of epaulettes on 8 July 1814 but no *aigrettes*, 216 pairs being purchased after 8 July and a further 30 in 1815, all being issued. Grenadiers furthermore had 216 copper grenades purchased for their *gibernes* in 1814, 188 being issued in 1814 and just 28 in 1815.

Voltigeurs were armed with dragoon muskets, we note, and to make their clothing, regimental accounts report in 1814 13m 75 chamois broadcloth was used to make collars for *voltigeur habits* and a further 8m 20 in 1815. Regimental records furthermore report that for *voltigeur gibernes* 216 copper hunting horn badges were purchased, 173 being issued in 1814 and 43 in 1815: presumably more of the same of those in use. Concerning *voltigeur aigrettes*, none existed on 8 July 1814, 216 were bought by 1 May 1815 and a further 10 after this date, all being issued, again more of the same.

For the centre companies, 950 fusilier *schakos* were purchased and 6 for *adjutant-sous-officiers* in the First Restoration. In addition, during the 100 Days 1,493 tricolour cockades were purchased for *schakos*, 470 being issued, while 1,067 bosses for chinscales were purchased, just 21 sets being issued. For *schakos*, 328 new *schako* plates were ordered in 1814 and 2,070 in 1815, of which just 73 were issued, so it seems the regiment never changed totally to the new designation. In 1815 579 sets of *schako* chinscales were purchased, none being issued. A standout reference in the archives is the purchase of 2,381 crowned 'N' devices in copper for *gibernes*, of which 550 sets were issued. No crowned 'N' devices existed in 1814, and this was the first purchase of such items.

Regimental accounts note that between 8 July 1814 and January 1815 593m of *livrée du Roi* was purchased, all of it being used to make new drummers' clothing. In the 100 Days the regiment purchased 18m 24 green broadcloth accompanied by 529m of what we assume to be Imperial Livery. Of the green broadcloth, 15m 15 was used – sufficient to make 12 *habits* – along with all 529m of drummers' lace – sufficient to make 35 *habits* – so we can be sure some drummers' had green *habits* with presumably Imperial Livery.

No *sapeurs*' equipment existed on 8 July, and before 1 May 1815 12 axes, 12 axe cases and belts, 12 aprons and 12 pairs of gauntlets were purchased. Headdress was surely a grenadier *schako*.[251]

92^e^ *de Ligne*

Inspected on 4 August 1814, as with all regiments in the army it had shortages of clothing, with, for example, 123 men having no *capote*, 105 no *bonnet de police*, and 91 no *giberne*.

We note that corporals, *sous-officiers*, and grenadiers carried the sabre, as did drummers and *cornets*, the latter having 274m 33 of unused drummers' lace in *dépôt*. We note 2 *voltigeur habits* were in store, presumably with chamois facings, alongside 14 grenadier *habits*, 229 fusilier *habits-vestes*, 70 *habits-longe*, 18 pairs of *pantalons de tricot*, 372 *bonnets de police*, 316 fusilier *schakos* as well as 170 *schakos* of the old model, 1,071 *schako* covers, 396 grenadier *aigrettes*, 444 *voltigeur aigrettes* and 1,110 fusilier *houpettes*.[252] In September 1815, not an inch of green broadcloth or drummers' lace existed in store, or any chamois broadcloth. Of the men under arms that summer, the grenadiers and *voltigeurs* had no *aigrettes* and no epaulettes lodged in the *dépôt* – we assume all those from 1814 were still in use.[253]

93e *de Ligne*

Inspected on 13 August 1814, the regiment mustered 897 rank and file, which were wearing clothing that was mostly in need of total replacement or was brand new. The inspection tells us that the men had been recently clothed in the new regulation, and some old-pattern items were in use that needed to be replaced.[254] The *dépôt* was sparsely furnished with materials, just 1m 29 of beige broadcloth for *capotes*, 0m 04 blue broadcloth, 0m 10 white broadcloth, 7m 48 scarlet broadcloth, 11m 30 chamois broadcloth, 340m

Opposite: This *vivandière* was drawn in 1816. Every battalion had two *vivandières* and two washerwomen. What they wore is the subject of much debate. For the 21e *de Ligne*, that debate is easily answered by regimental documents that detail the dress of these women. Catherine Maygnet died in in May 1811 and her effects were valued and sold off by the regiment. In ready cash she had the substantial sum of over 3,500fr! She possessed a four-wheeled cart valued at 45fr drawn by two horses valued together at 317fr. Inside the cart was a bed with blankets valued at 13fr 75. Her personal possessions included:

> 'A top hat with plume, 4 "shirts", two dresses made from printed Indian cotton, a set of clothes *déshabillé*, two corsets, two jupon (quilted petticoats), a double-breasted redingote made in blue broadcloth valued at 14fr 45, a black taffeta apron, a shawl, five handkerchiefs, a pair of stockings, a pair of cotton stockings and four pieces of spun cotton, a yard and a half of lace, two pairs of ladies' shoes, two embroidered pockets, a leather belt, hip pad (?), a man's blue broadcloth greatcoat, a gold hunter case watch with key on a necklace worth 110francs, two gold pocket watches, a pair of earrings and ring in gold worth 132francs, a serving spoon, four eating spoons, two forks and three coffee spoons in silver, totalling 44fr 38. Her net value was 4,294fr 12!'
>
> '*Deshabillé*' was an informal style of clothes in the eighteenth century. It's what people would wear when not dressed up, or when about to dress. It's somewhere between underwear/bathrobe and formal wear. People would not wear this outdoors, but it was not uncommon to receive friends at home in this. It also frequently appears in paintings. It seems clothing she was wearing or directly associated with her and not packed away in the cart were two dresses, one of which was in printed India cotton, a woman's greatcoat made from heavy broadcloth, a woman's *redingote*, a petticoat and corset, two shawls, one white, one 'colourful', four kerchiefs, two gilets. five pairs of stockings, a hurdy-gurdy mounted with silver, two clarinets and two small flutes. The *gilets*, I would guess, were sleeveless waistcoats with peplums fastened in front with laces or ties, likely quilted, worn under the gown or jacket for warmth. They were sometimes known in English as 'jumps'.

From the list of items we can paint a wonderful picture of her part of the camp, which would have been full of music, wine women and song. We also note a man's shirt and a small *portmanteau* in bad condition containing a copy of her birth certificate, her patent or licence, and an extract of her marriage certificate. The regimental archive reports that these items 'were sold on the 15th of September of the given year for a sum of 38 francs and 75 cents. The two shirts as well as the gilet (?) and the watch were given to the children on the orders of Mr le colonel, signed Guillaume [rest of name illegible]. Signed, members of the council of administration of the 21eme regiment d'infanterie de ligne.'

Her stock in trade had been sold for 600fr. In total, the estate was worth 4,572fr 87: her four children, presumably sons, were passed 4,352fr 87 and her daughter 204fr. The cotton dresses described as '*indienne*' were not necessarily from India: it was simply printed (or 'painted') with floral designs of Indian origin. *Indiennes* were produced in great quantities in France; among the most famous centres of production were Mulhouse, Jouy-en-Josas near Paris, and several cities in Provence – the famous Provençal prints. (The printing of traditional fabrics in Provence is still known as *indiennage*.) While obviously more expensive than plain or striped/checked fabrics, they were still much cheaper than authentic printed chintzes from India. This archive is a unique and wonderful snapshot of what these women were wearing.

70 white serge, 1m 05 white tricot, 1m of linen and 281m 80 of drummers' livery. Brand-new clothing in the *dépôt* included 383 *capotes*, 1 fusilier *habit de modèle*, 1 drummers' *habit de modèle*, 1 fusilier *gilet manches de modèle*, as well as model examples of a grenadier and a *voltigeur aigrette*. The *dépôt* held 1 *schako de grenadier de modèle*, 1 shirt de *modèle*, as well as *modèle* examples of a black stock, pair of linen socks, pair of shoes, grey and black gaiters, *sac à distribution* and *sac de peau*. The men's *capotes*, the inspecting general noted, had no lining.[255]

On 28 September 1815, when the *dépôt* was disbanded, we note it held 0m 60 green broadcloth, 5m 16 chamois broadcloth, 53 drummers' lace, four *sapeurs'* axes with cases, two *sapeurs'* aprons and a pair of pistols.[256] Regimental accounts show that 130fr had been spent purchasing 141 *schakos* with covers, epaulettes and *aigrettes* for grenadiers and *aigrettes* for *voltigeurs*. Furthermore, 8 aunes (1 aune = 116cm) of gold lace for the 2ᵉ and 3ᵉ *Porte-Aigle*, costing 8fr a metre and 18m of drummers' livery costing 90 centimes a metre had been obtained during the 100 Days.[257]

94ᵉ *de Ligne*

Inspected on 21 September 1814, the inspecting officer noted the clothing of the 953 other ranks on parade was worn out: for example, of the *habits*, 139 were in usable condition, 659 needed repairs, 95 needed total replacement and 61 men had no *habit*. Indeed, the inspector tells us:

> The men from the 1ᵉ and 2ᵉ battalion of the 94ᵉ, comprising the totality of the regiment, are dressed in *habits*, *vestes* and *culottes* of the old uniform. The majority of the *habits* have been in use for a minimum of 15 months and have been supplied from the *dépôt* at Bayonne.[258]

Looking in detail at the report, we see that only *sous-officiers* carried sabres, so too drummers and *cornets*. The drummers had green *habits*, some 10m 80 of green broadcloth being in *dépôt* and 377m 40 of drummers' lace. Clothing in the *dépôt* ready to be issued comprised 3 grenadier *habits*, 64 *voltigeur habits*, 175 *habits de fusilier*, 4 *habits de tambour*, and 4 *gilets de fusilier*. Also in stores were 106 grenadier *aigrettes*, and 69 voltigeur *aigrettes*. Classed as *demi-uses*, i.e., usable but not for long, were 30 *capotes*, 30 grenadier *habits*, and 30 grenadier *gilets*, among other items.[259]

Disbanded on 11 August 1815, the *dépôt* held precious little: 479m white serge, 50m linen, 5m 05 gold lace, 46m 90 yellow worsted lace, 21m 60 scarlet worsted lace, 195m drummers' lace, 7m 96 silver lace, 107 *capotes*, 1 pair of epaulettes for *adjutant-sous-officiers*, 45 *bonnets de police*, 184 *houpettes*, 1,189 *gibernes* with *porte-gibernes*, 463 musket slings, 24 drums, 22 drum carriages, 2 *voltigeur cornets* and 6 *sapeurs'* aprons, axe cases, gauntlets and axes, 25 infantry muskets, 83 dragoon muskets for *voltigeurs*, 108 bayonets and 575 bayonet scabbards.[260]

95[e] *de Ligne*

Inspected on 26 August 1814, the regiment mustered 103 officers and 834 other ranks. From the report we see grenadiers and *sous-officiers* carried sabres, and clothing was in an overall shabby condition. For example, 80 men had no *habit*, 133 *habits* needed immediate replacement, and 269 repairing, leaving just 352 in usable condition. The *voltigeur* companies had drummers. The men were also issued 1,405 shirts, 490 pairs of *pantalons de route*, 621 black stocks, 45 white stocks, 3 pairs of linen ankle socks, 1,030 pairs of shoes, 383 pairs of black gaiters, 280 pairs of grey gaiters, 48 *sacs à distribution* and 806 *sacs de peau*. The inspector noted 350 *porte-gibernes* and 74 muskets slings, and 4 drum carriages to be written off as they were made from blackened cow hide.[261] No *aigrettes* were in use it seems, and no epaulettes for grenadiers. We assume the men were wearing Bardin regulation.

A detailed inspection report dated 19 June 1815 gives us a lot of information about the regiment during the 100 Days. The report tells us that the 1e and 2e battalions mustered 994 *sous-officiers* and men. Two detachments of men, the first of 92 the other of 69, were sent to the *dépôt* of the Imperial Guard.

In terms of headdress, the grenadiers and *voltigeurs* had received in 1815 new *schako* and *aigrettes*. Does this mean new *voltigeur* 'pattern' *schakos* with lace? Or simply that the *voltigeurs* had new fusilier *schakos* issued? We cannot say for a fact which hypothesis is correct. Furthermore, the Administrative Council of the regiment had ensured that the men of the war battalions had been issued two pairs of shoes, and a further 350 pairs remained in the *dépôt*, the magazine as a whole holding 800 pairs. The *dépôt* of the regiment reported that they were in the process of equipping the 433 men in the *dépôt*. In terms of armament, the *dépôt* had 184 infantry muskets, 44 dragoon muskets for *voltigeurs* and 122 sabres.[262]

Regimental records reveal that during the 100 Days, 2 *sapeur* bearskins were purchased costing 104fr, two sabres for *sapeurs* costing 22fr 62, 16 grenadier *aigrettes* costing 56fr, 6 *voltigeur aigrettes* costing 15fr, 16 pairs of grenadier epaulettes costing 54fr 40, and 2,657 *schako* plates with eagle motif costing 1,856fr, of which 801 remained in *dépôt* and 664 had been lost in the Waterloo campaign; 15m 12 of green broadcloth was purchased.[263] The *dépôt* was inspected on 1 July 1815, when it held among other items 5m 19 chamois broadcloth,15m 12 green broadcloth, and 180m drummers' lace along with 56 grenadier *schakos* and 81 for fusiliers, 83 grenadier *aigrettes*, 59 *voltigeur aigrettes*, and 65 pairs of grenadier epaulettes.[264]

96e *de Ligne*

Inspected on 7 August 1814, the regiment had 94 officers and 1,210 other ranks, but the review tells us almost nothing. It reports that the *voltigeur* companies had drummers, yet we cannot say how they were dressed or the drummers in the other companies, or indeed the grenadiers or *voltigeurs*! The inspector did remark that all the *schakos* were very old, and that the clothing contained many items that were no longer regulation. The inspector ordered the regimental staff to read the regulations for clothing, and urged that all non-regulation items were to be replaced, adding that about three quarters of the regiment needed a new uniform. Black cross belts were in use.[265]

At the time of disbandment the *dépôt* held among other items 1m 47 chamois broadcloth, 3m 42 green broadcloth, 534 *gibernes*, 195 *porte-gibernes* in buff and 71 cut from blackened cow hide, 139 buff musket slings and 171 blackened cow hide examples, 1 sergeant's *giberne*, 1 *voltigeur cornet*, 92 *habits*, 263 *vestes*, 52 pairs of *pantalons de tricot*, 394 pairs of *caleçons*, 39 *capotes*, 109 grenadier *schakos*, 56 fusilier and *voltigeur schakos*, 1,001 fusilier *houpettes*, 94 pairs of grenadier epaulettes, 55 *voltigeur aigrettes*, 773 *schako* covers and 92 white cockades. Also in existence were three green drummers' *habits* with Imperial Livery. No grenadier *aigrettes* are listed and we assume they are counted with the grenadier-pattern *schakos*.[266]

100[e] *de Ligne*

Reviewed in February 1813, the men were all wearing, according to the inspector, 'the clothing described by the previous regulation'.[267] Therefore, we assume that the regiment was dressed either in part or entirely in pre-Bardin clothing in spring 1813.

Reviewed on 24 September 1814 by Joseph Duaxon, the regiment had 51 officers, 126 men in the grenadier company, viz 3 sergeant majors, 15 sergeants, 3 *fourriers*, 26 corporals, 7 drummers, 126 grenadiers, and 1,196 men in the centre companies. Overall, the clothing was in fairly good condition where it existed. For example, of the 1,196 *habits*, 785 were in serviceable condition, 150 needed repairs, and 261 needed to be replaced. Of those in use, 255 were of the old model. Equipment wise, *baudriers* were issued to grenadiers and *sous-officiers*, but still left a shortfall of 162 items. Clothing in the *dépôt* included 98 fusilier *habits-vestes*, 3 fusilier *gilets manches* and 45 old-pattern *habits-longe*. Hardly any cloth existed in the *dépôt*, just 0m 13 blue broadcloth, 0m 18 white broadcloth, 4m 07 scarlet broadcloth, and 236m 48 serge. The inspector noted money was needed urgently to buy cloth and items of equipment.[268]

At the time of disbandment in 1815, the *dépôt* held very little in terms of materials, clothing and equipment, including 18m 24 of green broadcloth, 30 pairs of grenadier epaulettes and 30 *aigrettes*, no doubt to supplement those already in use. A single model of *schako* was in use, presumably the fusilier model. We cannot say for a fact how *voltigeurs* were marked out. We assume they had chamois facings and the cloth was entirely used to make new items. We also note the following items of equipment on 16 September 1815:[269]

4 *sapeurs*' axes
4 axe cases and belts for *sapeurs*
5 *sapeurs*' sabres
5 *baudriers* for *sapeurs*

This document is interesting, as it is one of only two primary sources for the existence of *sapeurs'* sabres in the line in 1815. The sergeant clearly carried a sabre and not the axe.

101e *de Ligne*

In summer 1814 the regiment was reduced to 514 other ranks, who were mostly lacking their uniforms. For example, 239 men had no *pantalons de tricot*, 223 men had a *schako* fit only for the rubbish heap, 284 *habits* needed repairs and 36 immediate replacement, and 40 men had no *habit*: just 148 were in good condition. The men also issued 962 shirts, 514 pairs of *pantalons de route*, which every man was clearly wearing to make up for the lack of *pantalons de tricot*, 439 black stocks, 538 pairs of socks, 639 pairs of shoes, 316 pairs of black and 226 pairs of grey gaiters: clearly this was a mix and match approach to ensure that every man had a pair of gaiters as insufficient existed to have a pair of each. We also note 402 *havresacs* were issued and 305 canteens recorded as wicker-covered bottles. The inspector noted that the regiment's clothing did not accord to the decree of 19 January 1812, and had not yet enacted the decree of 23 April 1814 in removing Imperial iconography. We have no details about the dress of grenadiers, *voltigeurs*, drummers or *sapeurs*. We assume all the clothing and equipment to be Bardin regulation. The *dépôt* held no cloth or materials nor any clothing or equipment. The *dépôt* had been captured when the magazine at Gênes had been taken by the allies.[270]

No disbandment paperwork for the *dépôt* can be found for 1815, therefore we can say nothing else about the dress of the regiment.

102e *de Ligne*

Inspected on 1 September 1814, the regiment's clothing, despite several months of peace, was either in need of repairs, replacement or was simply missing in most cases: we note for the 980 men, 67 needed a *habit*, 409 a *veste*, 348 a pair of *pantalons de tricot*, and 221 *capotes* among other items needed. Of the men lucky enough to have a *habit*, 216 needed repairs and 290 total replacement; this pattern being the common thread of the regiment's clothing and equipment. The *dépôt* held virtually nothing: 24m 13 white broadcloth, 1,021m white serge, 33m 27 white tricot and 2,470m 37 of linen. Clothing in the *dépôt* was 40 *capotes*, either new or needing repairs, 8 new *gilets manches* and 77 pairs of *culottes en tricot*.[271] Grenadiers, we assume, had epaulettes as these had been bought in 1810 and 1811 according to regimental accounts. The regiment's clothing was described as old model, and the inspector noted that since 23 April, the clothing officer had been working hard to totally reclothe the unit as new by September 1814 according to the regulations. The officers had been observed when off duty wearing civilian clothing both in barracks and promenading in town. The inspector ordered that this was to be stopped forthwith.[272]

The regiment was finally wound up in January 1816. The *dépôt* still held a substantial amount of cloth, which included 2m 50 of chamois broadcloth. Clothing and equipment in the *dépôt* included 1 drum major's mace, 808 pairs of blue *pantalons de tricot*, 11 new pairs of white *pantalons de tricot*, 3 pairs of grenadiers' epaulettes, 54 grenadiers' *aigrettes*, 72 *voltigeur aigrettes*, 400 pairs of black half gaiters, 400 pairs of long grey *ancien modèle*, 200 *cols noir ancien modèle*, i.e., pre-Bardin black stocks, 381 brand-new blackened cow hide *giberne* belts, 187 *giberne* belts in buff, 272 blackened cow hide musket slings and 287 in buff leather, 104 *giberne* covers, 159 copper hunting horns for *gibernes*, 44 *fleur-de-lys* badges for *gibernes*, 43 sword knots, 31 pairs of chinscales and a further 89 pairs of grenadier epaulettes.[273]

No lace existed for drummers in 1814 or 1815 – was any purchased and used? Alas, without more information we cannot say. A letter of 28 March 1816 gives us some wonderful information about a unique regimental tradition:

> On April 1, 1691, the grenadiers of the Dauphin regiment, at the headquarters of Mons, armed with forks, carried away assault a horn work defended by Austrians, whom they took prisoners. Louis XIV, wishing to perpetuate such a glorious action, allowed the sergeants of grenadiers of the Dauphin regiment to carry these forks instead of muskets.
>
> The 102nd regiment being from the Dauphin regiment, its grenadiers continued to carry this weapon until today. We must help preserve from oblivion this feat of arms whose tradition has been preserved in the regiment for more than a century, despite the troubles of the Revolution.
>
> This armament was worn by non-commissioned officers of the 102nd infantry regiment during the Revolution and the Empire.[274]

Clearly the eagle guard still had these forks in 1815!

103e *de Ligne*

Reviewed on 28 August 1814, the regiment had 132 officers and 1,312 other ranks with 6 *enfants de troupe*. The clothing, as with all regiments at the end of the 1814 campaign, was either new or worn out. For example, 768 *habits* were in good condition, 162 needed repairs, 179 needed replacing and 93 men had no *habit*. Cloth in the *dépôt* included, 0m 10 green broadcloth and 0m 66 chamois broadcloth: no doubt all that was left from making drummer and *voltigeur* clothing. Brand-new clothing in the *dépôt* comprised 55 *capotes*, 168 fusilier *habits*, 120 pairs of *pantalons de tricot*, 11 grenadier *aigrettes*, 38 *voltigeur aigrettes*, 1,394 fusilier *houpettes* and 12 pairs of grenadier epaulettes. Also sat in stores, brand new and waiting to be issued, were 173 pairs of *pantalons de route*, 735 pairs of shoes, and remarkably 1,392 pairs of white gaiters.[275]

Disbanded on 7 August 1815, the *dépôt* for the war battalions held, among other items, 12m 21 chamois broadcloth to make *voltigeur* clothing. Grenadiers clearly had *aigrettes* as 92 were in *dépôt* accompanied by 85 *voltigeur aigrettes* and 541 fusilier *houpettes*. *Dépôt* also had 137 pairs of linen *pantalons*, 1 pair of black tricot gaiters, 23 pairs of grey gaiters and 1,380 pairs of white gaiters, of which just 12 pairs had been issued.[276]

104ᵉ *de Ligne*

The 104ᵉ was formed at Mayence (Mainz) on 1 January 1814 from the 3ᵉ battalion of the 52ᵉ *de Ligne*, 3ᵉ battalion 67ᵉ *de Ligne* and the 2ᵉ and 3ᵉ battalions of the 101ᵉ *de Ligne*. The regiment was organised by 1 March, but a matter of months later, on 21 August, was reorganised as the 85ᵉ *de Ligne*. It was disbanded in September 1815.[277] Reviewed on 22 August 1814, the regiment had been brought up to strength with the incorporation of the 1ᵉ and 2ᵉ battalion of the 137ᵉ *de Ligne* and elements from the 5ᵉ *regiment de Tirailleurs de la Garde Imperiale*. The clothing was considered to be 'good' by the inspector, General Comte Guillaminot, who observed it was well sewn, but was in need of repairs, especially the *capotes*. He noted that the uniform did not accord exactly with the decree of January 1812, and that it had many mistakes caused by the negligence of the officers overseeing production of uniforms.[278] Not an inch of cloth or lace was in stores, nor any items of clothing and equipment. The inspector ordered the *cantinière* cart, horses and harness sold and the proceeds put into the regimental funds.[279] We can say nothing about the appearance of *sapeurs*, drummers, *voltigeurs* or grenadiers.

Disbanded in 1815, the regimental *dépôt* held 2m 80 white broadcloth, 3m 63 scarlet broadcloth, 1m 40 chamois broadcloth, 122m 95 white tricot and 180m of drummers' lace. Clearly the *voltigeurs* had chamois collars, and also yellow *aigrettes* as 95 were held in *dépôt*, along with 96 grenadier *aigrettes* and 106 pairs of grenadier epaulettes.[280]

105ᵉ *de Ligne*

Inspected on 13 August 1814, as the 86ᵉ *de Ligne,* the regiment had its drummers in green *habits*, with Imperial Livery. The *dépôt* held 9m 05 of green broadcloth and 991m of drummers' livery: arguably a mix of Royalist and Imperial Livery. The *dépôt* held large quantities of brand-new clothing and equipment, notably 97 *capotes*, 180 fusilier *habits*, 3 grenadier *gilets manches*, 31 fusilier *gilets manches*, and we also note 7 *sapeurs*' axes with cases, 9 *sapeurs*' aprons, and 210 fusilier *houpettes*.[281] The inspector ordered 'the old innovations' in order of dress to be removed, and that the regulations 'were to be enforced with vigour'. Those men without clothing were to be equipped as speedily as possible.[282] We have no idea what these innovations were. The regiment was in the process of replacing non-Bardin kit with Bardin kit that summer.

No disbandment records can be found at the time or writing. We can say nothing about grenadiers or *voltigeurs*. We assume the regiment was dressed in Bardin kit at Waterloo, but we cannot prove it. Likewise, they may have carried 105 on the buttons and *schako* plates, or indeed a mix of 85 and 105.

106ᵉ *de Ligne*

The regiment was inspected on 21 July 1814; the 803 men under arms were wearing clothing that was 'past its best'; for example, of 803 habits in use, 388 needed repairs and 106 total replacement. Only 793 pairs of shoes were in use and clearly some men were on parade wearing *sabots*. There were just 28 canteens, described as wicker-covered glass bottles. The drummers certainly had Imperial Livery as 307m of '*Galons de tambours ancien modèle*' was in *dépôt*. Despite none being in stores, chamois had existed as we find 30 new *voltigeur habits* in *dépôt*. The *dépôt* held a considerable stock of new clothing ready to use in addition to those *voltigeur habits*: 658 *capotes*, 42 grenadier *habits*, 375 fusilier *habits*, 806 fusilier *gilets manches*, 742 pairs of *pantalons de tricot*, 728 *bonnets de police*, 342 pairs of *caleçons*, 306 fusilier *schakos*, 359 *schako* covers, 1,068 *gibernes* and 1,067 *porte-gibernes*, 81 musket slings and 571 sabre belts. For *sapeurs* the *dépôt* held 10 axes with cases, 10 aprons, and 10 pairs of gauntlets all waiting to be issued. Also, in *dépôt* were 191 grenadier *aigrettes*, 200 *voltigeur aigrettes* and 117 pairs of grenadier fringed epaulettes. The inspector noted that the colonel had worked hard in clothing the regiment, the *dépôt* taking deliveries on 23 July and 6 August of clothing, and was in the process of being totally re-dressed.[283] The inspector commented that the regulations of 19 January 1812 and the *circulaire* of 23 April 1814 concerning the colour, cut and dimensions of uniforms had been ignored.[284] Presumably drummers wore blue henceforth and Royalist Livery?

Disbanded on 16 November 1815, the 266 men were wearing 205 *habits*, 223 *vestes*, 232 pairs of *pantalons de tricot*, 52 pairs of *caleçons*, 266 *capotes* – every man had one – 207 *schakos*, 3 *bonnets de police*, 15 red *aigrettes*, 29 yellow *aigrettes*, 146 *sacs de peau*, and 20 *sacs à distribution*.[285] Alas, nothing is said about the appearance of drummers.

107e *de Ligne*

The regiment was formed on 1 January 1814 from the 3e battalion of the 6e *de Ligne*, the 4e battalion of the 10e *de Ligne*, 6e battalion 20e *de Ligne* and the 4e battalion of the 102e *de Ligne*. The regiment existed for a matter of months before it was disbanded on 21 July 1814 and became part of the 88e *de Ligne*, along with the former 149e *de Ligne*.[286] The 224 men of the 107e *de Ligne* in summer 1814 were wearing Bardin-regulation uniforms, but they were old and needed repairs. The *dépôt* was devoid of stocks of clothing, equipment and materials as it had not yet been formally established to produce clothing and equipment, and indeed, the inspector noted that the regiment was still in the process of formation at the time of disbandment.[287] We can say nothing about grenadiers, drummers or *voltigeurs*.

The war battalions were disbanded 12 September 1815 and the *dépôt*, which was devoid of materials, clothing and equipment, on 11 August 1815. The remaining men under arms carried away with them 144 *habits*, 27 *vestes*, 10 pairs of *pantalons de tricot*, 3 pairs of *caleçons*, 65 *capotes*, 142 *schakos*, 34 *bonnets de police*, 32 *gibernes* and belts, 28 *baudriers* with 28 sabres, and 32 muskets – just 14 had a musket sling.[288] We can say nothing for a fact about how the regiment was dressed: we presume Bardin regulation and drummers in Royalist Livery.

108[e] *de Ligne*

At the close of the 1814 campaign, as would be expected, the regiment's clothing was in very bad condition indeed, with more than three quarters needing to be repaired or totally replaced. The inspector noted the regiment had been clothed in new-regulation clothing during the third quarter of 1812, but had received nothing since! The regiment's *dépôt* had virtually no items to make good the items needed, holding just 18 *capotes* in need of repair, 9 new *gilets manches* for fusiliers, 278 pairs of *pantalons de tricot* and 7 pairs of *caleçons*. The *dépôt* did hold 112 new grenadier *aigrettes* and 88 pairs of grenadier epaulettes, 97 *aigrettes* for *voltigeurs* and 1,975 *houpette*s for fusiliers. To make new clothing and effect repairs to damaged clothing, the regiment had no stocks whatsoever of broadcloth, but it held 1,192m 89 of white serge and 139m 40 of drummers' livery.[289] The inspector noted that the regiment had been blockaded in Magdeburg and the men were wearing 'heavy winter *pantalon*s', which had to be replaced.[290] We assume these to be brown, or blue broadcloth or tricot. At disbandment in 1815, nothing was in stores that gives any idea about the appearance of the regiment.[291]

109[e] *de Ligne*

No regiment of this designation existed in the First Empire.

110[e] *de Ligne*

No regiment of this designation existed in the First Empire.

111e *de Ligne*

The regiment was created on 20 June 1808 from the *1er demi-brigade Piedmontese*. It became the 90e *de Ligne* on 1 August 1814.[292]

Regimental records reveal that in 1811 280fr was spent buying two spontoons from Habert et Popard of Paris. *Dépôt* held in August 1814 three pistols with cases. Here we have uncompromising evidence of the 2e and 3e *porte-aigle* armed with pistols and spontoons. Yet no helmets are listed, so we assume these men wore *schakos*.[293] By August 1814 the spontoons were AWOL as not listed in the regiment's care. We know *voltigeurs* had chamois facings as between 1 January 1812 and 1 January 1814 18m 54 of chamois broadcloth was purchased for 177fr 98. It had been almost entirely used by August 1814, as we shall see. In 1812 7,350fr was spent on new *schakos*, and 4,722fr on epaulettes, pompoms and *schakos*. At some stage in 1813, 80fr was expended buying two pack horses for the canteen of 1[e] battalion, while a single horse was obtained for 3[e] battalion costing 40fr

Partial regimental accounts report 4,722fr 50 was spent on *schakos*, *houpettes* and epaulettes for grenadiers on 5 October 1813. At the same time, the regiment purchased

300 sets of red *schako* cords! These are totally unexpected and totally non-regulation, and were accompanied by 25 sky blue pompoms and 25 white for the staff. On the same day, the regiment also ordered:[294]

63m lace for trumpeters – surely *voltigeur cornets*?
571m lace for drummers
12m gold lace for drum major

Inspected on 1 August 1814, the regiment mustered 59 officers, 231 other ranks and 7 *enfants de troupe*. As with all regiments in summer 1814, the clothing was either new or life expired. For example, 71 pairs of *pantalons de tricot* were in good condition, 130 needed total replacement and 26 men had none; 102 *gilets manches* were in good condition, 23 needed repairs, 6 total replacement and 96 men had no none. All ranks had *houpettes* and fusilier *schakos*.

Cloth and materials in the *dépôt* included 331m 63 blue broadcloth, 1,056m 86 white broadcloth, 58m 98 scarlet broadcloth, 3m 25 chamois broadcloth, 1,061m 79 white serge, 447m 33 white tricot, 473m 15 linen for lining, 29m gold lace, 113m 15 red worsted lace and 129m yellow worsted lace. Brand-new clothing and equipment in the *dépôt* included 198 *habits*, 132 *gilets manches*, 198 pairs of *pantalons de tricot*, 227 *bonnets de police*, 198 pairs of *caleçons*, 88 sets of braces, 2 *gibernes* with belts, 56 musket slings, and 331 fusilier *houpettes*. Worn-out clothing taken out of service awaiting disposal included 443 *capotes*, 3 grenadier *habits* – no doubt marked out as such by the scarlet epaulettes and cut-out grenades on the tails, 10 *voltigeur habits*, 43 fusilier *habits*, 5 drummers' *habits* noted as green with Imperial Livery, 12 *gilets manches*, and 4 pairs of *pantalons de tricot*. Clothing needing repairs included 572 *capotes*, 1 *voltigeur habit*, 66 fusilier *habits*, and 98 *gilets manches* among other items.[295]

Importantly for us, the inspector added that the regiment had not acted upon the Decree of 19 January 1812, nor the *circulaire* of 23 April 1814 to change the colour, lace, cut and dimensions of the regiment's clothing for the uniform of the *sous-officiers* and men.[296]

The regiment's archive presents a very clear picture of materials purchased and clothing made from August 1814 to September 1815. We note that the regiment used the cheaper rouge-garance facing cloth in lieu of scarlet, which cost 3fr 47 instead of 15fr 82 a metre. With the stinging words of the inspector no doubt ringing in the colonel's ears, he embarked on a programme of re-dressing his regiment. Clothing made following the inspection was as follows:[297]

	Habits-Vestes		Vestes		Pantalons		Underwear		Capotes		Bonnet de Police		Schako	
	Made	Issued	Made	Issued	Made	Issued	Made	Issued	Made	Issued	Made	Issued	Made	Issued
In Magazine 1 August 1814	198		232		198		198		0		227			
3rd and 4th Quarter 1814	162	334	160	371	146	337	14	212	0			227	41	41
1st and 2nd Quarter 1815	1,053	1,059	1,356	1,327	767	774	920	897	1,387	1,383	1463	1460	1520	1519
Total	1,413	1,393	1,748	1,698	1,111	1,111	1,132	1,109	1,387	1,383	1690	1687	1561	1560
In *Dépôt* 16 September 1815	20		50		0		23	4				3	1	

The *habits-vestes* in *dépôt* on 1 August were *habits-longe*. Seemingly these were issued out of necessity until sufficient numbers of *habits-vestes* came online to cloth the regiment entirely. After 8 January 1815 the regiment bought 2,421m 92 blue broadcloth, 237m 37 white broadcloth, 134m 74 red broadcloth, 2,913m 60 beige broadcloth, 12m 55 chamois broadcloth, 18m 84 green broadcloth, 142m 21 serge, 1,896m 48 white tricot, 33m 95 gold lace, 70m 80 yellow worsted lace, and 9m 45 red worsted lace.

For the drummers, 285m of Royalist Livery was obtained, and some used in 1815 making blue drummers' *habits*. There was sufficient for 18 *habits*. During the 100 Days 18m 84 of green broadcloth was purchased and used to make 18 *habits*, along with 465m of drummers' lace. Eighteen habits needed 285m of lace, ergo, the 180m left in *dépôt* in September 1815 was Imperial Livery. Clearly just the 12 drummers and 2 *cornets* of 1e battalion had drummers in Imperial Livery, plus the drum major, two drum masters and, we assume, band mast. Other battalions must have dressed their drummers and *cornets* as rank and file.

Some 3m 25 of chamois broadcloth was used in store in 1814, 3m 21 being used to make new *voltigeur habits* after August 1814, and a further 12m 55 purchased in 1815, of which 3m 32 was used, leaving 6m 53 in store. The paperwork also shows the regiment in January or August 1814 had no *aigrettes* or epaulettes for grenadiers, and no *aigrettes* for *voltigeurs*. These were all purchased in 1815 – likely arriving during the 100 Days – along with 10 pairs of *adjutant-sous-officier* epaulettes, 312 pairs of grenadier epaulettes, of which 254 pairs were issued, 337 grenadier *aigrettes* with 294 issued, and 322 *voltigeur aigrettes* with 315 issued.

Some 1,599 new *schako* plates were purchased after 8 January 1815 and all were issued, along with 1,136 new bossettes for chinscales, 1,156 dozen large buttons and 5,261 dozen small uniform buttons – arguably it was not until spring 1815 that the regiment adopted new Royalist buttons and emblems, thus we can argue that during the 100 Days the regiment was very much adorned in Royalist clothing, and not Imperial. Of course, several purchases of buttons, lace etc could have been made in 1815 of Royalist and Imperial pattern, and simply archived as 8 January 1815 to 26 September 1815, which is a distinct possibility, but the balance of evidence suggests purchases made before the 100 Days.[298]

The *dépôt* on 27 March 1816 held:

14 new *habits* valued at 364fr
6 *habits* cut out and needing to be sewn up, valued at 141fr 30
4 *capotes* cut out and needing to be sewn up, valued at 97fr 20
11 new *vestes* valued at 122fr 45
35 cut out *vestes* needing to be sewn up, valued at 349fr 30
4 *vestes* to be written off
23 pairs of *caleçons* valued at 56fr 12
3 *bonnets de police* valued at 23fr 33
1 *schako* valued at 8fr 60

2 *schako* covers to be written off
58 pairs of grenadier epaulettes valued at 3fr 40 each
18 new grenadier *aigrettes* valued at 63fr
25 grenadier *aigrettes* in good condition valued at 75fr
7 grenadier *aigrettes* valued at 21fr
100 pairs of chinscales valued at 70fr
500 new fusilier *houpettes* valued at 300fr
62 good condition fusilier *houpettes* valued at 24fr 80
541 sets of braces valued at 324fr 60

Cloth in *dépôt* included 660m 75 blue broadcloth, 152m 71 white broadcloth, 8m 71 red broadcloth, 376m 80 beige broadcloth, 9m 27 chamois broadcloth, 22m white serge, 876m 75 white tricot, 185m worsted lace and 180m of drummers' lace. We cannot tell the pattern of the drummers' lace as it could be unused Royalist Livery from making drummers' kit in the first quarter of 1815. Clearly, as the Empire fell, workmen were busy making new clothing.

Sapeurs were armed with light cavalry *mousquetons*. *Dépôt* held 33 of these. For *sapeurs* the regiment purchased in 1815 14 axes, 2 aprons, and 21 axe cases with belts. Of these, 13 axes with cases and belts, 13 aprons, and 13 pairs of gauntlets were issued during the 100 Days: the inference here is 12 *sapeurs* led by a corporal.[299]

112e *de Ligne*

Created on 9 September 1803, the regiment was disbanded on 12 May 1814, with the 1e and 4e battalions passed to the 7e *de Ligne*. The *dépôt* held no stocks of clothing or materials. The inspector ordered that the regiment had not acted upon the decree of 19 or 7 February 1812 nor the *circulaire* of 23 April, and the drummers were to have livery of the Royal Household.[300] Therefore, drummers were in green with Imperial Livery, yet the men had not a single piece of Bardin clothing in use.

113e *de Ligne*

Created on 23 May 1808 as the *régiment d'infanterie Toscan*. Officially the 113e *de Ligne* from 1 January 1810. The regiment was disbanded on 7 February 1814. The *dépôt* or 5e battalion passed to the 14e *de Ligne* in August 1814 held a huge stockpile of clothing, which included 287 brand-new *capotes*, 13 grenadier *habits* accompanied by 13 grenadier *gilets manches*, 16 *voltigeur habits* accompanied by the same number of *gilets manches*, 318 fusilier *habits* and *gilet manches*, plus 16 needing repairs, 7 drummers' *habits* – presumably green with the Imperial Livery – 1,401 pairs of *pantalons de tricot*, 431 *bonnets de police*, 1,401 pairs of *caleçons*, 1,201 sets of braces, and 847 fusilier *schakos* with 461 covers. Clothing needing repairs included 12 *capotes*, 16 fusilier *habits*, 20 fusilier *gilets manches*, 1 pair of *pantalons de tricot*, 17 *bonnets de police*, 20 fusilier *schakos*, 179 *gibernes* and belts,

13 drums and drum carriages, 4 drummers' aprons and 2 *voltigeur* horns. Equipment included 450 new *gibernes*, 270 musket slings, 17 *baudriers*, 7 drums and carriages that were brand new, 389 fusilier *houpettes*, 7 drummers' aprons, and 13 pairs of grenadier epaulettes. No *sapeurs'* equipment is listed yet we find in store 400 pairs of *pantalons de route*, 200 black stocks, 200 pairs of linen socks, 400 pairs of shoes, 200 pairs of black gaiters and 200 pairs of grey gaiters.[301]

114ᵉ *de Ligne*

Created on 7 July 1808 by merging the 1ᵉ and 2ᵉ *régiments provisoires des armées d'Espagne*, the regiment was mobilised at Miranda de Ebro in Spain on 30 August 1808. It was disbanded in summer 1814.

The 1ᵉ battalion's clothing was in remarkably good condition: the inspector noted that it had been re-dressed from the contents of the *dépôt* to the new regulation. Battalion stores held nothing beyond 600m of grey linen bought in Spain to make gaiters.[302] When inspected in summer 1814 the grenadier company of 2ᵉ battalion possessed, remarkably, 60 bearskins and had 2 *sapeurs*, as 2 axes, 2 axe cases and belts and 2 aprons were in use.[303] The 3ᵉ battalion passed to the 41ᵉ *de Ligne* 131m 20 blue broadcloth, 102m 10 white broadcloth and 525m 85 white serge.[304] Both battalions' clothing was pre-Bardin. The *dépôt* passed to the 56ᵉ *de Ligne*, among other items, 106m 81 red broadcloth, 17m 64 green broadcloth, 380m 55 drummers' livery and passed to the 5ᵉ *de Ligne* from the 1e battalion were 4 *schakos*, 87 *aigrettes* and 6 *gibernes*.[305]

115ᵉ *de Ligne*

Formed in 1808 from an amalgam of the 3ᵉ and 4ᵉ *régiments provisoires des armées d'Espagne*, with the decree of 7 July 1808. It was a collection of conscripts with very few veteran *sous-officiers* and officers. The *dépôt* was established on 16 August 1808 at camp d'Armiñon in Spain, and the regiment was disbanded in 1814.

The regimental *dépôt* held 627m 60 of drummers' lace, which was sufficient to make 41 *habits*! Clearly none had ever been used. Brand-new clothing in the *dépôt* included 3 *voltigeur cornets*, 30 pairs of grenadier epaulettes and 94m 34 of yellow worsted laced. Also tucked away in *dépôt* were 13 fusilier *habits*, as well as 203 linen *giberne* covers and 39 *schako* covers – all items being marked as non-regulation.[306] Not a single item of Bardin clothing was in use.

116ᵉ *de Ligne*

The regiment was formed on 7 July 1808 from the 5ᵉ and 6ᵉ *régiments provisoires des armées d'Espagne*. The formation process of the regiment is detailed very well in its paper archive.

The 1e battalion prior to incorporation into the 84e *de Ligne* was inspected on 1 August 1814. The unit was in rags: for example, of the 348 men on parade, 182 had *habits* in good condition, 166 men had *habits* in dire need of immediate replacement, 99 men had no *gilet manches* at all, ditto 16 men had no *pantalons de tricot*, 99 no *caleçons*, 181 no *capote*, 71 had no *schako* and 161 no *bonnet de police*, while 90 fusiliers had no *houpette*! The grenadiers had 62 pairs of epaulettes in use, but lacked *aigrettes*, and the *voltigeurs* had no *aigrettes*. The inspector noted that men were wearing grey linen pantalons, which is all the legwear they possessed. He had taken out of service heavy brown cloth *pantalons* as they were unsuitable for summer use. These had been made in Spain from captured cloth. Half the men were wearing *habits-longe* with no *vestes*, the pantalons being cut high enough to conceal the shirt, the inspector noted, and not one man had any Bardin-issue kit.[307]

Inspected on 7 August 1814, the stand-out item in the returns is the fact that the 2e battalion had its grenadiers wearing 39 bearskins and yet not a single pair of *pantalons de tricot*. Most men were wearing heavy brown cloth *pantalons*, which had been made in Spain being cut high enough to conceal the shirt. The stores held 4 brand-new green Imperial Livery drummers' habits.[308]

The men of the 5e battalion were wearing Bardin-regulation clothing that was either new or need repairs. In store were 147 brand-new fusilier *habits-vestes*, 249 *gilets*, 601 pairs of *pantalons de tricot*, 2 grenadier *aigrettes*, 7 *voltigeur aigrettes*, and 7 worn-out pairs of grenadier epaulettes among other items. Camping equipment in the *dépôt* included 4 marmites (water boiling cans) 12 hatchets, 3 *grand bidons* (large water cans) and with the war battalions 80 hatchets and 228 billhooks. Materials in *dépôt* included 70m white tricot, 691m 30 or Imperial Livery and 1m 60 gold lace. The battalion had in store, remarked the inspector '13 *habits a la chasseur*, 13 *vestes* of the same, 13 *pantalons* the same, 55 *gilets manches* cut the same and 8 *pantalons* the same'. We assume these are the short-tailed *habit-courte* of 1811.

The inspector also noted that the 116e *de Ligne* storeroom was 'filled to the rafters' with non-regulation clothing, recently taken out of use or that had not been issued.

Cloth and materials comprised:

74m 24 of *bleu de ciel* superfine broadcloth valued at 1,002fr 24
49m 92 *bleu de ciel* common broadcloth valued at 898fr 56
30m of yellow broadcloth valued at 347fr 06
54m 05 of red tricot valued at 262fr 14
71m 22mm wide gold lace valued at 497fr
23m 90 11mm wide gold lace valued at 129fr 50

Tricot was used to make *vestes* and *pantalons* – so do we imagine the band or drum major had red *pantalons and vestes*? The yellow broadcloth was, we assume, used for *voltigeurs'* distinctions? Or was it used with the *bleu de ciel* broadcloth to make uniforms for the band and or drummers? Other items in the *dépôt* included 1,000 dozen copper buttons for gaiters, 1,397 pairs of brown broadcloth *pantalons* – no doubt made from locally available materials –, 17 pairs *of bleu de ciel* broadcloth *pantalons*, 281 grenadier plumes, 15 *voltigeur* plumes, 11 sets of embroidered hunting horns for *voltigeur habits*, 371 pairs of black half gaiters, 23 grenadier sword knots, 29 *voltigeur* sword knots, 1 set of grenadier *schako* cords – these were in theory abolished in 1810! – 43 sets of *voltigeur schako* cords, 46 pairs of *voltigeur* epaulettes, and 24 pairs of grenadier epaulettes! Also, in the *dépôt* were 20 copper grenades for grenadier *gibernes*, and a further 40 were in use, likewise 22 copper hunting horns were allocated to *voltigeurs* in use and 20 remained in the *dépôt*. In use were 11 *giberne* covers in white linen and 80 in grey linen, 1,330 pairs of breeches knee buckles, 186 grenadier plumes of the old model, 214 *voltigeur* plumes of the old model, 260 old-model *schako* plates, 83 eagles in copper for the drum carriages, 233 scarlet collars for *habits*, 135 sets of scarlet *contre-epaulettes* for grenadier *gilets manches*, a box of instruments for the band, a bass drum, a tenor drum and a leather *portmanteau* containing music. We also note 2 *chapeaux* with carrying cases, 3 old pairs of ankle boots for the *sapeurs*, 7 bundles of green broadcloth, each weighing 1kg and 6 drum skins. The *dépôt* also held 7 *schakos* for officers, 40 officers' *gorgets*, 1 officer's sword knot, 11 white officers' plumes, 29 officers' sabres with waistbelts, 1,000 button sticks and 250 pairs of linen half gaiters![309]

117ᵉ *de Ligne*

Created with the decree of 7 July 1808 from the 9ᵉ and 10ᵉ *Regiment provisoires d'infanterie* for service in Spain. The *dépôt* was raised on 21 August 1808 at Haro in Spain. Disbanded in 1814, the 1ᵉ, 2ᵉ, 3ᵉ and 6ᵉ battalions passed to the 71ᵉ *de Ligne* and the 5ᵉ and 7ᵉ battalions to the 69ᵉ *de Ligne*.

Reviewed on 8 August 1814, the *dépôt* of the regiment held, among other items, 46 old-pattern *habits* and 1 *habit de tambour de modèle* – presumably green with Imperial Livery – for disposal, 24m chamois broadcloth, and 68m 55 of drummers' lace. Of the men on parade that day from the 5ᵉ and 7ᵉ battalions, 11 grenadiers had a pair of fringed epaulettes, and 7 had an *aigrette*, but the *voltigeurs* had no *aigrettes*.[310] The bulk of the two battalions' clothing was in good condition, but roughly 50 per cent needed repairs or total replacement as it was all pre-Bardin. There was not enough of every item to give each man his regulation allocation of clothing and equipment. We also see that just one man had service chevrons! This is not unexpected as the number of veterans in the army in 1814 with sufficient service for just a single chevron, some seven years, was very low indeed considering the losses of the 1812 and 1813 campaigns.[311]

118ᵉ *de Ligne*

Formed in 1808 for service in Spain, with the decree of 7 July from the 11ᵉ *Régiments Provisoire des Armées d'Espagne* and three battalions of conscripts from the *dépôt général*, it was disbanded 20 May 1814, the men being incorporated into the 10ᵉ, 44ᵉ, 105ᵉ and 108ᵉ *de Ligne*. The 4e battalion, 106 men, was disbanded into the 10e *de Ligne* in summer 1814. The men were wearing *schakos*, *gilets manches*, *pantalons de route*, *caleçons*, black gaiters and standard infantry equipment. The men had been issued 44 new *habits-vestes* prior to the inspection, and 16 brand-new fusilier *habits-vestes* were in stores accompanied by 110 *habit-longues*. The inspector further notes English items were in service but alas fails to identify what these were.[312]

The *dépôt* passed to the 102e *de Ligne* 1,133m 77 beige broadcloth, 591m blue broadcloth, 3m 10 white broadcloth, 44m 96 scarlet broadcloth, 10,335m 08 white serge and 257m of linen. Clothing in the *dépôt* included 12 new fusilier *habits-vestes*, 2 new *gilets manches*, 140 pairs of *pantalons de tricot*, 175 *bonnets de police*, 334 brand-new *gibernes*, accompanied by 260 belts, 203 muskets slings, 175 *baudriers*, 132 fusilier *houpettes* and 40 pairs of grenadier epaulettes – clearly grenadiers had epaulettes and no *aigrettes*. We can say nothing about *voltigeurs* or drummers.[313] Clearly the regiment was in the process of transitioning between pre-Bardin and Bardin kit in 1814.

119e *de Ligne*

Formed in 1808 to serve in Spain from the 13e and 14e *Régiments Provisoires de Infanterie*. The paper archive of the regiment is primarily concerned with officers' pay, officer vacancies in the regiment and officers' promotions and says literally noting about the dress of the regiment.[314] The 1e and 4e battalions were taken into the 74e *de Ligne* on 13 August 1814, the 2e and 3e battalions passed to the 78e *de Ligne* 22 September 1814 and the 5e battalion as well as the *dépôt* passed to the 63e *de Ligne* on 29 October 1814. The regiment's 2e and 3e battalions *dépôt* in September 1814 held stocks of clothing and equipment needing repair, notably 4 *capotes*, 175 fusilier *habits*, 4 drummers' *habits*, 158 pairs of *pantalons de tricot*, 57 *bonnets de police*, 20 *gibernes* with belts, 106 grenadier *aigrettes* and 69 *voltigeur aigrettes*.[315]

The revue inspector commented that the regiment had passed to the 67e *de Ligne* 300 *habits*, 300 *vestes*, 300 pairs of *pantalons de tricot*, and 300 pairs of *caleçons*, all of the old model, as well as cloth of diverse colours, and *schakos* of different dimensions – does this mean grenadier and fusilier models or 1806 and 1810 types? – garnished with plates of different types.[316] Clearly a mix of clothing patterns was in use.

120e *de Ligne*

Formed on 7 July 1808 to serve in Spain from the 17e and 18e *Régiments Provisoires de Infanterie*. The regiment's paper archive is remarkably complete for the pay, promotions and names of officers but says absolutely nothing about the dress of the regiment.[317] Reviewed on 28 August 1814, as with all regiments in 1814 the clothing was a mix of life expired, in desperate needs of repairs, good condition or entirely missing. Some 174 *habits* were in serviceable condition, 17 needed repairs, 57 total replacement and 9 men had no *habit*; 99 men out of the 259 on parade had no *gilet manches*, 234 men had no *bonnet de police*, no man had any *caleçons*, and 24 men lacked *pantalons de tricot*. Further, 28 men had no *giberne* and *porte-giberne,* while 44 had no musket sling. Not an inch of cloth or lace was in *dépôt* and not a single item of clothing.[318] We can say nothing about grenadiers, drummers or *voltigeurs*.

121ᵉ *de Ligne*

The regiment was formed on 1 January 1809 from the 1ᵉ and 2ᵉ *Légion de réserve*. The only inspection return is dated 26 July 1814 and concerns the 1ᵉ battalion. The inspection shows that the battalion had two *sapeurs*, along with two *voltigeur cornets*. Clothing was in moderately good condition; for example, 325 *habits* were in good condition: 5 needed repairs and 29 needed immediate replacement; not every man had a pair of *pantalons de tricot*, just 2 pairs were in good condition, 4 needed repairs and 76 total replacement – and the men were on parade wearing their linen *pantalons*. Of the *capotes*, 122 were in good condition, and 129 needed total replacement. In addition, a total of 29 grenadier *aigrettes* were in use and 21 were fit for disposal. Likewise, 38 *voltigeur aigrettes* were in good condition and 38 were fit for disposal. 286 fusilier *houpettes* were in use.[319] A second report reveals that the *dépôt* of the regiment held 343m 78 of beige broadcloth, 11,010m 48 of white serge, 627m 20 of drummers' livery and 1m 52 of white linen lace.[320] A third report records that the *dépôt* also held, amongst other items, 235 new *habits* of the old model, 42 used old-model *habits*, 198 brand-new *habits-vestes*, 2,335 pairs of *culottes* in good condition, 16 old bearskins for *sapeurs*, 25 pairs of long black gaiters and 81 pairs of long grey gaiters.[321]

122ᵉ *de Ligne*

The regiment was formed in 1809 from the 3ᵉ and 4ᵉ battalions *of the* 3ᵉ *Légion de réserve* and the 4ᵉ *bataillon* from the 4ᵉ and 5ᵉ *Légion de réserve*. The regiment's paperwork says nothing on clothing.[322]

Inspected on 22 August 1814, 255 other ranks of the regiment from 1ᵉ battalion were wearing a motley collection of clothing: for example, just 64 *habits* were in good condition, 14 needed repairs, and a whopping 158 needed replacement, while 24 men had no *habit*. The *pantalons de tricot* were likewise in terrible condition or missing entirely: 94 men were wearing brown broadcloth overalls, 134 men did have white *pantalons de tricot* that needed total replacement, 8 further pairs needed repairs and just 4 pairs were in good condition.[323] The battalion had seen service in Germany, seeing action at Bautzen and Leipzig, and had clearly picked up non-regulation kit during the winter of 1813.

The 2ᵉ battalion was dressed in all pre-Bardin and had been supplied from Bayonne, and the battalion had only arrived in France in January 1814 from Spain. We note 48 grenadier and *voltigeur houpettes* were issued. The battalion had three *sapeurs*, as three aprons, axes, axe cases with belts and three pairs of gauntlets were in use, as well as a single *voltigeur cornet* and five drummers. Most of the men lacked *pantalons de tricot*, and were wearing non-regulation brown cloth *pantalons*. In addition, 120 pairs of grey gaiters were in use and just sixty pairs of black – clearly not every man had a pair of gaiters and not enough existed to give each man his regulation issue.[324]

123e *de Ligne*

The regiment was created in 1810 from the 2e *Régiment d'infanterie Hollandaise* and the 2e *bataillon*, 6e *Régiment d'infanterie Hollandaise*. Archaeological evidence recovered from the mass grave at Vilnius shows that at least some of the men were wearing French uniforms in the Russian campaign. Reviewed in August 1814, the 2e battalion was wearing Bardin-regulation clothing. The 131 men in the battalion had 119 muskets and 40 sabres, 222 shirts, 115 pairs of *pantalons de route*, 122 black stocks, just 20 pairs of socks, 131 pairs of shoes, 112 pairs of black gaiters, 104 pairs of grey gaiters, 15 *sacs à distribution,* 11 grenadier *aigrettes*, 3 pairs of grenadier epaulettes, 12 *voltigeur aigrettes* and 122 *havresacs* – representing those items left over from issuing clothing and kit to the men.[325] The inspector noted that 'many of the *banderoles* are made from blackened cow hide'.[326]

Of all the regiments examined, the 123e *de Ligne* is one of the few to list colpacks. Under the terms of the Bardin regulation, drum majors received colpacks as headdress. We wonder therefore at the presence of two of these items, when in theory just one was needed. Are these for the *tambour-major* and *tambour-maître*, who wore one unofficially, or do they belong with the *sapeurs*' equipment in *dépôt*, of which 2 sets existed? The *dépôt* held in August 1814, 207 shirts, 98 pairs of linen *pantalons*, 100 black stocks, 100 white stocks, 168 pairs of shoes, 98 pairs each of grey and black gaiters, 1 *gilet manches*, 4 *bonnets de police*, 164 *gibernes*, 302 *porte-gibernes*, 54 musket slings, 10 sabre belts, 9 drums, 5 drum carriages, 2 *sapeurs*' aprons, 2 axes with cases, 2 pairs of gauntlets for *sapeurs*, and 10 *voltigeur aigrettes*.[327]

124e *de Ligne*

The regiment was created on 18 August 1810 from the 3e *Régiment d'infanterie Hollandaise* and the 1e bataillon of the 7e *Régiment d'infanterie Hollandaise.* We know very little about the regiment's clothing. We learn a little about the dress of the regiment from a letter from the War Ministry to the Emperor dated 19 February 1812:

> … by a letter dated October 8th from Utrecht, Your Majesty informed me of his intention to entirely dress the 124th Line Infantry Regiment with blue jackets. Based upon the regimental store reports I have been given, only 1,255 *habits* would have reached the end of their lifespan in 1812 and 1,280 would only need replacing in 1813.
>
> Since the Decree of January 19th has bought about great changes regarding regimental uniforms but these will not start to come into effect until 1 January

1813, I have thought that Your Majesty would agree with me to not supply the 124th with the old pattern clothing and to then entirely dress the regiment with the new uniform the following year.

I also thought it prudent not to follow Your Majesty's intentions on the basis that if we were to equip the entire regiment with blue jackets, its treasury would be unable to cover such an expense and that government would best be served by allowing their current uniforms to be used until their next regulated issue is due.[328]

We cannot tell if this was carried out due to the lack of archive sources. Reviewed on 1 April 1813, the 2e battalion was dressed in 1812 regulation clothing and needed 28 *habits*, *vestes*, *capotes* and pairs of *pantalons de tricot*. Likewise, 28 *schakos* were needed, 2 *gibernes* and belts, 94 sabres and belts, 3 musket slings, and 2 drums and carriages.[329] Regimental accounts report an epée and waistbelt for the adjutant costing 12fr was purchased in 1813, and a ball and chain for the condemned costing 19fr 95, while 315fr 75 was spent on epaulettes and *houpettes* for the grenadiers.[330]

When disbanded in summer 1814, the *dépôt* held no cloth or materials whatsoever. The men were wearing clothing that was mostly in good condition. The inspector noted 101 black stocks were in use – clearly of the 165 men on parade more than 60 had an improvised stock, just 1 pair of socks was issued along with 150 pairs of shoes – 15 men were wearing clogs. He also records 157 pairs of black gaiters, 146 pairs of grey gaiters in use: clearly an either-or situation was going on as insufficient pairs of either type existed for each man to have the regulation issue.[331] The inspector further noted that the regiment was wearing *habits a revers*, and that not all clothing, equipment, and *schakos* in use was made in accordance to the decree of 19 January 1812.[332]

125e *de Ligne*

Raised in August 1810 from the 4e *régiment d'infanterie de ligne hollandaise* and the 2e *bataillon du 7e régiment d'infanterie de ligne hollandaise,* the regiment existed for little over 18 months. The 1e, 2e and 3e battalions were given a shake-down inspection on 29 June 1812, when the inspector noted two companies were dressed in blue, and the remainder in white Dutch uniforms.[333] It was disbanded into the 123e *de Ligne* in January 1813 following the Russian campaign.

126e *de Ligne*

Raised with the decree of 18 August 1810 from the 5e *régiment d'infanterie de ligne hollandaise* and 1e *bataillon*, 8e *régiment d'infanterie de ligne hollandaise*, the *dépôt* was raised at Haarlem on 6 October 1810. The regiment existed for little over 18 months. Reviewed on 5 March 1812, all the clothing and equipment in the 1e battalion was well made, and the muskets were all Dutch.[334] The 2e and 3e battalions, when reviewed at Wesel 29 April 1812, were, according to the inspector, dressed in clothing of 'the Dutch model, it is white and well made' as was the equipment and muskets.[335] The inspector noted on 22 June 1812 that the 4e battalion, some 792 other ranks, were dressed in new, well-made clothing, so too the leather work and made from good-quality materials.[336] The war battalions marched to Russia wearing their Dutch 1801 model white uniforms, while the 4e and 5e battalions were equipped from new with French clothing which cost 2,286fr 87 to produce. We know the *voltigeurs* had French-pattern *cornets* as two costing 51fr 50 were obtained in 1812.[337] It was disbanded into the 123e *de Ligne* on 9 March 1813 following the Russian campaign. We note 565 men from the 123e, 124e, 125e and 126e *de Ligne* became part of the *bataillon de marche du Texel.* The major in charge noted that great insubordination existed because the officers were inexperienced or crippled old soldiers. The quality of the soldiers was described as 'good' but 'old the soldiers have slackened their discipline due to their long stay on board the ships'. The clothing was noted as:

> fairly good, even though many *habits* within the companies are worn out and many *gilets* are in a bad state. The equipment is fairly good but many *schakos* are lacking their chin-scales and the weapons are in bad condition for the most part. This situation is not surprising as sending soldiers to serve on board the navy's ships is a good way for the regiments to send their bad lot of men.[338]

We know nothing else.

Officers

A kit list of the effects of an officer that was auctioned off after he had died on return from the Russian campaign dated 3 January 1813 gives us a snapshot of how the officers looked:[339]

1 blue redingote, 5fr
1 white collet,[340] 5fr
1 uniform *frac*, 5fr 50
1 pair white *pantalons*, 11fr
1 pair grey *pantalons*, 2fr
2 pairs of boots, 11fr
1 bearskin, 1fr
2 shirts
1 pair of *pantalons*, and 1 pair of *culottes* in nankeen, 6fr 50
1 pair of woollen stockings, 2fr
1 epée and waistbelt

Clearly, the grenadier company had worn bearskins, which were no doubt Dutch issue of the 1801 types. Presumably the higher price paid for some items was because they were in good condition: we guess the bearskin was in terrible condition to be valued so low!

127e *de Ligne*

The 127e *Régiment d'infanterie de Ligne* was formed with the decree of 3 February 1811 from the *Garde de Hamburg* and *Garde de Lubeck*. The sum total of the regiment's archive concerning clothing is a review dated 16 August 1813, when the inspector noted that the regiment was dressed and equipped and the men had three pairs of shoes.[341] We know very little about the regiment's appearance. The first battalion passed to the 19e *de Ligne* and were wearing Bardin regulation. The unit had a solitary *sapeur*.[342]

The *dépôt* was taken into the 108e *de Ligne*. It held 1,192m 89 of white serge, 139m 40 of drummers' livery, 112 grenadier *aigrettes*, 97 *voltigeur aigrettes*, 88 pairs of grenadier epaulettes, 1,975 fusilier *houpettes*, 315 *schako* covers, 26m of gold lace, 125m 80 yellow worsted lace and 10m of red worsted lace, and not a single item of clothing. Needing repairs were 80 *gibernes* and belts, 4 drums and carriages, 2 *sapeurs*' axes and 2 *sapeurs*' aprons. Also in store were 377 brand-new shirts, 666 black stocks with buckles, 863 pairs of linen socks, 79 pairs of shoes, 672 pairs of black gaiters, 578 pairs of grey gaiters and 366 *havresacs*.[343]

128e *de Ligne*

The 128e *Régiment d'infanterie de Ligne* was created with the decree of 3 February 1811 from the *Garde de Breme* and recruits from the following departments: *Bouches du Wesser*, *Bouches de l'Elbe* and *l'Ems-Superieur*.

Reviewed on 16 July 1814, the *dépôt* of the 1e and 5e battalions was incredibly well stocked with clothing, yet half the regiment was dressed in rags – 652 men had a *habit-veste* in serviceable condition, 410 needed repairs and 652 needed total replacement as they were *habits-longe*! The men were split 50/50 between Bardin and pre-Bardin clothing. In the *dépôt* were 450 *capotes*, 57 grenadier *habits*, 64 *voltigeur habits*, 856 fusilier *habits*, 392 fusilier *gilets manches*, 146 grenadier *aigrettes*, 195 *voltigeur aigrettes*, 800 fusilier *houpettes*, and 160 pairs of grenadier epaulettes. The *dépôt* also held 10 pairs of *culottes* in doe hide from the regimental artillery along with 10 pairs of dragoon boots, as well as 11m 34 of green broadcloth and 476m 90 of drummers' livery, which we assume was Imperial Livery. Also, in *dépôt* were 3 axes with cases and belts, 3 *sapeurs*' aprons, and 3 pairs of *grenadier epaulettes pour sapeur*.[344]

The 2e and 7e battalion of the regiment were merged to the 13e *de Ligne*. Remarkably the grenadiers of the 2e battalion had clung to their bearskins: we assume some grenadiers wore *schakos* as insufficient bearskins existed for every man to have one. The battalion also had a single *sapeur*. The battalions lacked *pantalons de tricot* and the men must have been on parade wearing their linen *pantalons*, of which 392 pairs existed. In addition, 344 men had black gaiters, and only 83 had a pair of grey gaiters. The *sapeur* was armed with a light cavalry *mousqueton* and the *voltigeurs* with dragoon muskets. Only grenadiers, drummers, *cornets*, *sapeurs* and *sous-officiers* had sabres. The *dépôt* of the battalions held no cloth or materials, but it did have 30 fusilier *habits* fit only for disposal, 10 life-expired fusilier *schakos*, 185 brand-new pairs of tricot *culottes* and 233 pairs that were life expired, 16 life-expired bearskins and 2 brand-new *sapeurs*' axe cases.[345]

129ᵉ *de Ligne*

Created on 3 February 1811 from *Régiment d'Oldenbourg*, detachments from the *Garde de Westphaliens (Garde Royale* and Chasseurs), as well as detachments 2ᵉ, 3ᵉ, 4ᵉ, 5ᵉ and 6ᵉ *Régiments d'infanterie de Ligne Westphalien*, and the 1ᵉʳ *bataillon, Infanterie Légère Westphalien*. It ceased to exist following the Russian campaign and the remaining men were passed to the 127ᵉ and 128ᵉ *de Ligne* with the decree of 13 August 1813. The sum total of the regiment's archive concerning clothing is a review dated 16 August 1813, when the inspector noted that of the 181 men taken into the 127ᵉ *de Ligne* were dressed with new clothing, which was well made to the recent regulation, were fully equipped and the men had three pairs of shoes.[346] We can say nothing on the dress of the grenadiers, *voltigeurs* or drummers sadly unless more paperwork comes to light.

130ᵉ *de Ligne*

Created with the decree of 9 March 1811 from the 1ᵉʳ, 3ᵉ and 6ᵉ *bataillons auxiliaires de l'armée du nord* (which had been raised at Versailles on 1 January 1810), and the 2ᵉ *bataillon expéditionnaire de La Rochelle*. It served only in Spain. The regiment's archive is particularly complete for the period 1812–14, and shows the production of the following garments:

Year	Habits			Capotes		Vestes	Culottes	Pantalons	Bonnets de police	
	Habit de Fusilier		Drummers' Habit							
	2fr 45	2fr 90		1fr 50	1fr 90	1fr 20			40 centimes	60 centimes
1812	370	200	3	392	300	470	126	107	294	200
	200			200		200	200			
1813	1,602		45	2,280		2,753		1,779		1,166
1814	384			167		33		145		560
Total	2,378	200	48	3,059	300	3,445	326	2,191	294	1,926

The *habits* costing 2fr 45 are Bardin regulation, likewise the more expensive *capote* and *bonnet de police*. The *dépôt* had received from the War Ministry sealed pattern examples of a drummers' *habit*, so we assume, the garments made in 1813 were copied from this. Two battalions mustered 36 drummers and *cornets*, the drum major and two drum masters takes the tally to 39, leaving 7 men in the band.[347]

We gain something of the effect of campaign rigours on uniform when the regiment was given a shake-down inspection in September 1813. The clothing was in need of repair or replacement. Of 1,945 *habits*, 320 needed to be totally replaced, 299 needed to be replaced within six months, 237 within a year, the remainder between 18 and 24 months. A mix of Bardin and pre-Bardin clothing was in use. Of the 1,946 *vestes*, 417 needed immediate replacement, and a further 227 had to be replaced within six months. The *culottes*, of which 1,946 pairs existed, were basically life expired, and 1,379 pairs needed immediate replacement, with 461 having to be replaced within six months. The men were wearing in essence uniforms that were in tatters. Of the 1,946 *capotes*, 214 needed immediate replacement. The inspecting officer commented that the clothing was in bad condition, and that it was a matter of urgency that the regiment made preparations to obtain replacement items. The regiment had 1,946 *schakos*, some 397 needing immediate replacement, and 244 needed replacing within six months. Just 270 sabres and *baudriers* were issued, along with 270 sabres, while a further 118 *baudriers* and sabres were needed to equip the grenadiers. Of the *gibernes*, 820 were in good condition, 1,106 needed repairs.[348]

Inspected again a year later on 26 September 1814, the inspecting officer noted the remaining 488 men under arms had recently joined since January 1814 and the bulk of the regiment's clothing was either in need of repair, replacement or the men simply lacked most items. Of the 488 men on parade, just 16 had a *habit* in good condition, 19 needed repairs, 441 needed immediate replacement, and 18 men had none. No man had a *veste*, *bonnet de police*, and pair of *pantalons de tricot*, and only 76 men had a *schako* and 6 a *capote*. In addition, they possessed 925 shirts, 354 black stocks, 488 pairs of shoes and no gaiters or other items of clothing or equipment. We are left to wonder as to what exactly the men were wearing on parade! No clothing was in *dépôt*, but it did contain 5 sets of *sapeurs*' equipment, 50 *giberne* ornaments, and 2,185 pairs of *culottes*.[349] One gets a feeling that none of the clothing issues that existed in 1813 were ever resolved. The *dépôt* held the following stocks of material on 14 May 1814:[350]

23m 40 scarlet broadcloth
312m 94 white broadcloth
192m blue broadcloth
264m 50 beige broadcloth
21m 60 green broadcloth
11,759m 39 white tricot
346m 65 white milled serge
241m 71 linen for linings
42 pairs of *culottes de peau*
43 pairs of heavy cavalry boots.

The green cloth is an indicator that the regiment adopted Imperial Livery, the *culotte de peau* and heavy cavalry boots must surely be equipment from the regimental drivers. Of the 45 drummers' *habits* made, they are likely to be green. Nothing is listed in the returns for grenadiers or *voltigeurs*: no *aigrettes*, no epaulettes and no chamois broadcloth.

131[e] *de Ligne*

The regiment was formed on 24 January 1811 from runaway conscripts who had been caught and returned to the army. The regiment was disbanded in summer 1814.

1e battalion's clothing was described as very good by the inspecting officer and of the new model.[351]

2e battalion's clothing on transfer to the 17e *de Ligne* was totally life expired, according to the inspector, and of pre-Bardin models. The inspector noted that 'many of the *banderoles* are made from blackened cow hide'.[352]

The 3e battalion was taken into the 22e *de Ligne*, and the 248 men were dressed in brand-new clothing issued from the *dépôt* and of Bardin regulation, replacing life-expire kit. Every man had his regulation issue but were only issued 102 *petit bidons*.[353]

4e battalion, passed to the 34e *de Ligne*, had 206 examples of *habits*, *gilets manches*, *pantalons*, *caleçons*, *capotes*, *schakos* and *bonnets de police* in good condition, and exactly the same number needed total replacement as life expired. Everything was pre-Bardin.[354]

5e battalion held a considerable stock of new clothing, notably 318 *capotes*, 370 fusilier *habits*, 11 green drummers' *habits* and 1 needing repairs, 406 fusilier *gilets manches*, 11 green drummers' *gilets manches* and 1 needing repairs, 550 pairs of *pantalons de tricot*, 280 *bonnets de police*, 125 pairs of *caleçons*, 26 fusilier *schakos*, 1,480 *gibernes*, 1,495 *porte-gibernes*, 12 drum carriages, 60 drummers' aprons, 2 *voltigeur cornets*, 90m of gold lace and 88m 25 of yellow worsted lace. Cloth included 1,226m beige broadcloth, 1,421m 69 blue broadcloth, 648m 13 white broadcloth, 3m 41 chamois broadcloth, 1,328m 40 white serge and 2,912m 48 white tricot. Tucked away in stores were 1,133 pairs of knee buckles, 276 uniform brushes and 4m of gold lace.[355]

132e *de Ligne*

Created on 24 January 1811 from conscripts, it served in the campaigns of 1813 and 1814. The regiment was disbanded on 21 August 1814, when the men were sent to the 26e *de Ligne*. At the time of disbandment, the *dépôt* of the regiment held very little in terms of materials, notably a staggering 873m of drummers' lace! For such a huge amount to remain unused in the *dépôt* strongly suggests drummers never had Imperial Livery sewn to any garment. The *dépôt* was packed to the rafters with clothing and equipment. Brand-new unissued clothing included 404 *capotes*, 58 fusilier *habits*, 102 *bonnets de police*, and 689 pairs of *caleçons*. Items needing repairs included 23 fusilier *gilet* 13 *habits*, 2 *capotes*, 10 pairs of *pantalons de tricot* and a solitary *habit verte pour tambour modèle*, again needing repairs.[356]

133e *de Ligne*

Created on 11 March 1811 as 2e *Régiment de la Méditerranée*, it became the 133e *de Ligne* with the decree of 20 September 1812. An inspection return of 30 January 1812 records that:

> The men do not have a *capote*, the *habits* are cut extremely short and are extremely disagreeable for the 92ᵉ … the *habits* were delivered in October 1811, and the *vestes* in April and May.
>
> The *habits* and the *vestes* along with the *pantalons* have been made according to the instructions of his Excellency the Minister Director. The tricot for the *pantalons* and the broadcloth for *habits* is very low quality, the *schako* plates have no numbers …[357]

The regiment was reviewed on 11 August 1814, when it mustered 47 officers, 291 other ranks and 1 *enfant de troupe*. Clothing in use was all in good condition, and of 'the recent regulation', the inspector noted.[358]

The inspector noted 248 pairs of black gaiters and 255 pairs of grey gaiters were in use – not enough for a man to have a pair of each, so clearly a mix and match arrangement existed – and not a single pair of socks was in use, so shoes must have been worn over bare feet. The *dépôt* was moderately well stocked with materials, among which was 46m 50 green broadcloth, 272m 80 drummers' lace, 18m 35 green serge, 30m 68 green tricot, 219 brand-new fusilier *habits-vestes* and 38 needing repairs, 2 green drummers' *habits* with imperial livery needing repairs, 84 grenadier *aigrettes*, 97 *voltigeur aigrettes*, 1,051 fusilier *houpettes*, 1 pair of adjutant's epaulettes, and 89 pairs of grenadier epaulettes.[359]

Chapter 6

Conclusion Bardin, Myth or Reality?

So, what does this all mean? The book shows that the 1812 regulations as imagined by Vernet never made it off the drawing board and that 'Bardin' was not a single, comprehensive regulation: no single unifying regulation existed until summer 1814. The Bourbons, contrary to myth, during the First Restoration spent vast sums of money in remaking the army in its own image and creating order from chaos.

The mass inspections made from June to October 1814 allowed the War Ministry to identify what was going on with the army's clothing situation: the first audit since November 1807 to February 1808. It shows that 41 regiments wore *habits-longe* in summer 1814 and often not a single item of Bardin-regulation clothing, equating to 32 per cent of the army.[1] Indeed, 20 regiments wore *culottes* with *habits-vestes* and long gaiters![2] All of this work resulted in the now almost totally forgotten 1815 dress regulations, which were designed to remake the army in the royalist image: this process was hugely incomplete by the time Paris fell on 3 July 1815.

What this book shows is that by and large the army was dressed as fusiliers, few regiments had grenadiers and *voltigeurs* with epaulettes and *aigrettes*, and few had green-liveried drummers. The years 1813 to 1815 were times of improvisation – whatever kit was in *dépôt* was used. No money, or at least credit, existed to buy luxury items like green broadcloth, drummers' livery, epaulettes, costly chamois or scarlet cloth. Many regiments used much cheaper madder red and not scarlet, and dressed the men as economically as possible. Whatever the regulation stated, we note the regulation *schako de grenadier* was used by just 10 regiments out of 130.[3] Extant items add to this the 6ᵉ, 9ᵉ, 88ᵉ, and 122ᵉ *de Ligne*, making 15 regiments: this means 90 per cent of all regiments used fusilier *schakos* for their grenadiers. Indeed, we find eight regiments still wore bearskins in 1814![4] Under the original January decree, Bardin allowed grenadiers a pair of scarlet-fringed epaulettes, which were seemingly replaced by scarlet shoulder straps in November 1812: presumably these are the '*habit de grenadier*' we find listed in stores' inventories.[5] Indeed, the study of the 1814 inspection returns show that just 15 regiments had grenadiers with a distinctive *habit*, which presumably had epaulettes attached to it and red cut out tail grenades. Just three had the regulation *gilet manches* for grenadiers! Furthermore, we find only 23 regiments, making 38 regiments in total, with grenadiers with epaulettes, or 70 per cent of all line infantry regiments had grenadiers dressed as fusiliers![6] Sword knots, in red worsted lace for grenadiers, were authorised under the decree of September 1812 to be of the previous regulation, yet they were a luxury many regiments did not have. Just eight regiments had sword knots for grenadiers; ergo they were not in common use.[7] Yet as grenadiers and *voltigeurs* did not carry sabres under Bardin we see these regiments were

Archive documents tell us many regiments had Imperial Livery but no green broadcloth. This image, which slightly post-dates the epoch, in giving drummers and cornets blue *habits*, is therefore based on a degree of fact.

not adhering to the regulations concerning these men not to have sabres. The *giberne* was in theory adorned with a grenade, yet just eight regiments had these devices.[8]

Just 19 regiments had *voltigeur habits*, i.e., they had chamois collar and shoulder straps;[9] a further 21 regiments[10] had chamois cloth, representing the presence of more *voltigeur habits*; an additional 5 regiments had yellow broadcloth, which was allowed for in the April 1813 decree.[11] Thus we can add 26 regiments to the tally of those regiments that had *voltigeur habits*: just 45 regiments, or 30 per cent, had *voltigeurs* wearing their own pattern *habit*. *Voltigeurs* had been allowed to wear epaulettes from 19 September 1805, which were to be yellow.[12] We find in 1814–15 proof positive that seven regiments had these items.[13] Most *voltigeurs* were marked out by a yellow *houpette*, or if they were lucky an *aigrette*. Indeed, 45 regiments out of 130 had *voltigeurs* with yellow *aigrettes*. This still leaves 95 regiments, or 73 per cent of the regiments studied, with *voltigeurs* having no *aigrette*. Just six regiments had copper hunting horns on the *giberne*.[14] Some

At the First Restoration drummers, *cornets* and trumpeters were all to adopt Royalist Livery. It is neatly executed here in a naïve image from June 1814. For a grenadier, he oddly has white non-regulation *schako* cords.

regiments armed their *voltigeurs* with dragoon *mousquetons*. In the 19e *de Ligne*, officers of the *voltigeur* companies seem to have been issued An XI *mousqueton*, 10 being issued along with a single *carabine rayé*, i.e., a rifle.[15] The 28e *de Ligne* issued 10 *carabine rayé*, presumably to officers of *voltigeur* companies.[16] Thus, just two regiments had *voltigeur* officers armed with firearms as per the Bardin regulations. In the 95e *Ligne*, the dépôt had 184 infantry muskets, 44 dragoon muskets for *voltigeurs* and 122 sabres.[17]

In theory every regiment had *voltigeurs* with *cornets* in place of drummers, yet just 50 regiments ever adopted these.[18] Just 38 per cent of all line regiments had regulation *cornets*. Even more tellingly, just five regiments had *cornets* with identifiable clothing.[19] However, where regiments had drummers in Imperial Livery, the *cornets* would have followed. Of interest, the voltigeur *cornets* of the 17e, 65e, and 111e *de Ligne* were issued cavalry trumpets! Yet if one believed artists, wargamers, re-enactors and many books on the subject, one would believe every *voltigeur* in the army had yellow-fringed epaulettes, *aigrettes*, chamois collars and a specific type of *schako*. This is utterly and mendaciously wrong.

When we look at the data, 50 regiments, or fewer than 40 per cent of all line infantry regiments, had *sapeurs*![20] In theory every regiment had 18 *sapeurs* headed by a corporal: nope! By looking at the archive sources, we find 82 regiments had Imperial Livery. Yet this is a gross oversimplification of the data as it masks the fact that 17 regiments only adopted green *habits* with Imperial Livery in 1815.[21] Thus, in the 1e Empire 1813–14, just 65 regiments had drummers in green *habits* with Imperial Livery, or 40 per cent of all line infantry regiments we can prove beyond reasonable doubt had Imperial Livery drummers prior to summer 1814.

Technically every regiment had an eagle guard. Not a single helmet is listed anywhere in any documentation from 1814 or 1815. Spontoons existed in just the 19e, 48e and 111e *de Ligne*. If the paper archives are to be believed, the overwhelming majority post-1812 did not have eagle guards with distinctive clothing and weapons: we assume it was all lost in Russia and never replaced.

We note 16 regiments are recorded with blackened cow hide *giberne* belts, drum carriages, drummers' aprons, sabre belts, and musket slings.[22] Just three regiments had the crowned 'N' giberne plate.[23]

Napoleon's last Grande Armée was improvised and impoverished. As long as a soldier had a *giberne* and belt, musket, *schako*, *capote*, trousers and shoes as well as his *havresac*, this is all he needed. Bardin as decreed on 19 January 1812 is a myth – it never could have been adopted in full given that the army was at war and the state was in economic freefall.

Prior to the completion of this study, the understanding of the dress of the French Army of the epoch was based on the work of Lucien Rousselot and others. These men in their passion for the subject relied primarily on iconography to draw their conclusions, but did not on the whole use archive data. The invention of digital photography has transformed research: a task with film that would have taken days can be completed in under an hour. This has allowed the collation of hundreds of thousands of archive documents as copies to work from. The inspection returns that form the heart of this

This musician with his back to us and drummer are drawn by Major Jolly. The drummer with white epaulettes and Royalist Livery adornments to a fusilier *habit* is typical of how most drummers appeared from summer 1814 until disbandment of the Imperial Army in summer 1815. (*Collection KM*)

book offer a glimpse into a how a unit was dressed on a particular date, and may not be representative of the unit a year earlier. The returns report only matters of interest to the War Ministry: how money was spent, and if it was spent fraudulently. Of course, it is possible that when regiments were inspected the inspecting officer turned a blind eye to grenadier bearskins, chamois cloth etc, but it seems very improbable that a colonel and his officers went out of their way to hide paperwork, and squirrel away bearskins from usage for an inspection parade. We have to go with the official written records.

This is what Rousselot got wrong.

His studies were based on contemporary prints, regulations and then very limited research. His research was in essence conducted to verify the images. The starting point has to be regimental records to determine if regulations were put into practice. Regulations represent the idealised world; the archive research shows the reality. We must always rely upon archive research and not simply use others' research, and rely on pretty pictures and the regulations. We need to take a holistic approach, and allow the data to speak for itself. One of the big issues with reconstructing what soldiers of the past wore is the reliance on a minimal data set of extant items. By their very nature, items that exist made from degradable materials such as cloth and leather, or where the materials can be recycled, metal, leather, fabric etc, means that what exists are 'freaks' – the items that fell through the gaps. Museum collections contain an imbalance to officers' items – being private purchase and often kept in a wardrobe or drawer for decades in a private home, means that these items had less chance of being recycled or worn until they disintegrated. The clothing of the common soldier is largely missing, with very few items surviving. Therefore, why do they survive? What processes have enabled them to come down to us to the present day? Perhaps a half a million or more 1812 *habits vestes* were made for common soldiers, less than 20 can be found today, representing 1 per cent at most. Are they typical of what was worn? Of course not, and we cannot take them to be representative of the material culture of the army. These items are all atypical. But by an analysis of these garments we can gain an understanding of how things were done in terms of cut, and construction, which can be scaled up to represent the totality of material culture. Yet at the same time, we need to be cautious of museums. The Musée de l'Armée in Paris until recent years had many mannequins on display of complete sets of uniform. However, in most cases these had one or two original items, displayed on reconstructions, yet no museum guide ever mentioned that the bulk of the displays were from the 1960s and not the period of the First Empire. We need to understand what we are looking at rather than believing what we are told it is we are being shown in a museum display case.

Here is why we need to treat museum collections with care. Indeed, many items in the Musée de l'Armée have been heavily restored since accession and are thus no longer in their historical form, and are thus totally useless to use in reconstructing the material culture of the period. For example, the bearskin of the *grenadier à cheval* mannequin was re-covered in fur in the 1960s, as was that of grenadier Simplet – these items retaining little of their originality. The officer's *habit* of grenadiers a pied was 're-cut' in the 1960s – meaning that the item on display is little more than First Empire fabrics and buttons as the jacket has been irredeemably altered with no record made of what damage was done to the item in the name of conservation.

What is found in museums, moreover, is often used to apply what was unique to a specific regiment to the totality of the French Army. Not a single *voltigeur schako* has been found in any archive document from 1809 to 1815. They simply did not exist as part of the Bardin regulation. Yet despite this, examples of the '1812 pattern' *schako* adorned with yellow lace in the manner of grenadiers can be found in various museums for the 72^{e}, 75^{e} and the 79^{e}. On the balance of evidence, these are clearly atypical: 3 regiments out of 137 means that these items were not in common use. We also note that *schakos* with lace existed for 2^{e} *de Ligne* – green lace top band and yellow cords – and 3^{e} *de Ligne* – yellow lace top band and green cords. These may date from 1810 to 1812 and not be late Empire, of course, but on balance of evidence, *voltigeur schakos* simply did not exist in common usage in 1814 or 1815: these are atypical items unique to a regiment in a certain time and place. Rather than accepting these items at face value we need to ask, are these items actually genuine? Have they been altered post-epoch? Thirdly, we need to understand how items came to be in museum collections: that they exist is atypical, and we need to remember the danger of taking atypical artefacts as typical. Items in museums made from non-durable materials such as uniform coats, by their nature are freaks – and may not be typical of what was used. Items like muskets, sabres, and *cuirasses*, which are made from durable materials and of which several hundred exist, are typical. What we don't have is a corpus of organic material culture like regimental *habits*, and breeches. This process is called hermeneutics, which is the theory and methodology of interpretation, and is the same process by which archive paperwork has survived to the present day. Hermeneutics asks the questions: What is it? Why is it? How does it exist? What does it mean? How do we know what it is? Just like understanding the theory of history, we must understand the theory of material culture and how it comes to survive to present times. The questioning of things, both material culture and empirical data, is of essential importance if we are to reconstruct the material culture of the French Army.

This is why we need to think critically about what we are looking at. We must always question: did this happen? Was it really like that? How do we know? For too long, uniformology has been based on the study of pretty pictures, looking at museum collections and guesswork, cutting out the archive research conducted within a theoretical framework model. The Bardin regulations went through a multiplicity of changes: indeed, the Vernet plates are highly disingenuous and downright misleading as they show the regulations in theory and not as they were actually implemented by the War Ministry. If we based our understanding of the uniforms of Napoléon's army on the written and iconographic official representations of Bardin, we would generate an image of the army that would be fundamentally wrong. Bardin, as we have demonstrated, is more than one regulation. This is why it is important to conduct archive research into how the War Ministry implemented the regulation and, moreover, how colonels implemented it at battalion level. In addition, we need to look at pictorial sources, material culture and empirical written data to gain a fuller understanding of the dress of the army.

Grenadier in full dress, c.1815. Drawn from memory, Major Jolly presents many inconsistencies, but these may be a reflection of reality during the 100 Days. Our grenadier has a bayonet carried on his *giberne* belt – possible if he was transferred from a fusilier company and no grenadier *giberne* belts were spare – he has a white plume and *schako* cords, both of which are non-regulation. He also has a cover to his greatcoat: these were used by just one regiment in the period, the 36[e] *de Ligne*. This image should not give credence to the widespread use of these items in the 1[e] Empire. (*Collection KM*)

Any interpretation of the past is subject to change and evolution, and any interpretation is multi-vocal. As we said in the introduction, another researcher may well interpret the same data as used here in a different manner. The role of the interpreter is as important as the sources used. There are a multitude of competing discussions of the same data sets, the choice of a theory is based on the theoretical basis in which the interpreter works, the result is a vision of the past created through publication. The historian is concerned with the past, the historian creates a past, in turn the past once created becomes historical. Yet it is just one theory of the past as created by the interpreter. No historian is neutral, and how the past really was will always elude us. Into the hermeneutic circle and theory, we need to bring dialectics to bind real objects to theory.[24] Just because it is in a museum does not mean it is an original item, nor that the object is typical, or that the item is in the same condition we view it today as when it was accessioned. The most important question is, of course, 'How do we know what it is?' We must always seek to challenge what we see or are told what we are seeing is. The famous *cuirassier* trumpeters' coat at the Musée l'Empéri is actually made from original lace on a totally new *habit* made for Edouard Detaille, yet today the garment is understood to be authentic. As seen in earlier chapters, the evidence for *cuirassier* trumpeters actually having these *habits* and white epaulettes is actually very minimal indeed. We must use more than one point of reference. We must seek to unite pictorial, written empirical data and material culture into a single framework of reference if we are to truly understand the clothing of the Grande Armée.

This why archive documents are so very important in assessing the practice behind the theory. Of course, it could be easy to say that regimental adjutants simply counted up the number of *schakos* or *habits* regardless of type and submitted the basic numbers. Yet again this is a possibility, as indeed some adjutants simply wrote '*neant*' across all returns, meaning 'we have literally nothing', but it clearly cannot be the case that an entire regimental dépôt was totally empty. Some adjutants were clearly more careful administrators than others. Even accepting this, even in regiments that do declare grenadier *schakos*, the absence of *voltigeur schakos* is striking. The same argument can be used for green cloth and Imperial Livery – it was all used on clothing and thus none was in store, and the adjutant was lazy and just tallied up *habits*. Yes again, very plausible, but again in regiments with competent staff officers, green cloth and Imperial Livery is conspicuous by its absence both in 1814 and 1815. Some regiments declare they burnt what stocks they held, so we are sure some units did have it but not actually use it on clothing. Again though, the balance of evidence strongly suggests that Imperial Livery and green-coated drummers was a rare occurrence in the army of 1814 and 1815. Without more archive sources, we cannot assess the use of Imperial Livery in 1813 or earlier as most regiment's inspection returns have a large gap from 1808 through to 1814.

It is our task as historians to acknowledge that it may never be possible to fully align iconographic and written sources. We should work from quantifiable data – the regimental records – and go from there. Dress regulations, original items and iconography help us visualise what these items look like and how they were worn. Yet in many cases the iconography shows uniforms that simply cannot be reconstructed from official documents. Yet which is correct? Where more than one, independent eyewitness iconographic source presents similar information, we can be sure that the iconography is reliable, or where the iconographic source is backed up by eyewitness written testimony. I hope this study has shown, that if we are to reconstruct the past, we have to use all the sources available to us. The data we use, by its very nature is incomplete and irredeemably chaotic. That we have endeavored to draw a conclusion, where none can perhaps be drawn, is an error. The study has show the value into "going back to basics" and asking that most important question "how do we know?" The archive documentation, to some degree, answers this question; but the inspectors at the time knew what they were looking at, and did not record the details that we are seeking to obtain from these records. This conclusion is my best attempt to bring order to the chaos of the source material. I may be wrong. What is needed, is more research in the remaining 1,000 or so archive boxed at SHDDT concentrating on the supply of uniforms to the various Corps and Armies of the period, That more is yet to be learned and discovered is a given, and I hope researches use my own work as a spring board for further investigation in archive holdings.

Notes

Chapter 1

1. Archives Nationales de France [hereafter AN] AF/IV/1326/A.
2. AN, AF/IV/1326 comte de Cessac to Napoléon 18 Janvier 1811.
3. AN, AF/IV/1326 RAPPORT Sur le Projet relatif à une nouvelle Fixation de la Masse générale d'habillement. 10 Fevrier 1811.
4. Ibid.
5. AN, AF/IV/1179. RAPPORTS ET PROJET DE DÉCRET Relatifs à une nouvelle Fixation de la Masse générale d'habillement. 11 Mars 1811.
6. AN, AF/IV/1179. Bourcier to Berthier 30 Avril 1811.
7. AN AF/IV/1119.

Chapter 2

1. Bibliothèque Musée de l'Armée, Manuscripts and printed books, Volume 1 du projet de règlement sur l'habillement du major Bardin, pp.1–20.
2. Ibid., pp.27–31.
3. Ibid., p.30.
4. Ibid., pp.30–32.
5. Ibid., p.44.
6. Ibid., p.44.
7. Ibid., p.9.
8. Journal Militaire 2e Trimestre 1812, p.111.
9. Crowdy (2015), pp.87–88.
10. Bibliothèque Musée de l'Armée, Manuscripts and printed books, Volume 1 du projet de règlement sur l'habillement du major Bardin, p.45.
11. Ibid., p.48.
12. Crowdy (2015), p.79.

Chapter 3

1. Journal Militaire, 13 Mars 1812.
2. Journal Militaire 21 Mars 1812, p.124.
3. Service Historique de la Armée de Terre [hereafter SHDDT] Xs 525 *circulaire*, 2 Avril 1812.
4. Journal Militaire 12 Avril 1812.
5. SHDDT Xs 528 Ordre Comte de Cessac 21 Juillet 1812.
6. SHDDT Xs 525 Ordre 24 Juillet 1812.
7. SHDDT Xs 528 Décret 26 Juillet 1812.
8. Journal Militaire 2e tremestre 1812, p.111.
9. SHDDT Xb 477 65e *de Ligne* 1812 a 1815, Dossier 1815. Rapport 13 Avril 1819, citing a War Ministry circular of 11 January 1809, forbade the use of government money, i.e. the clothing fund and stoppages from the men's pay, to pay for sword knots and epaulettes for *voltigeurs*; ergo if colonels wanted them, the officers' corps had to foot the bill.
10. Journal Militaire 2e tremestre 1812, p.111.
11. Ibid.
12. SHDDT, Xs 525-526. Rapport 15 Septembre 1812.

13. AN AF/IV/1119. Lettre 23 7bre 1812.
14. SHDDT Xb 378 *16e de Ligne* 1812 a 1815. Dossier 1814. Rapport 26 7bre 1814.
15. SHDDT Xs 528 'Devis des quantités d'etoffes, toiles et boutons nécessaires pour confection des différentes parties de l'Habillement de l'Infanterie de la Ligne, rédige en exécution et conformément aux dispositions du Décret impérial du 19 Janvier 1812', p.3.
16. AN AF/IN/1179. Lettre a Napoleon 14 8bre 1812.
17. Ibid., rapport 24 Décembre 1812.
18. AN AF/IN/1179. Ordre [illegible]. The order states the reserves made in July 1812 were to be issued and replenished. From the sequence of orders, the paper in question is attached to, it must date from between 20 November 1812 and 6 January 1813.
19. AN AF/IN/1179 Comte de Cessac to Napoleon 20 9bre 1812.

Chapter 4

1. SHDDT C2 135 Rapport 7 Janvier 1813.
2. SHDDT Xb 460 57e *de Ligne* 1812 a 1815. Dossier 1814. Rapport 14 Fevrier 1821.
3. AN AF/IV/1179 rapport 18 Fevrier 1813.
4. AN AF/IV/1179, Comte de Cessac to Napoleon 14 Mars 1813.
5. AN AF/IV/1179. Comte de Cessac [illegible] 1813.
6. SHDDT Xs 525-526. Comte de Cessac to Napoléon 12 Avril 1813.
7. Ibid.
8. SHDDT Xs 525-526. Rapport 21 Avril 1813.
9. SHDDT Xs 525-526. Rapport 10 Mai 1813.
10. SHDDT Xs 525. Décret 22 Juin 1813.
11. SHDDT Xs 525 Décret 19 Aout 1813.
12. SHDDT Xb 449 52e *de Ligne* 1812 a 1815. Dossier 1814. Rapport 14 7bre 1814.
13. SHDDT C2 110 Oudinot a Ministre de Guerre, 2 Juillet 1813.
14. SHDDT Xs 525 Décret 17 Novembre 1813.
15. SHDDT Xs 525-526.
16. Journal Militaire. 4e tremestre 1813, p.274.
17. AN AF/IN/1179 Comte de Cessac to Napoleon 27 Xbre 1813.
18. SHDDT Xs 525 Décret 8 Janvier 1814.
19. SHDDT Xs 528 Décret 17 Avril 1814.
20. SHDDT Xs 528 Décret 22 Avril 1814.
21. SHDDT C15 39 Decrets 1815.
22. SHDDT C15 39 Decrets 1815.
23. AN AF/IV/1941, Rapport fait l'Empereur par le ministre de la Guerre, le 26 mars 1815.
24. AN AF/IV/1941, Davout, *Rapport à Sa Majesté l'Empereur*, 5 avril 1815. See also Davout à Mollien, *Correspondance du maréchal Davout*, 17 avril 1815.
25. SHDDT, C16 fol 11, *Correspondance militaire générale pendant les Cent-Jours, Bureau de l'habillement, Circulaires, ministre de la Guerre*, 2 mai 1815.
26. AN, AF/IV/1941, Davout, *Rapport à Sa Majesté l'Empereur*, 5 avril 1815. See Also AN, AF/IV/1941, Davout, *Rapports à Sa Majesté l'Empereur*, 4, 11 et 13 mai 1815.
27. SHDDT C16 11, *Correspondance militaire générale pendant les Cent-Jours, Bureau de l'habillement, Circulaires, ministre de la Guerre*, 2 mai 1815.
28. AN/AF/IV/1941, Davout, *Rapport à Sa Majesté l'Empereur*, 5 avril 1815. See Also AN/AF/IV/1941, Davout, *Rapports à Sa Majesté l'Empereur*, 4, 11 et 13 mai 1815.
29. AN/AF/IV/1941, Davout, *Rapport à Sa Majesté l'Empereur*, 5 avril 1815. See also Davout à Mollien, *Correspondance du Maréchal Davout*, 17 avril 1815.
30. AN/AF/IV/1941, Davout, *Rapports à Sa Majesté l'Empereur*, 4, 11 et 13 mai 1815.
31. *Correspondance de Napoléon 1er*, n° 21891, 11 mai 1815.
32. AN/AF/IV/1941, Davout, *Rapport à Sa Majesté l'Empereur*, 5 avril 1815. See also Davout à Mollien, *Correspondance du Maréchal Davout*, 17 avril 1815.

33. AN/AF/IV/1941, A Daru, *Correspondance du Maréchal Davout*, 15 avril 1815.
34. SHDDT C16 fol 11, *Correspondance militaire générale pendant les Cent-Jours, Bureau de l'habillement, Circulaires, ministre de la Guerre*, 2 mai 1815.
35. AN/AF/IV/1941, Davout, *Rapport à Sa Majesté l'Empereur*, 5 avril 1815. See also Davout à Mollien, *Correspondance du Maréchal Davout*, 17 avril 1815.
36. SHDDT C15 fol. 4, *Daru to Soult* 2 juin 1815. See also SHDDT, C16 fol. 21, lieutenant général commandant le 6e corps au ministre de la Guerre, 12 juin 1815.
37. AN/AF/IV/1938, *Rapport à Sa Majesté l'Empereur sur la situation des différends services de l'armée au 12 juin 1815.*
38. SHDDT C15 35 Situation Rapports Armée du Nord. Rapport 21 Mai 1815.
39. SHDDT C15 39 Decrets 1815. Décret 1 Avril 1815.
40. Ibid., Décret 17 Juin 1815.

Chapter 5

1. SHDDT Xb 343 1e de Ligne 1814 a 1815. Dossier 1814. Rapport 27 7bre 1814.
2. SHDDT Xb 343 1e de Ligne 1814 a 1815. Dossier 1814. Rapport 27 7bre 1814.
3. SHDDT Xb 346 2e *de Ligne* 1814–1815. Dossier 1814. Rapport 23 Aout 1814.
4. Ibid.
5. SHDDT Xb 346 2e *de Ligne* 1814–1815. Dossier 1814. Rapport 23 Aout 1814.
6. SHDDT Xb 346 2e *de Ligne* 1814–1815. Dossier 1815. Rapport 25 août 1819.
7. SHDDT Xb 346 2e *de Ligne* 1814–1815. Dossier 1815. Rapport 25 7bre 1815.
8. SHDDT Xb 346 2e *de Ligne* 1814–1815. Dossier 1815. Rapport 25 août 1819.
9. SHDDT Xb 346 2e *de Ligne* 1814–1815. Dossier 1815. Rapport 25 août 1819.
10. Ibid.
11. SHDDT Xb 346 2e *de Ligne* 1814–1815. Dossier 1815. Rapport 25 7bre 1815.
12. SHDDT Xb 346 2e Ligne 1814–1815. Dossier 1815. Rapport 25 7bre 1815
13. SHDDT Xb 346 2e Ligne 1814–1815. Dossier 1815. Rapport 25 7bre 1815.
14. Ibid.
15. SHDDT Xb 348 3e *de Ligne*. Dossier 1814. Rapport 16 Juillet 1814.
16. SHDDT Xb 348 3e *de Ligne*. Dossier 1815. Rapport 21 7Bre 1815.
17. SHDDT Xb 350 4e *de Ligne* 1812 a 1815. Dossier 1814. Rapport 28 Juillet 1814.
18. SHDDT Xb 350 4e *de Ligne* 1812 a 1815. Dossier 1815. Rapport 26 Septembre 1815.
19. SHDDT Xb 352 5e *de Ligne* 1813 a 1815. Dossier 1814. Rapport 29 Juillet 1814.
20. Ibid.
21. SHDDT Xb 352 5e *de Ligne* 1813 a 1815. Dossier 1815.
22. Ibid.
23. SHDDT Xb 355 6e *de Ligne* 1812 a 1815. Dossier 1815. Rapport 5 Fevrier 1821.
24. Ibid.
25. SHDDT Xb 355 6e *de Ligne* 1812 a 1815. Dossier 1814. Rapport 13 Aout 1814.
26. SHDDT Xb 355 6e *de Ligne* 1812 a 1815. Dossier 1815. Rapport 7 Aout 1815.
27. SHDDT Xb 357 7e *de Ligne* 1812 a 1815. Dossier 1814. Rapport 1 7bre 1814.
28. SHDDT Xb 357 7e *de Ligne* 1812 a 1815. Dossier 1814. Résumé de la revue 1 7bre 1814.
29. SHDDT Xb 357 7e *de Ligne* 1812 a 1815. Dossier 1815. Rapport 3 Aout 1815.
30. SHDDT Xb 359 8e *de Ligne* 1812 a 1815.Dossier 1814. Rapport 21 Juillet 1814.
31. SHDDT Xb 359 8e *de Ligne* 1812 a 1815.Dossier 1812. Rapport 25 Septembre 1815.
32. SHDDT Xb 391 9e *de Ligne* 1812 a 1815. Dossier 1814. Rapport 20 7bre 1814.
33. SHDDT Xb 391 9e *de Ligne* 1812 a 1815. Dossier 1815. Rapport 25 9bre 1815.
34. SHDDT Xb 391 9e *de Ligne* 1812 a 1815. Dossier 1815. Rapport 26 Avril 1819.
35. SHDDT Xb 364 10e *de Ligne* 1813 a 1815. Dossier 1814. Rapport 1 7bre 1814.
36. SHDDT Xb 364 10e *de Ligne* 1813 a 1815. Dossier 1815. Rapport 25 7bre 1815.
37. SHDDT Xb 366 11e *de Ligne* 1813 a 1815. Dossier 1814. Rapport 26 Juillet 1814.

38. SHDDT Xb 366 11e *de Ligne* 1813 a 1815. Dossier 1815.Rapport 12 7bre 1815.
39. SHDDT Xb 369 12e *de Ligne*. Dossier 1814. Rapport 30 Juillet 1814.
40. SHDDT Xb 369 12e *de Ligne*. Dossier 1815. Rapport 20 7bre 1815.
41. SHDDT Xb 372 13e *de Ligne* 1812 a 1815. Dossier 1815. Rapport 6 Aout 1820.
42. SHDDT Xb 372 13e *de Ligne* 1812 a 1815. Dossier 1814. Rapport 6 octobre 1814.
43. Ibid.
44. SHDDT Xb 372 13e *de Ligne* 1812 a 1815. Dossier 1815. Rapport 6 Aout 1820.
45. SHDDT Xb 374 14e *de Ligne* 1812 a 1815. Dossier 1814. Rapport 19 Aout 1814.
46. SHDDT Xb 374 14e *de Ligne* 1812 a 1815. Dossier 1815. Procès-verbal 3e et 4e bataillon.
47. SHDDT Xb 374 14e *de Ligne* 1812 a 1815. Dossier 1813. Lettre 12 Octobre 1813.
48. SHDDT Xb 376 15e *de Ligne* 1812 a 1815. Dossier 1814. Rapport 16 septembre 1814.
49. SHDDT Xb 376 15e *de Ligne* 1812 a 1815. Dossier 1815. Rapport 9 9bre 1815.
50. SHDDT Xb 378 16e *de Ligne* 1812 a 1815. Dossier 1814. Rapport 26 7bre 1814.
51. SHDDT Xb 378 16e *de Ligne* 1812 a 1815. Dossier 1815. Rapport 16 7bre 1815.
52. SHDDT Xb 382 17e *de Ligne*. Dossier 1814. Rapport 25 Aout 1821.
53. SHDDT Xb 382 17e *de Ligne*. Dossier 1814. Rapport 7 Juillet 1814.
54. SHDDT Xb 382 17e de Ligne. Dossier 1814. Résumé de revue 7 Juillet 1814.
55. SHDDT Xb 382 17e *de Ligne*. Dossier 1815. Rapport 27 7bre 1815.
56. SHDDT Xb 385 18e *de Ligne* 1812 a 1815. Dossier 1814. Rapport 16 Juillet 1814.
57. SHDDT Xb 385 18e *de Ligne* 1812 a 1815. Dossier 1815. Rapport 25 7bre 1815.
58. SHDDT Xb 387 19e *régiment de Ligne*. Dossier 1814. Rapport 26 Juillet 1814.
59. Ibid.
60. SHDDT Xb 387 19e *régiment de Ligne*. Dossier 1815. Rapport 25 7bre 1815.
61. SHDDT Xb 387 19e *régiment de Ligne.* Dossier 1815. Rapport 24 7bre 1815.
62. Ibid.
63. SHDDT Xb 387 19e *régiment de Ligne*. Dossier 1815. Rapport Xbre 1815.
64. SHDDT Xb 387 19e *régiment de Ligne*. Dossier 1815. Rapport 24 7bre 1815.
65. Ibid.
66. SHDDT Xb 387 19e *régiment de Ligne*. Dossier 1815. Rapport 24 7bre 1815.
67. Ibid.
68. SHDDT Xb 387 19e *régiment de Ligne*. Dossier 1815. Rapport 24 7bre 1815.
69. SHDDT Xb 390 20e *régiment d'infanterie de la Ligne* 1812 a 1815. Dossier 1814. Rapport 16 Aout 1814.
70. SHDDT Xb 390 20e *régiment d'infanterie de la Ligne* 1812 a 1815. Dossier 1814. Rapport 6 8bre 1814.
71. Ibid.
72. SHDDT Xb 390 20e *régiment d'infanterie de la Ligne* 1812 a 1815. Dossier 1815. Rapport 15 Septembre 1815.
73. SHDDT Xb 392 21e *de Ligne*. Dossier 1813. Rapport 26 Janvier 1813.
74. SHDDT Xb 392 21e *de Ligne*. Dossier 1811. Résume d'Inspection 1814.
75. SHDDT Xb 392 21e *de Ligne*. Dossier 1815.
76. SHDDT Xb 394 22e *de Ligne* 1812 a 1815. Dossier 1814. Rapport 12 Aout 1814 .
77. Ibid.
78. SHDDT Xb 394 22e *de Ligne* 1812 a 1815. Dossier 1815. Rapport 19 septembre 1815.
79. SHDDT Xb 396 23e *de Ligne* 1809 a 1815. Dossier 1814. Rapport 24 Juillet 1814.
80. SHDDT Xb 396 23e *de Ligne* 1809 a 1815. Dossier 1815. Rapport 21 7bre 1815.
81. SHDDT Xb 398 24e *de Ligne* 1809 a 1815. Dossier 1814. Rapport 1 Juillet 1814.
82. SHDDT Xb 398 24e *de Ligne* 1809 a 1815. Dossier 1815. Rapport 3 Aout 1815.
83. SHDDT Xb 400 25e *de Ligne* 1812 a 1815. Dossier 1814. Procès-verbal, 1 Aout 1814.
84. SHDDT Xb 400 25e *de Ligne* 1812 a 1815. Dossier 1814. Rapport 1 Aout 1814.
85. SHDDT Xb 400 25e *de Ligne* 1812 a 1815. Dossier 1814. Procès-verbal 1 Aout 1814.

86. SHDDT Xb 400 25e *de Ligne* 1812 a 1815. Dossier 1815. Rapport 1 Janvier 1816.
87. SHDDT Xb 402 26e *de Ligne* 1812 a 1815. Dossier 1814. Rapport 5 Aout 1814.
88. SHDDT Xb 402 26e *de Ligne* 1812 a 1815. Dossier 1815. Procès-verbal 8 8bre 1815.
89. SHDDT Xb 404 27e *de Ligne* 1813 a 1815. Dossier 1814. Rapport 1 Aout 1814.
90. SHDDT Xb 404 27e *de Ligne* 1813 a 1815. Dossier 1815. Rapport 8 Fevrier 1816.
91. SHDDT Xb 406 28e *de Ligne*. Dossier 1814. Rapport 1 Aout 1814.
92. SHDDT Xb 406 28e *de Ligne*. Dossier 1815. Rapport 30 septembre 1815.
93. SHDDT Xb 406 28[e] *de Ligne*. Dossier 1815. Rapport 30 septembre 1815.
94. SHDDT Xb 408 29[e] *de Ligne*. Dossier 1814. Rapport 1 Aout 1814.
95. SHDDT Xb 408 29[e] *de Ligne*. Dossier 1814. Rapport 1 Aout 1814. See also SHDDT Xb 408 29[e] *de Ligne*. Dossier 1815. Rapport 21 Janvier 1816.
96. SHDDT Xb 408 29[e] *de Ligne*. Dossier 1815. Rapport 26 7bre 1815.
97. SHDDT Xb 410 30[e] *de Ligne* 1812 a 1815. Dossier 1814. Rapport 15 Juillet 1814.
98. SHDDT Xb 410 30[e] *de Ligne*. Dossier 1815. Rapport 21 Septembre 1815.
99. SHDDT Xb 410 30[e] *de Ligne*. Dossier 1815. Rapport 21 Septembre 1815.
100. Ibid.
101. SHDDT Xb 410 30e *de Ligne*. Dossier 1815. Proces Verbal.
102. SHDDT Xb 412 32e *de Ligne*. Dossier 1814. Rapport 1 Aout 1814.
103. SHDDT Xb 412 32e *de Ligne*. Dossier 1814. Rapport 1 Aout 1814.
104. SHDDT Xb 412 32e *de Ligne*. Dossier 1814. Résume Rapport 1 Aout 1814.
105. SHDDT Xb 412 32e *de Ligne*. Dossier 1814. Rapport 1 Aout 1814.
106. SHDDT Xb 412 32e *de Ligne*. Dossier 1815. Rapport 7 Aout 1815.
107. SHDDT Xb 415 33e *de Ligne* 1814 a 1815. Dossier 1814. Résumé de la Revue d'Organisation 13 Aout 1814.
108. SHDDT Xb 415 33e *de Ligne*. Dossier 1815. Rapport 21 Septembre 1815.
109. SHDDT Xb 417 34e *de Ligne* 1812 a 1815. Dossier 1814. Rapport 29 Juillet 1814.
110. SHDDC 15 Correspondance Armée du Nord 11 Juin a 20 Juin 1815. Dossier 20 Juin. Rapport du 20 Juin.
111. Ibid.
112. SHDDT Xb 417 34e *de Ligne* Armée a 1815. Dossier 1812. Rapport 7 Mai 1812.
113. SHDDT Xb 419 35e *de Ligne* 1812 a 1815. Dossier 1814. Rapport 16 Juillet 1814.
114. SHDDT Xb 419 35e *de Ligne* 1812 a 1815. Dossier 1814. Rapport 16 Juillet 1814.
115. SHDDT Xb 419 35e *de Ligne*. Dossier 1815. Rapport 3 Aout 1815.
116. SHDDT Xb 419 35e *de Ligne*. Dossier 1815. Rapport 21 Novembre 1815.
117. SHDDT Xb 421 36e *de Ligne*. Dossier 1815. Rapport 1 décembre 1815.
118. SHDDT Xb 421 36e *de Ligne*. Dossier 1815. Rapport 1 décembre 1815.
119. SHDDT Xb 421 36e *de Ligne* 1812 a 1815. Dossier 1814. Rapport 1 7bre 1814.
120. SHDDT Xb 421 36e *de Ligne* 1812 a 1815. Dossier 1814. Résume de la Revue 1 7bre 1814.
121. SHDDT Xb 421 36e *de Ligne*. Dossier 1815. Rapport 1 Décembre 1815.
122. SHDDT Xb 421 36e *de Ligne*. Dossier 1815. Rapport 1 Décembre 1815.
123. SHDDT /GR 21 YC 324 36e *régiment d'infanterie de ligne*, 16 mai 1811–22 avril 1813 (matricules 8 376 à 10 175).
124. Bibliothèque Musée de l'Armée. Fonds Rousselot. Infanterie de la Ligne.
125. SHDDT Xb 421 36e *de Ligne*. Dossier 1815. Rapport 1 Décembre 1815.
126. SHDDT Xb 424 37e *de Ligne* 1812 a 1815. Dossier 1814. Rapport 4 Aout 1814.
127. SHDDT Xb 424 37e *de Ligne* 1812 a 1815. Dossier 1815. Rapport 25 7bre 1815.
128. SHDDT Xb 426 39e *de Ligne* 1812 a 1815. Dossier 1814. Rapport 11 Aout 1814.
129. SHDDT Xb 426 39e *de Ligne* 1812 a 1815. Dossier 1815. Rapport 11 Mai 1819.
130. SHDDT Xb 426 39e *de Ligne* 1812 a 1815. Dossier 1815. Rapport 21 7bre 1815.
131. SHDDT Xb 428 40e *de Ligne* 1812 a 1815. Dossier 1814. Rapport 16 Aout 1814.
132. SHDDT Xb 428 40e *de Ligne* 1812 a 1815. Dossier 1814. Résume de la revue 16 Aout 1814.

133. SHDDT C15 Correspondance Armée du Nord 11 Juin a 20 Juin 1815. Dossier 19 Juin. Rapport du 19 Juin.
134. SHDDT Xb 430 42e *de Ligne* 1812 a 1815. Dossier 1814. Rapport 17 Aout 1814.
135. SHDDT Xb 430 42e *de Ligne* 1812 a 1815. Dossier 1815. Rapport 24 Septembre 1815.
136. SHDDT Xb 342 43e *de Ligne* 1812 a 1815. Dossier 1814. Rapport 16 Juillet 1814.
137. SHDDT Xb 342 43e *de Ligne* 1812 a 1815. Dossier 1814. Rapport 21 décembre 1819.
138. SHDDT Xb 432 43e *de Ligne* 1814 a 1815. Dossier 1815. Rapport 26 7bre 1815.
139. SHDDT Xb 434 44e *de Ligne* 1812 a 1815. Dossier 1814. Rapport 1 Octobre 1814.
140. SHDDT Xb 436 45e *de Ligne* 1812 a 1815. Dossier 1814. Rapport 1 Aout 1814.
141. SHDDT Xb 436 45e *de Ligne* 1812 a 1815. Dossier 1814. Rapport fait au Ministre 1 Aout 1814.
142. SHDDT Xb 436 45[e] *de Ligne*. Dossier 1815. Rapport 26 7bre 1815.
143. Ibid.
144. Royal Collection Trust, RCIN 915075 French Army. Picquet of the 45th Regiment of the Line, 1814.
145. SHDDT Xb 436 45e *de Ligne*. Dossier 1815. Rapport 1814.
146. SHDDT Xb 438 46e *de Ligne* 1812 a 1815. Dossier 1814. Rapport 1 Aout 1814.
147. Ibid.
148. Ibid.
149. SHDDT C 15 Correspondance Armée du Nord 11 Juin a 20 Juin 1815. Dossier 19 Juin. Rapport du 19 Juin.
150. SHDDT Xb 438 46e *de Ligne*. Dossier 1815.
151. SHDDT Xb 438 46e *de Ligne*. Dossier 1813. Rapport 1 8bre 1813.
152. SHDDT Xb 440 47e *de Ligne* 1812 a 1815. Dossier 1814. Rapport 1 Octobre 1814.
153. SHDDT Xb 440 47e *de Ligne* 1812 a 1815. Dossier 1814. Résumé de la Revue 1 Octobre 1814.
154. SHDDT Xb 442 48e *de Ligne*. 1811 a 1815. Dossier 1814. Rapport 20 7bre 1814.
155. Ibid.
156. SHDDT Xb 442 48e *de Ligne*. Dossier 1815. Rapport 1 Décembre 1815.
157. SHDDT Xb 442 48e *de Ligne*. Dossier 1815. Rapport 1 décembre 1815.
158. SHDDT Xb 444 50e *de Ligne*. 1811 a 1815. Dossier 1814. Rapport 28 Septembre 1814.
159. SHDDT Xb 444 50e *de Ligne* 1811 a 1815. Dossier 1815. Rapport 7 Aout 1815.
160. SHDDT Xb 457 51e *de Ligne*. 1809 a 1815. Dossier 1814. Rapport 15 Septembre 1814.
161. SHDDT Xb 457 51e *de Ligne*. 1809 a 1815. Dossier 1815. Rapport 24 Janvier 1820.
162. SHDDT Xb 447 51e *régiment d'infanterie de Ligne*. Dossier 1815.
163. SHDDT Xb 449 52e *de Ligne* 1812 a 1815. Dossier 1814. Résume d'inspection 4 Aout 1814.
164. SHDDT Xb 449 52e *de Ligne* 1812 a 1815. Dossier 1814. Rapport 14 7bre 1814.
165. SHDDT Xb 449 52e *de Ligne* 1812 a 1815. Dossier 1815. Rapport 23 7bre 1815.
166. SHDDT Xb 451 53e *de Ligne* 1811 a 1815. Dossier 1814. Rapport 20 Aout 1814.
167. SHDDT Xb 451 53[e] *de Ligne* 1811 a 1815. Dossier 1815. Rapport 21 Septembre 1815.
168. SHDDT Xb 451 53[e] *de Ligne* 1811 a 1815. Dossier 1815. Rapport 20 Septembre 1815.
169. SHDDT Xb 444 50[e] *de Ligne* 1811 a 1815. Dossier 1814. Rapport 21 Juillet 1814. NB the 54[e] *de Ligne* became the 50[e] *de Ligne* in May 1814, hence why this report is misfiled in the box of the 50[e] *de Ligne* and not under the 54[e] *de Ligne*.
170. SHDDT Xb 453 54[e] *de Ligne*. Dossier 1815. Rapport 25 8bre 1815.
171. SHDDT Xb 455 55[e] *de Ligne* 1812 a 1815. Dossier 1814. Rapport 1 Aout 1814.
172. SHDDT Xb 455 55[e] *de Ligne*. Dossier 1815. Rapport 1 8bre 1815.
173. SHDDT Xb 455 55[e] *de Ligne*. Dossier 1815. Rapport 29 7bre 1815.
174. SHDDT Xb 449 52[e] *de Ligne* 1812 a 1815. Dossier 1814. Rapport 14 7bre 1814. The 56[e] became the 52[e] in the 1814 Amalgam, hence the 1814 inspection paperwork being in the archive of the 52[e] *de Ligne*.
175. SHDDT Xb 449 52e *de Ligne* 1812 a 1815. Dossier 1815. Rapport 1 8bre 1815.
176. SHDDT Xb 458 56e *de Ligne* 1810 a 1815. Dossier 1815. Rapport 31 Aout 1815.

177. SHDDT Xb 460 57e *de Ligne* 1812 a 1815. Dossier 1814. Rapport 16 Juillet 1814.
178. SHDDT Xb 460 57e *de Ligne* 1812 a 1815. Dossier 1814. Résume de la revue 16 Juillet 1814.
179. SHDDT Xb 460 57e *de Ligne* 1812 a 1815. Dossier 1814. Rapport 14 Fevrier 1821.
180. SHDDT Xb 560 57e *de Ligne* 1810 a 1815. Dossier 1815. Rapport 25 7bre 1815.
181. SHDDT Xb 560 57e *de Ligne* 1810 a 1815. Dossier 1815. Rapport 17 7bre 1815.
182. SHDDT Xb 560 57[e] *de Ligne* 1810 a 1815. Dossier 1815. Rapport 25 7bre 1815.
183. SHDDT Xb 462 58[e] *de Ligne* 1812 a 1815. Dossier 1815. Rapport 25 7bre 1815.
184. SHDDT Xb 462 58[e] *de Ligne* 1812 a 1815. Dossier 1815. Rapport 23 7bre 1815.
185. SHDDT Xb 462 58e *de Ligne* 1812 a 1815. Dossier 1815. Rapport 29 7bre 1815.
186. SHDDT Xb 462 58e *de Ligne* 1812 a 1815. Dossier 1814. Rapport 16 Juillet 1814.
187. SHDDT Xb 462 58e *de Ligne* 1812 a 1815. Dossier 1815. Rapport 23 7bre 1815.
188. SHDDT Xb 465 59e *régiment de Ligne*. Dossier 1814. Rapport 16 Aout 1814.
189. Ibid.
190. SHDDT Xb 467 60e *de Ligne* 1812 a 1815. Dossier 1815. Rapport 27 7bre 1815.
191. SHDDT Xb 467 60e *de Ligne* 1812 a 1815. Dossier 1814. Rapport 27 Septembre 1821.
192. Regiment accounts report 5m 16 of green broadcloth was bought in the 100 Days. Furthermore, some 17m 16 of green broadcloth had been inherited from the 114[e] *de Ligne* in 1814, which combined with the 380m of Imperial Livery from the same regiment provided a veritable stockpile of materials to make new Imperial Livery garments during the 100 Days.
193. SHDDT Xb 467 60e *de Ligne* 1812 a 1815. Dossier 1815. Rapport 26 juin 1816.
194. SHDDT Xb 469 61e *régiment de Ligne*. Dossier 1813. Rapport 21 Juin 1813.
195. SHDDT Xb 469 61e *régiment de Ligne*. Dossier 1815. Rapport 3 9bre 1815.
196. SHDDT Xb 469 61e *régiment de Ligne*. Dossier 1815.
197. Ibid.
198. SHDDT Xb 471 62e *de Ligne* 1810 a 1815. Dossier 1814. Rapport 21 7bre 1814.
199. SHDDT Xb 471 62e *de Ligne* 1810 a 1815. Dossier 1814. Rapport 21 7bre 1814.
200. SHDDT Xb 471 62e *de Ligne* 1812 a 1815. Dossier 1815. Rapport 7 août 1815.
201. SHDDT Xb 473 63[e] *de Ligne* 1811 a 1815. Dossier 1815. Rapport 25 7bre 1815.
202. SHDDT Xb 475 64[e] *de Ligne* 1812 a 1815. Dossier 1814. Rapport 16 août 1814.
203. SHDDT Xb 475 64[e] *de Ligne* 1812 a 1815. Dossier 1815. Rapport 21 7bre 1815.
204. SHDDT Xb 477 65[e] *de Ligne* 1812 a 1815, Dossier 1814. Rapport 1 août 1814.
205. SHDDT Xb 477 65[e] *de Ligne* 1812 a 1815, Dossier 1815. Rapport 13 Avril 1819.
206. These are likely to be bearskin cords.
207. SHDDT Xb 479 66[e] *de Ligne* 1812 a 1815. Dossier 1814. Rapport 21 Juillet 1814.
208. SHDDT Xb 481 67[e] *de Ligne* 1812 a 1815. Dossier 1815. Rapport 25 7bre 1815.
209. SHDDT Xb 481 67[e] *de Ligne* 1812 a 1815. Dossier 1815. Rapport 1 Mars 1815.
210. SHDDT Xb 481 67[e] *de Ligne* 1812 a 1815. Dossier 1815. Rapport 25 7bre 1815.
211. SHDDT Xb 484 69[e] *de Ligne* 1812 a 1815. Dossier 1814. Rapport 6 7bre 1814.
212. SHDDT Xb 484 69[e] *de Ligne* 1814 a 1815. Dossier 1815. Rapport 25 7bre 1815.
213. SHDDT Xb 486 70[e] *de Ligne* 1811 a 1815. Dossier 1814. Rapport 16 7bre 1814.
214. SHDDT Xb 486 70[e] *de Ligne* 1811 a 1815. Dossier 1814. Rapport 15 7bre 1814.
215. SHDDT Xb 486 70[e] *de Ligne* 1811 a 1815. Dossier 1814. Rapport 16 7bre 1814.
216. SHDDT Xb 486 70[e] *de Ligne* 1811 a 1815. Dossier 1815. Rapport 21 7bre 1815.
217. SHDDT Xb 488 72[e] *de Ligne* 1811 a 1815. Dossier 1815. Rapport 14 8bre 1821.
218. SHDDT Xb 488 72[e] *de Ligne* 1811 a 1815. Dossier 1813. Rapport 14 Mars 1813.
219. SHDDT Xb 488 72[e] *de Ligne* 1811 a 1815. Dossier 1813. Rapport 30 Aout 1813.
220. SHDDT Xb 488 72e *de Ligne* 1811 a 1815. Dossier 1813. Rapport 10 9bre 1813.
221. SHDDT Xb 488 72e *de Ligne* 1811 a 1815. Dossier 1814. Rapport 12 Aout 1814.
222. SHDDT Xb 488 72e *de Ligne* 1811 a 1815. Dossier 1814. Rapport 12 Aout 1814.
223. SHDDT Xb 488 72e *régiment de Ligne*. Dossier 1815. Rapport 11 Aout 1815.
224. SHDDT Xb 488 72e *régiment de Ligne*. Dossier 1815. Rapport 11 Aout 1815.

225. SHDDT Xb 488 *72e de Ligne* 1811 a 1815. Dossier 1815. Rapport 15 8bre 1821.
226. SHDDT Xb 490 *75e de Ligne* 1811 a 1815. Dossier 1814. Rapport 26 7bre 1814.
227. Ibid.
228. SHDDT Xb 490 *75e de Ligne* 1811 a 1815. Dossier 1815. Rapport 14 7bre 1815.
229. SHDDT Xb 490 *75e de Ligne* 1811 a 1815. Dossier 1815. Rapport 14 8bre 1821.
230. SHDDT Xb 492 *76e de Ligne* 1811 a 1815. Dossier 1814. Rapport 26 7bre 1814.
231. Ibid.
232. SHDDT Xb 492 76e *de Ligne* 1811 a 1815. Dossier 1814. Rapport 16 Aout 1814.
233. SHDDT C 15 Correspondance Armée du Nord 11 Juin a 20 Juin 1815. Dossier 19 Juin. Rapport du 19 Juin.
234. SHDDT Xb 492 76e *de Ligne* 1811 a 1815. Dossier 1815. Rapport 15 Avril 1817.
235. SHDDT Xb 492 76e *de Ligne* 1811 a 1815. Dossier 1815. Rapport 26 7bre 1815.
236. SHDDT Xb 492 76e *de Ligne* 1811 a 1815. Dossier 1814. Rapport 8 février 1817.
237. SHDDT Xb 484 69e *de Ligne* 1812 a 1815. Dossier 1814. Rapport 8 Aout 1814. The 79e *de Ligne* became the 69e *de Ligne* under the 1814 amalgam, thus it is no surprise this report was misfiled in the box for the 69e *de Ligne*.
238. SHDDT Xb 496 81e *de Ligne* 1812 a 1815. Dossier 1814. Rapport 18 7bre 1814.
239. SHDDT Xb 498 82e *de Ligne* 1812 a 1815. Dossier 1814. Rapport 30 7bre 1814.
240. SHDDT Xb 498 82e *de Ligne* 1812 a 1815. Dossier 1815. Rapport 16 novembre 1819.
241. SHDDT Xb 498 82e *de Ligne* 1812 a 1815. Dossier 1815. Rapport 30 7bre 1814.
242. SHDDT Xb 500 84e *de Ligne*. 1814 a 1815. Dossier 1814. Rapport 1 Aout 1814.
243. SHDDT Xb 500 84e *de Ligne*. 1814 a 1815. Dossier 1815. Rapport 25 7Bre 1815.
244. SHDDT Xb 502 85e *de Ligne.* 1812 a 1815. Dossier 1814. Rapport 16 7bre 1814.
245. SHDDT Xc 502 85e *de Ligne*. Dossier 1815 Rapport 25 7bre 1815.
246. SHDDT Xc 502 85e *de Ligne*. Dossier 1815. Rapport 1 Avril 1816.
247. SHDDT Xb 504 86e *régiment d'infanterie de la Ligne* 1813 a 1815. Dossier 1814. Rapport 13 Aout 1814.
248. SHDDT Xb 504 86e *régiment d'infanterie de la Ligne* 1813 a 1815. Dossier 1814. Livre de detail 1e compagnie, 1e bataillon 86e *de Ligne*.
249. SHDDT Xb 506 88e *de Ligne* 1811 a 1815. Dossier 1815. Rapport 28 7bre 1815.
250. SHDDT Xb 506 88e *de Ligne* 1811 a 1815. Dossier 1814. Rapport 8 Juillet 1814.
251. SHDDT Xb 506 88e *de Ligne* 1811 a 1815. Dossier 1815. Rapport 28 7bre 1815.
252. SHDDT Xb 508 92e *de Ligne* 1812 a 1815. Dossier 1814. Rapport 4 Aout 1814.
253. SHDDT Xb 508 92e *régiment de Ligne* 1814 a 1815. Dossier 1815.
254. SHDDT Xb 510 93e *de Ligne* 1812 a 1815. Dossier 1814. Résume de la revue 11 Aout 1814.
255. SHDDT Xb 510 93e *de Ligne* 1812 a 1815. Dossier 1814. Rapport 13 7bre 1814.
256. SHDDT Xb 511 93e *de Ligne* 1813 a 1815. Dossier 1815. Rapport 28 7be 1815.
257. SHDDT Xb 511 93e *de Ligne* 1813 a 1815. Dossier 1815.
258. SHDDT Xb 513 94e *de Ligne* 1811 a 1815. Dossier 1814. Rapport 21 7bre 1814.
259. SHDDT Xb 513 94e *de Ligne* 1811 a 1815. Dossier 1812. Rapport 30 Avril 1812.
260. SHDDT Xb 513 94e *de Ligne* 1811 a 1815. Dossier 1815. Rapport 11 Aout 1815.
261. SHDDT Xb 515 95e *de Ligne* 1812 a 1815. Dossier 1814. Rapport 26 Aout 1814.
262. SHDDC 15 Correspondance Armée du Nord 11 Juin a 20 Juin 1815. Dossier 19 Juin. 95e *régiment de Ligne*.
263. SHDDT Xb 515 95e *de Ligne* 1812 a 1815. Dossier 1815. Rappsort 29 Aout 1821.
264. SHDDT Xb 515 95e *de Ligne* 1812 a 1815. Dossier 1815. Rapport 25 7bre 1815.
265. SHDDT Xb 517 96e *de Ligne* 1812 a 1815. Dossier 1814. Résume de la revue 7 Aout 1814.
266. SHDDT Xb 517 96e *de Ligne* 1812 a 1815. Dossier 1815. Rapport no date 1815.
267. SHDDT Xb 417 34e *de Ligne* 1812 a 1815. Dossier 1813. Rapport 20 Fevrier 1813.
268. SHDDT Xb 519 100e *de Ligne* 1812 a 1815. Dossier 1814. Rapport 24 7bre 1814.
269. SHDDT Xb 519 100e *de Ligne* 1813 a 1815. Dossier 1815. Rapport 16 7bre 1815.

270. SHDDT Xb 521 101e *régiment d'infanterie de la Ligne* 1813 a 1815. Dossier 1814. Rapport 1 août 1814.
271. SHDDT Xb 523 102e *de Ligne* 1812 a 1815. Dossier 1814. Rapport 1 7bre 1814.
272. SHDDT Xb 523 102e *de Ligne* 1812 a 1815. Dossier 1814. Résumé de la revue 1 7bre 1814.
273. SHDDT Xb 523 102e *de Ligne* 1812 a 1815. Dossier 1815. Rapport 15 janvier 1816.
274. SHDDT Xb 523 102e *de Ligne* 1812 a 1815. Dossier 1815. Letter fait au committee central d'artillerie 28 Mars 1816.
275. SHDDT Xb 525 103e *de Ligne* 1812 a 1815. Dossier 1814. Rapport 28 Aout 1814.
276. SHDDT Xb 525 103e *de Ligne* 1812 a 1815. Dossier 1815. Rapport 7 Aout 1815.
277. SHDDT GR 21 YC 760 à 762 104e *régiment d'infanterie de ligne*. 1814–1815.
278. SHDDT XB 526 104e *de Ligne* 1791 a 1815. Dossier 1814. Resume de la Revue 22 Aout 1814.
279. Ibid.
280. SHDDT XB 526 104e *de Ligne* 1791 a 1815. Dossier 1815. Rapport 8 7bre 1815.
281. SHDDT Xb 528 105e *de Ligne* 1812 a 1815. Dossier 1814. Rapport 13 Aout 1815.
282. SHDDT Xb 528 105e *de Ligne* 1812 a 1815. Dossier 1814. Résumé de la revue 13 Aout 1815.
283. SHDDT Xb 528 105e *de Ligne* 1812 a 1815. Dossier 1814. Rapport 8 Aout 1815.
284. SHDDT Xb 528 105e *de Ligne* 1812 a 1815. Dossier 1814. Résumé de la revue 8 Aout 1815.
285. SHDDT Xb 530 106e *de Ligne* 1812 a 1815. Dossier 1815. Rapport 16 novembre 1815.
286. SHDDT GR 21 YC 780 107e *régiment d'infanterie de ligne*.
287. SHDDT Xb 531 107e *de Ligne*. Dossier 1814. Rapport 1 7bre 1814.
288. SHDDT Xb 531 107e *de Ligne*. Dossier 1813. Rapport 12 Mars 1813.
289. SHDDT Xb 533 108e *de Ligne*. Dossier 1814. Rapport 9 7bre 1814.
290. SHDDT Xb 533 108e *de Ligne*. Dossier 1814. Résumé de la revue 9 7bre 1814.
291. SHDDT Xb 533 108e *de Ligne*. Dossier 1815. Rapport 25 7bre 1815.
292. SHDDT GR 21 YC 792.
293. SHDDT Xb 535 111e *de Ligne* 1812 a 1815. Dossier 1815. Rapport 29 Janvier 1816.
294. SHDDT Xb 535 111e *de Ligne* 1812 a 1815. Dossier 1815. Rapport 20 janvier 1820.
295. SHDDT Xb 535 111e *de Ligne* 1812 a 1815. Dossier 1814. Rapport 1 Aout 1814.
296. SHDDT Xb 535 111e *de Ligne* 1812 a 1815. Dossier 1814. Résume de la revue 1 Aout 1814.
297. SHDDT Xb 535 111e *de Ligne* 1812 a 1815. Dossier 1815. Rapport 29 Janvier 1816.
298. SHDDT Xb 535 111e *de Ligne* 1812 a 1815. Dossier 1815. Rapport 19 7bre 1815.
299. Ibid.
300. SHDDT Xb 357 7e *de Ligne* 1812 a 1815. Dossier 1814. Résume de la revue 1 7bre 1814.
301. SHDDT Xb 374 14e *de Ligne* 1812 a 1815. Dossier 1814. Rapport 29 Aout 1814.
302. SHDDT Xb 352 5e *de Ligne* 1813 a 1815. Dossier 1814. Rapport 29 Juillet 1814.
303. SHDDT Xb 364 10e *de Ligne* 1813 a 1815. Dossier 1814. Rapport 1 7bre 1814.
304. SHDDT Xb 539 114[e] *de Ligne* 1808 a 1814. Dossier 1814. Rapport 24 Aout 1815.
305. SHDDT Xb 467 60[e] *de Ligne* 1812 a 1815. Dossier 1814. Rapport 1 septembre 1814.
306. SHDDT Xb 517 96[e] *de Ligne* 1812 a 1815. Dossier 1814. Rapport 7 Aout 1814.
307. SHDDT Xb 500 84[e] *de Ligne* 1814 a 1815. Dossier 1814. Rapport 1 août 1814.
308. SHDDT Xb 508 92[e] *de Ligne* 1812 a 1815. Dossier 1814. Rapport 4 Aout 1814.
309. SHDDT Xb 372 13[e] *de Ligne* 1812 a 1815. Dossier 1814. Rapport 6 octobre 1814.
310. SHDDT Xb 484 69[e] *de Ligne* 1812 a 1815. Dossier 1814. Rapport 8 Aout 1814. The 117[e] *de Ligne* along with the 79[e] *de Ligne* became the new 69[e] *de Ligne* under the 1814 amalgam, thus it is no surprise this report was misfiled in the box for the 69[e] *de Ligne* rather than the box for the 79[e] *de Ligne*.
311. SHDDT Xb 484 69[e] *de Ligne* 1812 a 1815. Dossier 1814. Rapport 8 Aout 1814. The 117[e] *de Ligne* along with the 79[e] *de Ligne* became the new 69[e] *de Ligne* under the 1814 amalgam, thus it is no surprise this report was misfiled in the box for the 69[e] *de Ligne* rather than the box for the 79[e] *de Ligne*.
312. SHDDT Xb 364 10[e] *de Ligne* 1813 a 1815. Dossier 1814. Rapport 1 7bre 1814.

313. SHDDT Xb 523 102[e] *de Ligne* 1812 a 1815. Dossier 1814. Rapport 1 7bre 1814.
314. SHDDT Xb 544 119[e] *de Ligne* 1808 a 1814.
315. SHDDT Xb 513 94[e] *de Ligne* 1811 a 1815. Dossier 1814. Rapport 21 7bre 1814.
316. SHDDT Xb 481 67[e] *de Ligne* 1812 a 1815. Dossier 1815. Rapport 1 Mars 1815.
317. SHDDT Xb 545 120[e] *de Ligne* 1808 a 1814.
318. SHDDT Xb 525 103[e] *de Ligne* 1812 a 1815. Dossier 1814. Rapport 28 Aout 1814.
319. SHDDT Xb 366 11[e] *de Ligne* 1813 a 1815. Dossier 1814. Rapport 26 Juillet 1814.
320. SHDDT Xb 546 121[e] *de Ligne* 1808 a 1814. Dossier 1814. Rapport 15 Janvier 1816.
321. SHDDT Xb 546 121[e] *de Ligne* 1808 a 1814. Dossier 1814. Rapport 15 Janvier 1816b.
322. SHDDT Xb 548 122[e] *de Ligne* 1809 a 1814.
323. SHDDT Xb 343 1e *de Ligne* 1814 a 1815. Dossier 1814. Rapport 22 Aout 1814.
324. SHDDT Xb 488 72e *de Ligne* 1811 a 1815. Dossier 1814. Rapport 12 Aout 1814.
325. SHDDT Xb 382 17e *de Ligne*. Dossier 1814. Exercise 1814. Rapport 7 Juillet 1814.
326. SHDDT Xb 382 17e *de Ligne.* Dossier 1814. Résume de revue 7 Juillet 1814.
327. SHDDT Xb 406 28e *de Ligne*. Dossier 1814. Rapport 1 Aout 1814.
328. AN AF/IV/1179. Comte de Cessac to Napoléon 19 Fevrier 1812.
329. SHDDT Xb 550 124e *de Ligne* 1811 a 1814. Dossier 1813. Rapport 1 Avril 1813.
330. SHDDT Xb 550 124e *de Ligne* 1811 a 1814. Rapport 12 Juin 1820.
331. SHDDT Xb 400 25e *de Ligne* 1812 a 1815. Dossier 1814. Rapport 1 Aout 1814.
332. SHDDT Xb 400 25e *de Ligne* 1812 a 1815. Dossier 1814. Rapport 1 Aout 1814.
333. SHDDT Xb 551 Dossier 125[e] *de Ligne*. Dossier 1812. Rapport 29 Juin 1812.
334. SHDDT Xb 551 Dossier 126[e] *de Ligne*. Dossier 1812. Rapport 5 Mars 1812.
335. SHDDT Xb 551 Dossier 126[e] *de Ligne*. Dossier 1812. Rapport 29 Avril 1812.
336. SHDDT Xb 551 Dossier 126e *de Ligne*. Dossier 1812. Rapport 22 Juin 1812.
337. SHDDT Xb 551 Dossier 126e *de Ligne*. Dossier 1812. Rapport 22 Juin 1812.
338. SHDDT C2 135 Rapport 5 Janvier 1813.
339. SHDDT Xb 551 Dossier 126e *de Ligne.* Rapport 5 Décembre 1820.
340. Collet = jacket i.e., habit.
341. SHDDT Xb 548 122e *régiment de Ligne* 1811–1814. Dossier 1814. Rapport 16 Aout 1813. This report is misfiled in the box of the 122e.
342. SHDDT Xb 387 19e *régiment de Ligne*. Dossier 1814. Rapport 26 Juillet 1814.
343. SHDDT Xb 533 108e *de Ligne* 1812 a 1815. Dossier 1814. Rapport Aout 1814.
344. SHDDT Xb 460 57e *de Ligne* 1812 a 1815. Dossier 1814. Rapport 16 Juillet 1814.
345. SHDDT Xb 372 13e *de Ligne* 1812 a 1815. Dossier 1814. Rapport 6 octobre 1814.
346. SHDDT Xb 548 122e *régiment de Ligne* 1811–1814. Dossier 1814. Rapport 16 Aout 1813. This report is misfiled in the box of the 122e *de Ligne*!
347. SHDDT Xb 555 130e *de Ligne* 1811 a 1814. Dossier 1815. Procès-verbal 25 8bre 1814.
348. SHDDT Xb 555 130e *de Ligne* 1811 a 1814. Dossier 1813. Rapport 23 7bre 1813.
349. SHDDT Xb 490 75e *de Ligne* 1811 a 1815. Dossier 1814. Rapport 26 7bre 1814.
350. SHDDT Xb 555 130e *de Ligne* 1811 a 1814. Dossier 1815. Procès-verbal 25 8bre 1814.
351. SHDDT Xb 556 131e *de Ligne* 1812 a 1815. Dossier 1814. Rapport 29 Juillet 1814.
352. SHDDT Xb 382 17e *de Ligne*. Dossier 1814. Résumé de revue 7 Juillet 1814.
353. SHDDT Xb 394 22e *de Ligne* 1812 a 1815. Dossier 1814. Rapport 12 Aout 1814.
354. SHDDT Xb 417 34e *de Ligne* 1812 a 1815. Dossier 1814. Rapport 29 Juillet 1814.
355. SHDDT Xb 506 88e *de Ligne* 1811 a 1815. Dossier 1815. Rapport 28 7bre 1815.
356. SHDDT Xb 402 26[e] *de Ligne* 1812 a 1815. Dossier 1814. Rapport 5 Aout 1814.
357. SHDDT Xb 508 92[e] *de Ligne* 1812 a 1815. Dossier 1812. Rapport 30 Janvier 1812.
358. SHDDT Xb 426 39[e] *de Ligne* 1812 a 1815. Dossier 1814. Rapport 11 Aout 1814.
359. SHDDT Xb 426 39[e] *de Ligne* 1812 a 1815. Dossier 1814. Rapport 11 Aout 1814.

Chapter 6

1. Regiments with *habits-longe* when inspected 1814: 2e *de Ligne*, 4e *de Ligne*, 6e *de Ligne*, 7e *de Ligne*, 8e *de Ligne*, 10e *de Ligne*, 30e *de Ligne*, 32e *de Ligne*, 33e *de Ligne*, 34e *de ligne*, 35e *de Ligne*, 36e *de Ligne*, 37e *de Ligne*, 44e *de Ligne*, 45e *de Ligne*, 46e *de Ligne*, 50e *de Ligne*, 53e *de Ligne*, 60e *de Ligne*, 61e *de Ligne*, 65e *de Ligne*, 66e *de Ligne*, 69e *de Ligne*, 82e *de Ligne*, 85e *de Ligne*, 88e *de Ligne*, 92e *de Ligne*, 94e *de Ligne*, 100e *de Ligne*, 114e *de Ligne*, 115e *de Ligne*, 117e *de Ligne*, 118e *de Ligne*, 119e *de Ligne*, 121e *de Ligne*, 122e *de Ligne*, 124e *de Ligne*, 128e *de Ligne*, 132e *de Ligne*, 133e *de Ligne*, 140e *de Ligne*.
2. 8e *de Ligne*, 10e *de Ligne*, 11e *de Ligne*, 27e *de Ligne*, 34e *de Ligne*, 36e *de Ligne*, 37e *de Ligne*, 44e *de Ligne*, 50e *de Ligne*, 53e *de Ligne*, 65e *de Ligne*, 75e *de Ligne*, 82e *de Ligne*, 88e *de Ligne*, 94e *de Ligne*, 102e *de Ligne*, 116e *de Ligne*, 121e *de Ligne*, 128e *de Ligne*, 130e *de Ligne*.
3. Summer 1814 and 1815 the following regiments had grenadier *schakos*: 5e *de Ligne*: 36 grenadier *schakos*, 24e *de Ligne*: 3 grenadier *schakos*, 32e *de Ligne*: 96 grenadier *schakos*, 35e *de Ligne*: 548 grenadier *schakos*, 59e *de Ligne*: 97 grenadier *schakos* of non-regulation pattern, 61e *de Ligne*: 47 grenadier *schakos*, 76e *de Ligne*: 63 grenadier *schakos*, 84e *de Ligne*: 41 grenadier *schakos*, 88e *de Ligne*: 220 grenadier *schakos* for three battalions, 95e *de Ligne*: 56 grenadier *schakos*.
4. Summer 1814 the following regiments had bearskins: 35e *de Ligne*: 52 new bearskins, 36e *de Ligne*: 52 bearskins, 46e *de Ligne*: 194 bearskins in 2 battalions, 62e *de Ligne*: 220 bearskins in use in 3 battalions, 114e *de Ligne*: 60 bearskins, 116e *de Ligne*: 39 bearskins, 121e *de Ligne*: 16 bearskins, 128e *de Ligne*: 48 bearskins.
5. In summer 1814 and 1815 the following regiments had '*habits de grenadiers*' and or '*gilets de grenadiers*': 9e *de Ligne*: 14 grenadier *habits*, 10e *de Ligne*: 45 grenadier *habits*, 19e *de Ligne*: 132 grenadier *habits*. 46 grenadier *vestes* in broadcloth, 18 grenadier *vestes* in tricot, 45e *de Ligne*: 7 grenadier *habits*. 6 grenadier *gilets manches*, 57e *de Ligne*: 10 grenadier *habits*, 58e *de Ligne*: 7 grenadier *habits*, 60e *de Ligne*: 16 grenadier *habits*, 61e *de Ligne*: 59 grenadier *habits* in dépôt 1814, 175 made 1814–1815 with red serge tail facings, 69e *de Ligne*: inventoried but none existed, 92e *de Ligne*: 14 grenadier *habits*, 94e *de Ligne*: 365 grenadier *habits*, 128 grenadier *gilets manches*, 106e *de Ligne*: 42 grenadier *habits*, 111e *de Ligne*: 3 grenadier habits, 113e *de Ligne*: 13 grenadier *habits*, 128e *de Ligne*: 57 grenadier *habits*.
6. Regiments with grenadier epaulettes in 1814 or 1815: 2e *de Ligne*: 1,200 pairs grenadier epaulettes. Worn by grenadiers and fusiliers, 3e *de Ligne*: 81 pairs grenadier epaulettes, 11e *de Ligne*: 121 pairs grenadier epaulettes, 12e *de Ligne*: 12 pairs grenadier epaulettes, 17e *de Ligne*: 77 pairs grenadier epaulettes, 20e *de Ligne*: 20 pairs grenadier epaulettes, 21e *de Ligne*: 10 Pairs, 23e *de Ligne*: 32 pairs, 29e *de Ligne*: 268 pairs grenadier epaulettes, 35e *de Ligne*: 99 pairs grenadier epaulettes, 48e *de Ligne*: 50 pairs grenadier epaulettes, 50e *de Ligne*: 216 pairs grenadier epaulettes, 58e *de Ligne*: 44 pairs grenadier epaulettes, 60e *de Ligne*: 495 pairs grenadier epaulettes, 72e *de Ligne*: 108 pairs grenadier epaulettes, 85e *de Ligne*: 4 pairs grenadier epaulettes, 86e *de Ligne*: 25 pairs grenadiers epaulettes, 95e *de Ligne*: 16 pairs grenadier epaulettes, 100e *de Ligne*: 100 pairs grenadier epaulettes, 103e *de Ligne*: 12 pairs grenadier epaulettes, 111e *de Ligne*: 312 pairs grenadier epaulettes, 118e *de Ligne*: 40 pairs grenadier epaulettes,133e *de Ligne*: 89 pairs of grenadiers epaulettes.
7. Regiments with sword knots 1814–1815 were: 7e *de Ligne*: grenadier sword knot, 27e *de Ligne*: grenadier sword knot, 32e *de Ligne*: grenadier sword knot, 35e *de Ligne*: grenadier sword knot and also *voltigeur* sword knot, 50e *de Ligne*: grenadier sword knot, 55e *de Ligne*: grenadier sword knot, 102e *de Ligne*: grenadier sword knot, 116e *de Ligne*: grenadier sword knot and also *voltigeur* sword knot.
8. Regiments with copper grenades for gibernes in 1814–1815: 5e *de Ligne*, 36e *de Ligne*, 39e *de Ligne*, 28 copper grenades costing 28fr, 45e *de Ligne*, 47e *de Ligne*, 88e *de Ligne*, 91e *de Ligne*, 116e *de Ligne*.
9. The following regiments are recorded as possessing *voltigeur habits*: 9e *de Ligne*: 6 *voltigeur habits*, 10e *de Ligne*: 53 *voltigeur habits*, 11e *de Ligne*: 16 *voltigeur habits*, 13e *de Ligne*: 4 *voltigeur habits*, 18e *de Ligne*: *voltigeur habits* listed on inventory, none present, but 250 pairs of *voltigeur* epaulettes were in use by summer 1815, 42e *de Ligne*: 2 *voltigeur habits*, 57e *de Ligne*: 25 *voltigeur habits*, 60e

de Ligne: 100 *voltigeur habits*, 61e *de Ligne*: 52 *voltigeur habits*, 76e *de Ligne*: 17 *voltigeur habits*, 84e *de Ligne*: 8 *voltigeur habits*, 86e *de Ligne*: 150 *voltigeur habits*, 92e *de Ligne*: 2 *voltigeur habits*, 94e *de Ligne*: 64 *voltigeur habits*, 106e *de Ligne*: 30 *voltigeur habits*, 111e *de Ligne*: 10 *voltigeur habits*, 113e *de Ligne*16 *voltigeur habits*, 116e *de Ligne*: 11 *voltigeur habits*, 128e *de Ligne*: 64 *voltigeur habits*.

10. Regiments with chamois broadcloth were as follows: 1e *de Ligne*, 17e *de Ligne*, 19e *de Ligne*, 22e *de Ligne*, 23e *de Ligne*, 34e *de Ligne*, 35e *de Ligne*, 36e *de Ligne*, 47e *de Ligne*, 51e *de Ligne*, 58e *de Ligne*, 59e *de Ligne*, 64e *de Ligne*, 69e *de Ligne*, 85e *de Ligne*, 93e *de Ligne*, 95e *de Ligne*, 100e *de Ligne*, 104e *de Ligne*, 123e *de Ligne*, 131e *de Ligne*.
11. Regiments with yellow broadcloth were as follows: 6e *de Ligne*, 18e *de Ligne*, 59e *de Ligne*, 103e *de Ligne*, 116e *de Ligne*.
12. SHDDT Xs 525. *Circulaire* 27 10bre 1807.
13. Regiments with epaulettes for *voltigeurs*: 2e *de Ligne*: 360 pairs, 18e *de Ligne*: 250 pairs, 20e *de Ligne*: 87 pairs, 32e *de Ligne*: 140 pairs, 61e *de Ligne*: 25 pairs, 72e *de Ligne*: 178 pairs, 116e *de Ligne*: 46 pairs.
14. Regiments with copper hunting horns for gibernes were 5e *de Ligne*, 36e *de Ligne*, 47e *de Ligne*, 88e *de Ligne*, 102e *de Ligne*, 116e *de Ligne*.
15. SHDDT Xb 387 19e *régiment de Ligne*. Dossier 1815.
16. SHDDT Xb 406 28e *de Ligne*. Dossier 1815.
17. SHDDT C15 Correspondance Armée du Nord 11 Juin a 20 Juin 1815. Dossier 19 Juin. 95e *régiment* de Ligne.
18. Regiments with *cornets* in 1814 were: 3e, 5e, 6e, 7e, 9e, 11e, 13e, 14e, 16e, 17e, 21e, 32e, 35e, 36e, 37e, 39e, 45e, 46e, 48e, 53e, 55e, 56e, 57e, 60e, 61e, 65e, 72e, 76e, 79e, 81e, 82e, 84e, 85e,8 6e, 93e, 94e, 96e, 100e, 111e, 114e, 115e, 128e, 131e.
19. Regiments where archive evidence shows the existence of *cornets* clothing: 6e, 19e, 35e, 85e and 111e.
20. The following regiments had *sapeurs* in 1814–1815: 1e *de Ligne*: 12 *sapeurs*, 2e *de Ligne*: 17 *sapeurs*, 3e *de Ligne*: 4 *sapeurs*, 7e *de Ligne*: 13 *sapeurs*, 11e *de Ligne*: 12 *sapeurs*, 12e *de Ligne*: 17 *sapeurs*, 13e *de Ligne*: 12 *sapeurs*, 19e *de Ligne*: 2 *sapeurs*, 26e *de Ligne*: 4 *sapeurs*, 29e *de Ligne*: 2 *sapeurs*, 34e *de Ligne*: 9 *sapeurs*, 35e *de Ligne*: 7 *sapeurs*, 36e *de Ligne*: 16 *sapeurs*, 37e *de Ligne*: 9 *sapeurs*, 43e *de Ligne*: 8 *sapeurs*, 44e *de Ligne*: 4 *sapeurs*, 45e *de Ligne*: 13 *sapeurs*, 46e *de Ligne*: 13 *sapeurs*, 48e *de Ligne*: 4 *sapeurs*, 50e *de Ligne*: 10 *sapeurs*, 53e *de Ligne*: 13 *sapeurs*, 56e *de Ligne*: 12 *sapeurs*, 58e *de Ligne*: 13 *sapeurs* with colpack headdress and *sapeur habit*, 59e *de Ligne*: 5 *sapeurs*, 60e *de Ligne*: 12 *sapeurs*, 65e *de Ligne*: *sapeurs* in bearskins, 67e *de Ligne*: 5 *sapeurs*, 70e *de Ligne*4 *sapeurs*, 75e *de Ligne*: 6 *sapeurs*, 76e *de Ligne*: 7 *sapeurs*, 79e *de Ligne*: 6 *sapeurs*, 81e *de Ligne*: 4 *sapeurs*, 82e *de Ligne*: 3 *sapeurs*, 84e *de Ligne*: 13 *sapeurs*, 85e *de Ligne*: 12 *sapeurs* in bearskin, corporal *sapeur* in colpack, 86e *de Ligne*: 9 *sapeurs*, 88e *de Ligne*: 12 *sapeurs*, 93e *de Ligne*: 4 *sapeurs*, 94e *de Ligne*: 6 *sapeurs*, 95e *de Ligne*: 2 *sapeurs* wearing bearskins with Imperial Guard pattern sabres, 100e *de Ligne*: 5 *sapeurs* with Imperial Guard model axes and sabres, 105e *de Ligne*: 9 *sapeurs*, 106e *de Ligne*: 10 *sapeurs*, 108e *de Ligne*12 *sapeurs*, 111e *de Ligne*: 12 *sapeurs*?, 114e *de Ligne*: 2 *sapeurs*, 121e *de Ligne*: 2 *sapeurs* wearing bearskins, 122e *de Ligne*: 3 *sapeurs*, 123e *de Ligne*: 2 *sapeurs*, 128e *de Ligne*: 3 *sapeurs*.
21. 2e *de Ligne*, 4e *de Ligne*, 5e *de Ligne*, 13e *de Ligne*, 20e *de Ligne*, 21e *de Ligne*, 33e *de Ligne*, 35e *de Ligne*, 42e *de Ligne*, 46e *de Ligne*, 52e *de Ligne*, 62e *de Ligne*, 64e *de Ligne*, 76e *de Ligne*, 88e *de Ligne*, 95e *de Ligne*, 96e *de Ligne*.
22. Regiments with blackened cow hide equipment in 1814 were as follows: 16e *de Ligne*, 17e *de Ligne*, 19e *de Ligne*, 24e *de Ligne*, 25e *de Ligne*, 30e *de Ligne*, 42e *de Ligne*, 44e *de Ligne*, 46e *de Ligne*, 67e *de Ligne*, 70e *de Ligne*, 75e *de Ligne*, 96e *de Ligne*, 102e *de Ligne*, 123e *de Ligne*, 131e *de Ligne*.
23. 36e *de Ligne*, 47e *de Ligne*, 88e *de Ligne*.
24. Michael Shanks and Christopher Tilly (2017) *Re-constructing Archaeology: Theory and Practice*, 2nd Edition, Routledge, London, Chapter 5.

Bibliography

Printed Sources

Anon (1779) *Reglement Arête pour le Roi pour l'habillement et l'equipment des ses troupes*. Paris: Imprimerie Royale

Anon (1787) *Instruction pour servir a expliquer les principes d'après lesquels on ete executes les différends modeles de coiffure, Habillement & equipment envoys a chacun des Regiments d'infanterie*. Paris: Imprimerie Royale

Etienne Alexandre Bardin (1813) *Mémorial de l'officier d'infanterie*. Chez Magimel Paris. 2 Volumes

Etienne Alexandre Bardin (1813) *Manuel d'infanterie, ou Résumé de tous les règlements, décrets, usages, renseignements concernant l'infanterie, dans lequel se trouve renfermé tout ce que doivent savoir les sergents et caporaux*. Paris: Chez Magimel

Etienne Alexandre Bardin (1850) *Dictionnaire de l'armée de terre, ou Recherches historiques sur l'art et les usages militaires des anciens et des modernes*. Paris. 17 volumes

Honoré Hugues Berriat (1812) *Législation militaire* Paris: A. Alexandrie

Pierre Charrie (2004) '*Lettres de Gueres 1792–1815*' Nantes: Editions du Cannonier

Terry Crowdy (2015) Napoleon's *Infantry Hand Book* Barnsley: Pen & Sword

Paul Lindsay Dawson (2019) *Napoleon's Imperial Guard Uniforms and Equipment: The Infantry*. Barnsley, Frontline

Les Gupil (1812) *Administrations du Masses*, Paris, Chez Magimel

Malibran (1904) *Guide a l'Usage des Artistes et des Costumiers Contenant la Description Des Uniformes de l Armée Française de 1780 à 1848*. Paris: Combet & Cie.,

Bibliothèque Musée de l'Armée

Fonds Rousselot. Infanterie de la Ligne

Manuscripts and printed books, Volume 1 projet de règlement sur l'habillement du major Bardin

Archives Nationales

AN, AF/IV/1326

AN, AF/IV/1179

Bibliothèque Service Historique Armée de Terre

Volume II, III, IV du projet de règlement sur l'habillement du major Bardin

Archives Service Historique Armée de Terre

C2 Correspondence Militaire Fevrier 1813

Xb 342 1e *régiment d'infanterie de la Ligne*

Xb 343 1e *régiment d'infanterie de la Ligne* 1814 a 1815

Xb 345 2e *régiment d'infanterie de la Ligne* An XII a 1812

Xb 346 2e *régiment d'infanterie de la Ligne* 1814 a 1815

Xb 347 3e *régiment d'infanterie de la Ligne* An XII a 1810

Xb 348 3e *régiment d'infanterie de la Ligne* 1811 a 1815

Xb 349 4e *régiment d'infanterie de la Ligne* An XII a 1811

Xb 350 4e *régiment d'infanterie de la Ligne* 1812 a 1815

Xb 352 5e *régiment d'infanterie de la Ligne* 1813 a 1815

Xb 355 6e *régiment d'infanterie de la Ligne* 1812 a 1815
Xb 356 7e *régiment d'infanterie de la Ligne* An 12 a 1810
Xb 357 7e *régiment d'infanterie de la Ligne* 1812 a 1815
Xb 358 8e *régiment d'infanterie de la Ligne* 1792 a 1811
Xb 359 8e *régiment d'infanterie de la Ligne* 1812 a 1815
Xb 361 9e *régiment d'infanterie de la Ligne* 1810 a 1815
Xb 364 10e *régiment d'infanterie de la Ligne* 1813 a 1815
Xb 366 11e *régiment d'infanterie de la Ligne* 1813 a 1815
Xb 368 12e *régiment d'infanterie de la Ligne* 1809 a 1812
Xb 369 12e *régiment d'infanterie de la Ligne* 1813 a 1815
Xb 374 14e *régiment d'infanterie de la Ligne* 1811 a 1815
Xb 377 15e *régiment d'infanterie de la Ligne* 1812 a 1815
Xb 379 16e *régiment d'infanterie de la Ligne* 1812 a 1815
Xb 381 17e *régiment d'infanterie de la Ligne* 1808 a 1812
Xb 382 17e *régiment d'infanterie de la Ligne* 1813 a 1815
Xb 384 18e *régiment d'infanterie de la Ligne* 1812 a 1815
Xb 387 19e *régiment d'infanterie de la Ligne* 1813 a 1815
Xb 390 20e *régiment d'infanterie de la Ligne* 1812 a 1815
Xb 391 21e *régiment d'infanterie de la Ligne* An XII a 1811
Xb 392 21e *régiment d'infanterie de la Ligne* 1812 a 1815
Xb 393 22e *régiment d'infanterie de la Ligne* An XII a 1811
Xb 394 22e *régiment d'infanterie de la Ligne* 1812 a 1815
Xb 397 24e *régiment d'infanterie de la Ligne* An XII a 1811
Xb 398 24e *régiment d'infanterie de la Ligne* 1812 a 1815
Xb 399 25e *régiment d'infanterie de la Ligne* An XII a 1811
Xb 400 25e *régiment d'infanterie de la Ligne* 1812 a 1815
Xb 402 26e *régiment d'infanterie de la Ligne* 1812 a 1815
Xb 404 27e *régiment d'infanterie de la Ligne* 1812 a 1815
Xb 406 28e *régiment d'infanterie de la Ligne* 1812 a 1815
Xb 408 29e *régiment d'infanterie de la Ligne* 1812 a 1815
Xb 410 30e *régiment d'infanterie de la Ligne* 1812 a 1815
Xb 412 32e *régiment d'infanterie de la Ligne* 1812 a 1815
Xb 414 33e *régiment d'infanterie de la Ligne* 1812 a 1815
Xb 417 34e *régiment d'infanterie de la Ligne* 1812 a 1815
Xb 419 35e *régiment d'infanterie de la Ligne* 1812 a 1815
Xb 421 36e *régiment d'infanterie de la Ligne* 1812 a 1815
Xb 423 37e *régiment d'infanterie de la Ligne* 1812 a 1815
Xb 428 40e *régiment d'infanterie de la Ligne* 1812 a 1815
Xb 430 42e *régiment d'infanterie de la Ligne* 1812 a 1815
Xb 432 43e *régiment d'infanterie de la Ligne* 1812 a 1815
Xb 434 44e *régiment d'infanterie de la Ligne* 1812 a 1815
Xb 435 45e *régiment d'infanterie de la Ligne* An XII a 1811
Xb 436 45e *régiment d'infanterie de la Ligne* 1812 a 1815
Xb 437 46e *régiment d'infanterie de la Ligne* An XII a 1811
Xb 438 46e *régiment d'infanterie de la Ligne* 1812 a 1815
Xb 440 47e *régiment d'infanterie de la Ligne* 1812 a 1815
Xb 442 48e *régiment d'infanterie de la Ligne* 1812 a 1815
Xb 444 50e *régiment d'infanterie de la Ligne* 1812 a 1815
Xb 447 51e *régiment d'infanterie de la Ligne* 1814 a 1815
Xb 449 52e *régiment d'infanterie de la Ligne* 1812 a 1815
Xb 451 53e *régiment d'infanterie de la Ligne* 1812 a 1815

Xb 452 54e *régiment d'infanterie de la Ligne* An XII a 1811
Xb 453 54e *régiment d'infanterie de la Ligne* 1812 a 1815
Xb 454 55e *régiment d'infanterie de la Ligne* An XII a 1811
Xb 455 55e *régiment d'infanterie de la Ligne* 1812 a 1815
Xb 457 56e *régiment d'infanterie de la Ligne* 1810 a 1812
Xb 458 56e *régiment d'infanterie de la Ligne* 1812 a 1815
Xb 459 57e *régiment d'infanterie de la Ligne* An XII a 1811
Xb 460 57e *régiment d'infanterie de la Ligne* 1812 a 1815
Xb 461 58e *régiment d'infanterie de la Ligne* An XII a 1811
Xb 462 58e *régiment d'infanterie de la Ligne* 1812 a 1815
Xb 465 59e *régiment d'infanterie de la Ligne* 1812 a 1815
Xb 467 60e *régiment d'infanterie de la Ligne* 1812 a 1815
Xb 469 61e *régiment d'infanterie de la Ligne* 1812 a 1815
Xb 471 62e *régiment d'infanterie de la Ligne* 1812 a 1815
Xb 472 63e *régiment d'infanterie de la Ligne* An XII a 1811
Xb 473 63e *régiment d'infanterie de la Ligne* 1812 a 1815
Xb 475 64e *régiment d'infanterie de la Ligne* 1812 a 1815
Xb 477 65e *régiment d'infanterie de la Ligne* 1812 a 1815
Xb 479 66e *régiment d'infanterie de la Ligne* 1812 a 1815
Xb 481 67e *régiment d'infanterie de la Ligne* 1812 a 1815
Xb 483 69e *régiment d'infanterie de la Ligne* 1809 a 1813
Xb 484 69e *régiment d'infanterie de la Ligne* 1814 a 1815
Xb 486 70e *régiment d'infanterie de la Ligne* 1812 a 1815
Xb 488 72e *régiment d'infanterie de la Ligne* 1812 a 1815
Xb 489 75e *régiment d'infanterie de la Ligne* An XII a 1811
Xb 490 75e *régiment d'infanterie de la Ligne* 1812 a 1815
Xb 492 76e *régiment d'infanterie de la Ligne* 1812 a 1815
Xb 496 81e *régiment d'infanterie de la Ligne* 1812 a 1815
Xb 498 82e *régiment d'infanterie de la Ligne* 1812 a 1815
Xb 500 84e *régiment d'infanterie de la Ligne* 1812 a 1815
XB 501 85e *régiment d'infanterie de la Ligne* An XII a 1811
Xb 502 85e *régiment d'infanterie de la Ligne* 1812 a 1815
Xb 505 88e *régiment d'infanterie de la Ligne* An XII a 1811
Xb 506 88e *régiment d'infanterie de la Ligne* 1812 a 1815
XB 508 92e *régiment d'infanterie de la Ligne* 1812 a 1815
XB 510 93e *régiment d'infanterie de la Ligne* 1809 a 1813
Xb 511 93e *régiment d'infanterie de la Ligne* 1812 a 1815
Xb 513 94e *régiment d'infanterie de la Ligne* 1812 a 1815
Xb 514 95e *régiment d'infanterie de la Ligne* An XII a 1811
Xb 515 95e *régiment d'infanterie de la Ligne* 1812 a 1815
Xb 516 96e *régiment d'infanterie de la Ligne* An XII a 1811
Xb 517 96e *régiment d'infanterie de la Ligne* 1812 a 1815
Xb 518 100e *régiment d'infanterie de la Ligne* An XII a 1811
Xb 519 100e *régiment d'infanterie de la Ligne* 1812 a 1815
Xb 521 101e *régiment d'infanterie de la Ligne* 1812 a 1815
Xb 523 102e *régiment d'infanterie de la Ligne* 1812 a 1815
Xb 524 103e *régiment d'infanterie de la Ligne* An XII a 1811
Xb 525 103e *régiment d'infanterie de la Ligne* 1812 a 1815
Xb 528 105e *régiment d'infanterie de la Ligne* 1812 a 1815
XB 530 106e *régiment d'infanterie de la Ligne* 1812 a 1815
Xb 531 107e *régiment d'infanterie de la Ligne* 1812 a 1815

Xb 533 108e *régiment d'infanterie de la Ligne* 1812 a 1815
Xb 535 111e *régiment d'infanterie de la Ligne* 1812 a 1815
Xb 539 114e *régiment d'infanterie de la Ligne* 1808 a 1814
Xb 540 115e *régiment d'infanterie de la Ligne* 1808 a 1814
Xb 541 116e *régiment d'infanterie de la Ligne* 1808 a 1814
Xb 542 117e *régiment d'infanterie de la Ligne* 1808 a 1814
Xb 543 118e *régiment d'infanterie de la Ligne* 1808 a 1814
Xb 544 119e *régiment d'infanterie de la Ligne* 1808 a 1814
Xb 545 120e *régiment d'infanterie de la Lign*e 1808 a 1814
Xb 546 121e *régiment d'infanterie de la Ligne* 1808 a 1814
Xb 547 122e *régiment d'infanterie de la Ligne* 1808 a 1814
Xb 548 122e *régiment d'infanterie de la Ligne* 1811 a 1814
Xb 549 123e *régiment d'infanterie de la Ligne* 1808 a 1814
Xb 549 124e *régiment d'infanterie de la Ligne* 1811 a 1814
Xb 550 125e *régiment d'infanterie de la Ligne* 1811 a 1814
Xb 551 126e *régiment d'infanterie de la Ligne* 1811 a 1814
Xb 552 127e *régiment d'infanterie de la Ligne* 1811 a 1814
Xb 553 128e *régiment d'infanterie de la Ligne* 1811 a 1814
Xb 554 129e *régiment d'infanterie de la Ligne* 1811 a 1814
Xb 555 130e *régiment d'infanterie de la Ligne* 1811 a 1814
Xb 564 1e *Légère* An XII a 1811
Xb 565 1e *Légère* 1812 a 1815
XB 567 2e *Légère* 1812 a 1815
Xb 572 4e *Légère* 1812 a 1815
Xb 575 6e *Légère* 1812 a 1815
Xb 577 7e *Légère* 1812 a 1815
Xb 580 8e *Légère* 1812 a 1815
XB 583 9e *Légère* 1812 a 1815
XB 585 10e *Légère* 1812 a 1815
XB 586 11e *Légère* 1812 a 1815
Xb 587 11e *Légère* An XII a 1811
Xb 588 11e *Légère* 1812 a 1815
XB 590 13e *Légère* 1812 a 1815
XB 594 15e *Légère* 1812 a 1815
Xb 595 16e *Légère* An XII a 1811
Xb 596 16e *Légère* 1812 a 1815
Xb 598 17e *Légère* 1812 a 1815
Xb 602 21e *Légère* 1812 a 1815
Xb 608 24e *Légère* 1812 a 1815
XB 611 25e *Légère* 1812 a 1815
Xb 613 26e *Légère* 1812 a 1815
Xb 615 27e *Légère* 1812 a 1815
XB 617 28e *Légère* 1812 a 1815
XB 622 33e *Légère* 1812 a 1815
XB 623 34e *Légère* 1812 a 1815

Xs 525 Habillement
Xs 526Habillement
Xs 527 Service d'Habillement 1770–1870

GR 21 YC 31 3e régiment d'infanterie de ligne dit régiment du Dauphin, 16 juillet 1814–17 décembre 1814 (matricules 1 à 1 800).

GR 21 YC 32 3e régiment d'infanterie de ligne dit régiment du Dauphin, 17 décembre 1814–1er juillet 1815 (matricules 1 801 à 2 135)

GR 21 YC 309 33e régiment d'infanterie de ligne (ex 34e régiment d'infanterie de ligne), 19 juillet 1814–4 novembre 1814 (matricules 1 à 1 800)

GR 21 YC 310 33e régiment d'infanterie de ligne (ex 34e régiment d'infanterie de ligne), 19 juillet 1814–21 juillet 1815 (matricules 1 801 à 2 572)

GR 21 YC 324 36e régiment d'infanterie de ligne, 16 mai 1811–22 avril 1813 (matricules 8 376 à 10 175)

GR 21 YC 602 75e régiment d'infanterie de ligne, 1er thermidor an XIII [20 juillet 1805]–25 octobre 1808 (matricules 3 001 à 5 976)

GR 21 YC 918 136e *régiment d'infanterie de ligne*. 1813–1814

GR 21 YC 923 138e *régiment d'infanterie de ligne*. 1813–1814

GR 21 YC 926 139e *régiment d'infanterie de ligne*. 1813–1814

GR 21 YC 929 140e *régiment d'infanterie de ligne*. 1813–1814

GR 21 YC 932 à 933bis 141e *régiment d'infanterie de ligne*. 1813–1814

GR 21 YC 934 142e *régiment d'infanterie de ligne*. 1813–1814

GR 21 YC 936 143e *régiment d'infanterie de ligne*. 1813–1814

GR 21 YC 940 144e *régiment d'infanterie de ligne*, 14 mars 1813–3 juillet 1813 (matricules 1 à 3 000)

GR 21 YC 940 144e *régiment d'infanterie de ligne*, 14 mars 1813–3 juillet 1813 (matricules 1 à 3 000)

GR 21 YC 146e *régiment d'infanterie de ligne*

GR 21 YC 147e *régiment d'infanterie de ligne*

GR 21 YC 944 148e *régiment d'infanterie de ligne*. 1813

GR 21 YC 945 149e *régiment d'infanterie de ligne*. 1813–1814

GR 21 YC 947 150e *régiment d'infanterie de ligne*. 1813–1814

GR 21 YC 949 151e *régiment d'infanterie de ligne*. 1813–1814

GR 21 YC 954 153e *régiment d'infanterie de ligne*. 1813–1814

GR 21 YC 957 154e *régiment d'infanterie de ligne*. 1813–1814

Dear Reader,

We hope you have enjoyed this book, but why not share your views on social media? You can also follow our pages to see more about our other products: facebook.com/penandswordbooks or follow us on X @penswordbooks

You can also view our products at www.pen-and-sword.co.uk (UK and ROW) or www.penandswordbooks.com (North America).

To keep up to date with our latest releases and online catalogues, please sign up to our newsletter at: www.pen-and-sword.co.uk/newsletter

If you would like a printed catalogue with our latest books, then please email: enquiries@pen-and-sword.co.uk or telephone: 01226 734555 (UK and ROW) or email: uspen-and-sword@casematepublishers.com or telephone: (610) 853-9131 (North America).

We respect your privacy and we will only use personal information to send you information about our products.

Thank you!